Joan [illegible] ly for over twenty-five years and her work has been published widely in both the UK and Canada. An interest in the theatre and history led to a series of historical plays and books for young children, including *The Princess in the Tower*. She has also recently completed a social evocation of working lives in Edwardian England and a survey of the evidence for death survival, *The Golden Shore*.

A long-standing interest in parapsychology gave rise to a series of books on the subject: *Haunted East Anglia, The Haunted South, Haunted Royal Homes* and a study of the extraordinary nature of time, *The Mask of Time*. The last book formed the basis of two BBC Television series on 'Timeslips', while *Haunted East Anglia* was featured in an Anglia Television programme in 1986.

Joan Forman is known, too, for her journalism, book reviewing and educational writings. She also lectures for the Eastern Arts Association and is a regular broadcaster on radio and television. She is currently working on a novel with a wildlife background.

JOAN FORMAN

Royal Hauntings

FONTANA/Collins

First published in Great Britain
in 1987 by Fontana Paperbacks,
8 Grafton Street, London W1X 3LA

Made and printed in Great Britain by
William Collins Sons & Co. Ltd, Glasgow

To
Peggy Bell and Christine Vernon,
without whose kindness and shelter
this book would not have been written

Contents

Acknowledgements

I am glad to acknowledge help given in the preparation of this book. In particular, my thanks are due to Mr and Mrs E. J. Barker of Westhorpe, Suffolk, for showing me the Westhorpe site of the Mary Rose hauntings.

Also thanks to Vivien and Donald Ferrier of West Newton, Norfolk, for their kindness in offering hospitality, information and encouragement. And to the late, irreplaceable Tom Litchfield for his further thoughts on Barnwell Castle. To Mrs Fay Scott of Edinburgh, for her assistance; and to Miss A. Cornish and Mrs S. Marsh, both of London, for clear accounts of personal experiences.

Renee Burgess of Bembridge, Isle of Wight, supplied a splendid Catherine Howard incident; Miss L. Dessau of London provided a fine timeslip-cum-haunting; Mrs A. Corcoran of Hartlepool gave me the oldest historical incident in the book.

To the many other correspondents, my warmest thanks for their assistance, interest and patience.

Thanks also are due to Peggy Bell and Christine Vernon, who proved friends indeed when book and author fell victims to the house-moving chain.

To Pauline Merchant thanks and appreciation for her impeccable typing. And to Sue Merchant and Ann Hanson for kindly allowing themselves to be staging-posts for the work during the year of its writing.

Finally to the staffs of the Norwich City Library and the Library of the University of East Anglia for their patience in supplying the many research needs.

Acknowledgements are also made to Evans Bros. for the use of a short extract from the *Memoirs* of Princess Marie-Louise; and to Constable & Co. Ltd. for use of a quotation from *Melbourne* by Lord David Cecil.

Introduction

In recent years, the idea of hauntings has developed from an initial frivolity into a subject to be taken seriously. Ghost stories are no longer mere tales to be told by a winter fireside, but are regarded as symptoms of a huge and hidden field of human experience, whose margin touches many lives.

Hauntings may represent that margin, a fringe area where the extrasensory, paranormal aspect of earthly life produces curious echoes of the past, whether aural, visual, tactile or olfactory; and occasional glimpses of the future, which are referred to as precognition rather than haunting.

It seems likely that there is some scientific basis for the genuine cases, for the method of hauntings tends to fall into a pattern and to relate consistently to the use of some form of energy. More interestingly, hauntings and ghostly encounters are not limited to any one sector of society, but are experienced across the human spectrum without regard to class, colour, sex, creed, age, rank, occupation, nationality or degree of intelligence or education. Thus, a paranormal happening is as likely to occur to a crowned head as to one wearing a cloth cap, to a duke's son as to the lad in the dole queue. The only factor which does appear to govern the ability is a certain type of sensitivity, probably deriving from a particular brain pattern found in a large proportion of the human race.

Ghosts, which seem to be the commonest form of paranormality, may be human or animal, of landscape, building or machine. There are ghostly aeroplanes, for instance, and spectral freight lorries; there are ghosts of castles, churches and cottages; and of horses as well as the horsemen riding them. Perhaps most often, hauntings relate to the great events of history, or to some part of them in which individuals were involved in high drama. Emotion seems to be a key factor in the production of hauntings, in that it appears to create a type of electrical impression upon the surroundings and to be capable of later replay, in the manner of a tape recording.

It is not surprising to find royalty featuring strongly in such phenomena. The moments of national and international drama involved them; conflict and warfare, as well as social violence and murder, were a constant feature of royal lives in the earlier reaches of history. The fifteenth and sixteenth centuries produced a plethora of ghosts; this was a time when royalty both exercised and suffered from unfettered power.

This book begins further back, however, at the time of Boudicca, the forceful Queen of the Iceni, whose glittering image is still sometimes seen in Lincolnshire driving her chariot out of a mist to some warlike rendezvous; through Arthur, the Celtic king, to the Saxon monarchs in England, and Malcolm II in Scotland. Guinevere's funeral procession appears occasionally along the Ridgeway's ancient track, and an Irish princess whose origins lie deep in myth is said to haunt a Scottish castle some fifteen hundred years after the incident which fixed her sorrow to the place. For grief is as much an instigator of haunting as is fear, and love may impress itself on surroundings as deeply as hate. All emotion calls for expenditure of energy, and evidence suggests that it is forms of energy which are the key to these strange occurrences.

After the Conquest, and the rise of the hot-tempered Plantagenets, the incidence of ghosts increases; the turbulent fourteenth and fifteenth centuries are crammed with the spectral records of violent events. The sixteenth century finds the Elizabethans – Mary, Queen of Scots, Lady Jane Grey, and the magnificent Elizabeth herself – with their fragments of life still recorded and repeating themselves in the places they once occupied. Often it is the royal residences which are haunted; the dreaded Tower remained an occasional royal home for centuries, and produces ghosts of both royal and nonroyal vintage. Hampton Court, too, carries its imprints of commoner and king – or more usually queen, for Catherine Howard and Anne Boleyn both walk there.

The Stuarts dominate the seventeenth and eighteenth centuries, gradually giving place to their Hanoverian relatives. Guy Fawkes, Strafford, Charles I and his son, and that son's mistresses; then the Young Pretender and sad Farmer George, have all been seen, heard or sensed over the centuries in places familiar to them in life. If the nineteenth century recorded less, perhaps it is because the royals were happier or felt safer in their earthly lives; certainly they lived less violently than their forebears. However, Queen Victoria seems to have made one extraordinary and inexplicable appearance in a family living-room in recent years.

In modern times, the recordings are mainly of experiences by royal personages of actual hauntings, but since royal families generally live in dwellings whose age and historical background produce the conditions required, it is not surprising that their occupants have occasionally encountered ghosts. Through the ages several royal personages seem to have possessed psychic ability, and it is they who have experienced parapsychological phenomena. The ability seems still to operate in the present generation, for there have been several instances in the twentieth century.

Royal hauntings, then, come in three types; ghosts of those who were royal; sites associated with royalty; and actual experiences by royal observers, but of course hauntings are not limited to royalty.

CHAPTER ONE
From Rome to the Norman Conquest

The idea of hauntings, the presence among the living of spirits of the dead, is of great antiquity, and probably arose in human consciousness about the same time as the first glimmerings of religion. It is even possible that the two ideas, both immensely powerful as motivators of human action throughout history, had similar origins, springing in each case from dread of the unknown.

The emerging human, his brain beginning to register the differences between various types of natural phenomena and their often disastrous effect, experienced much that was outside his control or power to influence. Great gales, floods, earthquakes, drought, thunder and lightning – all no doubt seemed to him the work of supernatural beings, who must be appeased if he were to survive. Why did vegetation appear and disappear, changing a season of rich plenty to one of starvation and death? Were all-powerful beings at work here, too? So, perhaps, began the first simple idea of religion.

The knowledge of death may have produced the second branch of human thought, which for thousands of years would be only slightly subsidiary to the first – belief in the supernatural. One suspects that the fact of death may sometimes prove puzzling to animals; how much more then to the developing human consciousness which, after a few years spent in its small family group, hunting, gathering, cave- or shelter-dwelling, would witness the death of one of its members. Alive and working, even communicating in a fashion, and then at once reduced to lifelessness, a few feet of cooling clay. Such realization must have caused terror in the beholders. Where had that individual gone? What had become of the vital aspect of their companion, which had responded to them and given him a life like their own? Surely he – his living essence – must have departed elsewhere at the moment of death, and would now be in a place set aside for the newly dead or with his friends still, in the place he had occupied in life – alive but invisible. So the idea of ghosts may have begun.

Certainly hauntings were accepted by the Egyptians, the Greeks, the Romans, and peoples even earlier still, and although the strength of belief in ghosts has ebbed and flowed over the centuries, it has never wholly disappeared, merely retreated temporarily in the face of science and rationalism, only to advance again as soon as its opponents began to weaken.

It would seem then that belief in the subject is almost as old as humanity itself, so it can never be regarded entirely as frivolity or idle superstition. The belief represents qualities of experience and perhaps of fact. It may have an important role to play in our life upon earth.

The beginning of British history has its own ghostly records, but they are now few and faded. However, by Roman times, information was being laid down in a form which would remain valid for centuries, recording events and people in such a way that some of them remain active into the present time.

In the middle of the first century AD, the Celts who had occupied Britain when the Romans invaded were living in uneasy compromise with their conquerors. Indeed, they probably thought of themselves less as a conquered people than as the rightful owners of a land they were temporarily forced to share with foreigners. At that time Britain was populated by a number of tribes which, though Celtic in origin, had arrived in the islands at different times and from different sources so that, although they shared a distant ancestry, there was no real unity between them. In some cases, fierce rivalry broke out into open tribal warfare.

The eastern part of the country, now known as East Anglia, was populated by three powerful tribes, the Catuvellauni, the Trinovantes and the Iceni, the latter with its stronghold somewhere in modern Norfolk. The tribes had met Roman military supremacy in different ways: the more hostile had withdrawn into their territories to await the next Roman move; those overrun in the southeastern corner had submitted to Roman terms; while those in some neighbouring territories – and this included the Iceni – had offered Rome qualified friendship and been accepted as 'client kingdoms'. They could keep their own kings and customs, but were expected to govern their lands on Rome's behalf, and to subordinate their interests where necessary to that of the Empire. Thus the client kingdoms could continue to think themselves independent while actually doing Rome's administrative work. It was a convenient arrangement so long as each side trusted the other and did not feel threatened by encroachment or betrayal.

In the case of the Iceni, it worked well so long as its king, Prasutagus, lived. Unfortunately, prior to his death, he had tried to secure his tribe's position with Rome by willing half his personal fortune (the Iceni were notably rich) to the then Emperor, Nero. On Prasutagus's death, his widow, Boudicca, his daughters and tribal subjects were descended upon by Nero's financial agent and numerous attendant plunderers bent on sharing the Iceni spoils. When the queen resisted the blatant looting, she was brutally flogged and her two daughters raped; the Iceni chieftains were stripped of their possessions and the remainder of the royal family treated as though they were Roman slaves. This was not to be borne, and the tribe at once began to plan revolt.

The outcome is history. The Iceni, under their ferocious, outraged queen, with several allied tribes, went to war against Rome. They wiped out the Roman town and inhabitants of

Colchester before visiting the same bloody doom on London.

Boudicca is described by the Roman historian, Dio Cassius, as being very tall, with flashing eyes, a harsh voice, a mane of red hair falling to her hips and a torque around her neck of twisted gold. She was a warrior queen whose status in the tribe was almost that of goddess. She was not, however, a trained strategist, and was bound to be outclassed in the kind of warfare practised by the Romans. Not surprisingly her forces were eventually defeated and broken by the Roman general Suetonius, probably between Watling Street and the Fosse Way. Rather than suffer the humiliation of being exhibited in a Roman triumph, Boudicca took poison. The site of her grave is unknown. Echoes of the queen remain, however, recurring through that strange faculty of awareness which seems able to tune in to time past with ease.

The small village of Cammeringham lies on the B1398 road between Ingham and Brattleby in Lincolnshire, not far from the old Roman Ermine Street. One of its residents, a man named Lucas, had risen early as he usually did to reach his work just after daybreak. Dawn one morning found him walking to his job through areas of mist which congregated, here in patches, there in banks and layers, promising a fine warm day ahead. As the sun rose and the light grew brighter, Lucas's attention focussed on an exceptionally large bank of vapour which was drifting slowly towards him. After a few seconds, there emerged from it a chariot pulled by two horses, one black, one white, and driven by a woman. He gazed at her in astonishment, for she wore a long flowing dress, and her mass of hair lay loose over her shoulders. Then she whipped the horses, and the movement, catching the sunlight, showed a quantity of gold jewellery about her neck. For a minute or two she remained in full view, then vanished as she had come, back into the mist. The whole incident took place in absolute silence, and Lucas was left astounded by what he had seen.

The 'Cammeringham Light', as it is known, has been seen several times over the centuries, the local opinion (which accorded with that of Lucas) assumes the figure to be that of Queen Boudicca. Iceni territory ran to the South Lincoln shire borders, and may occasionally have extended even farther north, into the territory of the tribe occupying Lincolnshire, the Coritani. It is feasible that the queen may have visited the area and used a convenient Roman road for her journey, in this case Ermine Street.

Boudicca is also said to haunt the ancient hill fort of Ambresbury in Essex, and there has been some speculation that she was buried there. However, although unknown, her burial place is more likely to be in the heartland of Icenian territory, central Norfolk, than in an outlying district. Perhaps one day some farm worker in the Thetford area will plunge a spade into the ground and find the redhaired queen, and the great treasure said to be buried with her.

Long before the Romans established themselves in Britain, the Celtic races which inhabited it had developed a majestic and exciting mythology, which was in part stories of ancient Celtic heroes and in part stories of their gods. Since the Celts had probably moved westward from Middle Eastern and Mediterranean sources, many of their traditions and legends had factors in common with those of Greece and Egypt. The Gaels of Ireland had developed sagas to rival those of the Norsemen, and the Ulster cycle contains three fine stories, of which one, the *Fate of the Sons of Uisneach*, has left echoes in twentieth-century Scotland.

Its central figure is Deirdre, whom Cathbadh the druid prophesied would be of marvellous beauty but would bring ruin and disaster upon all Ulster. Many advised that the baby be exposed at once and left to die, but the king, Conchobhar (pronounced Connor), ordered that she be brought up apart from the rest of her race, where she could influence no man and cause no harm. In time she grew into a beautiful girl. One day as she watched her fosterfather kill a calf on the winter snow, she saw a raven drinking the spilt blood. She wished that she might love a man whose hair was raven-black, whose skin was white as snow, whose cheek was red as blood. She was immediately told that there was such a man, Naoise, one of the three sons of Uisneach, and in time Deirdre and Naoise met and love grew between them. Naoise, however, knew that Deirdre had been promised as wife to the king, and his allegiance to Conchobhar at first inhibited him from wooing her.

Eventually, of course, neither loyalty nor gloomy prophecy prevented the lovers eloping to Alba (Scotland) taking with them Naoise's brothers, Ainle and Ardan. Once on Alba they made their way to Glen Etive, where they settled for several years, building a bower for Deirdre on the west side of the loch, and a hunting lodge among the pine trees at the foot of the cliffs running back to the Glen. They were wonderfully happy, although in time Naoise began to resent his exile and long for his homeland.

Meanwhile, in Ulster, King Conchobhar had been planning to retrieve his lost bride and exact vengeance on Uisneach's sons, particularly on Naoise. He needed an agent who would be sufficiently trusted by Naoise to be accepted as an honest messenger, and eventually chose Fergus Mac Roich to bring the fugitives home. When, in due course, Fergus sailed up the loch, calling to Naoise as he came, Deirdre was filled with foreboding and tried to dissuade her lover from believing Conchobhar's message of forgiveness. Not surprisingly, she was overruled; the three brothers and the princess returned under Fergus's protection to Ulster. As they left Loch Etive forever, Deirdre mourned her lost happiness and sang in lamentation:

Glenn Da-Ruad!
My love to every man who hath it as a heritage!
Sweet the cuckoo note on bending bough,
On the peak over Glenn Da-Ruad.

Once they were back on Ulster soil, the treacherous Conchobhar ambushed and killed the three brothers, taking the unhappy Deirdre by force. At this point there are two versions of the story. One has it that Deirdre, unable to tolerate life with King Conchobhar, flung herself from a chariot, dashing out her brains on a rock. The second version states that she survived for many years in sad desolation. Few of the great sagas offer happy endings!

I encountered this story first in my schooldays, by sneaking into the school library when I should have been doing gymnastics. Books, and in particular the myths and legends of the ancient races, were of much more attraction than parallel bars and vaulting horses. However, I had forgotten Deirdre of the Sorrows until a few years ago, when a copy of the Hebridean song, 'Deirdre's Lament for the Highlands', came into my possession. Something in its lilting sadness and plaintive word melody still captures the imagination.

> Glen-da-Rua! Glen-da-Rua!
> Where I built my bridal bower,
> From a cliff-tree called a cuckoo,
> And I think I hear him now.
> Glen-da-Rua!
> Glen-da-Rua!

The final line has a dying fall, a breath of wind over the loch, fading at last into silence. But this was not the last word on Princess Deirdre. During the research for this book, Mrs Anne Corcoran of Hartlepool wrote to tell me of a strange experience she had had in a remote Highland hotel in 1965.

> Two years ago I went for a holiday with a friend to Scotland. The hotel was like a castle and very isolated.
>
> We were given a large room which had two double beds and one single and had two windows.
>
> We decided to take a double bed each, either side of the

room. As there was only one centre light and the switch was by the door and my bed was nearest I put out the light and we were soon asleep as we'd had a day's journey.

I was awakened by my friend crying out, 'Anne, Anne, someone has hold of my throat'. I jumped out of bed to put on the light but the room was quite bright and the light seemed to be going out of one of the windows. We put on the light and observed that it was quite dark outside, not even the moon shining. My friend decided she must have been overtired and had imagined it.

The next night we decided to put something against the door as the lock did not work properly. In the room was an oak carver chair, very heavy – in fact it took the two of us to lift it and put it against the door. I couldn't sleep very well and during the night I felt a draught. I called my friend to shine her torch which we had bought as the light was away from our beds and we found the door was partly open. We pushed the chair back again and then decided to sleep together in the one double bed. We didn't say anything to the other guests but the next day bought some candles and candlesticks, determined to have a light at night. The next night at 3.30 am (with our candle on), we were both awakened by what we did not know and both at the same time. We looked at the door and saw the chair slowly moving and the door opening. No one we could see came in, but a light seemed to be in the room and floated out of the far window. We plucked up courage and looked out on the landing but no one was about. After the same experience the next night we told the other guests of it and were given one solution.

The hotel was, as I said, like a castle, and it was indeed a castle once and the owner married an Irish princess and brought her to live there. She had four brothers and they did not approve and they came to take her back to Ireland which they did, but in the fighting the husband was killed, and now she comes back crying and looking for her lost love, but I wish she had not chosen our room to do it in. As I said, the chair was very heavy and there was no wind so it must have been a ghost.

There are factors in this story which suggest the Deirdre legend. The site of the haunted hotel/castle is in the area said to have been the scene of Deirdre's and Naoise's homestead. The place named in two of the several versions of Deirdre's Lament (Glenn-da-Ruad or Glen-da-Rua) is obviously similar to that of the site of Mrs Corcoran's hotel Highland Hotel, or Glendarual. And the legend of an Irish princess who had lived in the area with a much-loved husband ties in well with the Ulster legend of Deirdre of the Sorrows.

On the negative side, there are discrepancies. Mrs Corcoran and her friend were shown the grave of the 'Irish princess', which would have been an impossibility unless Deirdre's body had been transported back from Ulster to Scotland. Local rumours do not fit the hotel's story either. Deirdre, if she were the Irish princess, did not marry a Scottish chieftain, nor did she bring her four brothers with her. The fighting and killing took place in Ireland not Scotland, and it is unlikely that any castle existed on Loch Etive's shore so early in history.

Ancient legend (and the facts of history) become distorted with time and ultimately all that remains is a garbling of the essence of a story, plus a handful of detail. This particular tale crystallized around the second century AD and might have related to even earlier events. It is hardly surprising that the passage of seventeen centuries has seen a corruption of its truth and incidents. The wonder is that anything has remained at all.

What did Mrs Corcoran and her friend experience? A feeling by the friend that someone was attempting to strangle her; a door ajar which had been shut and barred by heavy furniture; the chair moving and the door slowly opening, although no one entered; and, perhaps most significantly of all, on both nights a light which appeared to have no natural origin. On the second night this light actually moved across the room and out of the window.

These incidents bear all the hallmarks of the classic ghost story. What they do not have is characteristics identifying them specifically with the Deirdre legend. Yet this area of Scotland is full of allusions to the story; several of the buildings and landmarks round about carry names associated with it. It is unlikely that two such similar traditions should exist in the same district, and one is inclined to think that the Highland Hotel, Glendarual, may well be built on a site connected with the Sons of Uisneach. But we must also consider that the activities which disturbed Mrs Corcoran and her friend may arise from a different haunting entirely.

Long after the foundations of the Deirdre legend were laid, one of even greater power began in mainland Britain, that of Arthur, who may have his origins in the person of a Romano-British chieftain, and who was almost certainly a Celt who assimilated the Roman culture and wished to perpetuate it.

During the fourth century AD Britain was attacked by three different barbarian tribes at once – the Anglo-Saxons from across the North Sea, the Scotti from Ireland and the Picts from beyond the wall which stretched across northern Britain. With Roman power withdrawing from the island, the Britons found themselves standing alone against the invaders. For a time it seemed that they would be overwhelmed by the heathen war bands. Then the rout was halted, the defeats reversed. The invaders retreated and were held back for some thirty years, from 514 to 547. It is possible that thirty-three years may be the length of one man's reign, and that man a Romanized Celt known as Artorius or Arthur.

Whatever the truth, Arthur appears to have existed as a Celtic ruler. Legend has it that he was brought up in a cave beneath the cliff on which Tintagel Castle stands; that his mother was Ygraine, wife of Gorlois, Duke of Cornwall, and that Uther Pendragon, who desired her, gained access to her bed through a trick of Merlin, the druid magician. Uther was disguised as Gorlois, and Ygraine innocently accepted him as her husband. The product of this curious affair was Arthur, who became Merlin's pupil and eventually King of Britain: the once-and-future king. Much of this is folklore, to be taken with a large helping of salt. However, *some* chieftain did beat back the Saxons and impose peace on part of Britain for a third of a century, and Welsh accounts confidently name him as Arthur.

Tintagel is marvellously set on a wild headland jutting into the Atlantic. Not only set, but beset, for the waves batter it incessantly on three sides, almost severing it from the mainland. Access is by steep flights of steps which take the visitor up among the gulls and kittiwakes and to the high cliffs' edge. The foam gnaws at the distant foot of your standing place as though determined on your destruction. The castle itself is a windswept ruin, open to the crying winds and all the ocean's storm voices. It is a haunted place. But is it haunted by Arthur? Was there ever a Guinevere, a Lancelot, a magician named Merlin? Was the Round Table fact, fiction or allegory? Who occupied this seagirt collection of walls and what spirit inhabits them now?

It is fairly certain that what remains has little to do with King Arthur. On the headland there is a mixture of the ruins of a twelfth-century castle, once the property of the Black Prince, and even earlier monastic buildings. However, there are traces of earlier occupation still. Coins, ornaments and pottery of the fourth century have been found on the headland, and a Roman coin of the Emperor Magnentius (345–361 AD) was discovered in a well near the castle. It is an old, old site, and Artorius may well have had a stronghold here. Whatever the facts, Arthur's spirit is said to return to wild Tintagel at intervals, though I know of no evidence to support the claim.

More interestingly, a local tradition insists that twice each year the whole castle vanishes and materializes briefly in some fairy realm. Not a Cornish Brigadoon, I think, but a recognition of the mist-haunted and magical nature of this supremely beautiful site.

Not far from Tintagel is the little town of Camelford, named, one supposes, for the River Camel. Many have claimed this as King Arthur's Camelot, though another strong claimant is Cadbury Castle, the prehistoric hill fort in Somerset, the scene of this second Arthurian ghost story.

An ancient causeway runs between the villages of South and North Barrow, and on Midsummer's Eve the spectral procession of King Arthur and his knights has been seen riding along it, as though on a hunting expedition. Cadbury Castle is in direct line with the causeway and Marc Alexander tells a curious story of a woman and her friend driving home towards Cadbury late at night, just after the First World War. The women noticed a string of lights, almost processional, moving down the imposing mound and, as the travellers approached, they saw that what had seemed to be lights were flames illuminating the lance-points of a troop of mounted soldiers, whose leader was a tall, majestic man. All advanced silently for a while and then abruptly disappeared. This apparition has been seen frequently over the centuries and would appear to be connected with whatever respected chieftain once occupied the Dark Age site of Cadbury. Arthur is certainly a likely candidate. Marc Alexander puts forward the theory that the flames on the lance-tips were merely the result of summer lightning flashing on the mail and weapons of cavalrymen. But, if the hunting procession is ghostly, then so must be the lightning. An interesting idea, for it must constitute the 'recording' of an *actual* procession at a time when *actual* summer lightning was flashing. More of this theory later.

Local tradition still refers to an old path between Cadbury Castle and Glastonbury as King Arthur's Hunting Causeway.

Where such folk names have existed for a long time, they may relate to historical fact, finally incorporated into the woven coat of legend.

Arthur and his queen are said to have been buried in Glastonbury Abbey, and in 1190 the monks exhumed two bodies there which they asserted were those of Arthur and Guinevere. A leaden cross found in the tomb was inscribed: *Hic jacet septultus inclytus Rex Arthurus in Insula Avalonia* (Here lies the renowned King Arthur, interred in the Island of Avalon). The inscription does not mention Guinevere. But there are echoes of Guinevere elsewhere. A few miles east of Glastonbury runs the Wansdyke, from the edge of Savernake Forest to Bath. Wansdyke – originally Woden's Dyke – may once have been a tribal boundary between the Belgae and the Atrebates, intended as a defence against invaders. Wansdyke links up with that other ancient track, the Ridgeway, and may have served as a protection for the great pagan religious centre, Avebury, although Woden's name probably became attached to it at a later date.

Occasionally there have been sightings of a funeral cortège, travelling along the Wansdyke, the coffin carried by pall-bearers and bearing on top a crown-circlet of gold. This is said to be that of Guinevere, escorted on her last journey by Lancelot and her followers. If, as seems likely, the procession is a 'recording' of an actual event in time past, its subject is probably royal. Who else but a king or queen would rate a gold crown on the coffin? If Guinevere were indeed buried at Glastonbury, the latter is near enough to Wansdyke to confirm rather than contradict the funeral train's destination.

* * *

Almost four centuries would elapse before other royal ghosts made an imprint on the environment.

Dacre Castle stands hard by a village of that name in Cumberland, and was built by Ranulf Dacre in the thirteenth century. An earlier fortification had occupied the site and, as was common practice at the time, a later edifice grew upon it. A room in the Norman tower is still referred to as the Kings' Room to commemorate an historic meeting.

In 924 AD Athelstan had succeeded his father, Edward the Elder, son of Alfred 'the Great', as ruler. These Saxon kings, whose people had originally invaded and conquered or assimilated the Romano-Celtic peoples, were now under threat from the Danes. There had been wholesale Danish settlement in the north and midlands during the previous generation, and the English had come to accept the permanent presence of the Norsemen, though not their turbulent desire for expansion. When Athelstan, following his father's example, declared himself king of the Anglo-Saxons, he laid claim to virtually the whole of England. A kingdom of *all* the English, of whatever origin, was a new concept, and would ultimately change the history of these islands.

Athlestan temporarily cemented good relations with the Norse kingdom of Northumbria by marrying his sister to Sihtric, its Danish ruler, in York. However, Sihtric died in 927 and his son Olaf was supported by Guthfrith, Sihtric's brother, who came over from Ireland with a sizeable army. Athelstan at once pursued and defeated the pair of them and entered York in triumph, the first English king to take possession of Northumbria. England was growing.

At Eamont, near Penrith, Athelstan received the homage of the two northern kings who had supported Olaf and Guthfrith. They were King Constantine of Scotland, a hardy old warrior, and King Donal of Strathclyde. The meeting must have generated strong feelings. These two rulers would have posed a constant threat to Athelstan's intention to defeat the Danes and impose unity upon embryonic England. However, their submission led not to a lasting peace but to a renewal of war, in which Athelstan was opposed by a coalition of Norsemen and armies from Scotland and Strathclyde. It says much for his generalship (and great Alfred's blood) that he defeated them in a stupendous battle at Brunanburgh. The

Anglo-Saxon Chronicle states that 'the black and horn-beaked raven . . . and the dun-feathered eagle' presided over the warriors' corpses after the battle was over.

It is the meeting near Penrith, rather than the great battle, which has left its psychic imprint. At intervals during the ten centuries since, their three ghosts have been seen walking the grounds surrounding Ranulph Dacre's castle. Three kings, whose passions registered an incident of significance for the kingdom which would later be known as England. Dacre, as it happens, is adjacent to Eamont, so from the viewpoint of the ghost story they may be considered identical.

If Dacre Castle did not exist in its present form when the incident took place, the same may be said of a castle at the opposite end of the country – Corfe Castle in Dorset. The castle was not built until the twelfth and thirteenth centuries, and lasted until the Civil War when it was besieged and fiercely slighted by the Cromwellian forces. However, over a century before the foundations of the Norman keep, a royal palace stood on the site.

The Saxon king, Edgar, a firm ruler and lawgiver, died in 975, aged thirty-two, leaving two sons by different women. The mother of the elder boy, Edward, had been betrothed but not married to the king when she died; but betrothal in the Middle Ages was regarded as a legal bond, and thirteen-year-old Edward succeeded his father to the throne. Unfortunately, the mother of the younger son, Ethelred, had actually been married to Edgar and was legally queen. She seems to have been none too scrupulous about achieving her ambitions. Although Edward had the reputation of being a youth of 'intolerable violence in speech and behaviour', according to Professor D. M. Stenton, he was the anointed king and should have been able to count on the loyalty of his father's followers. Yet in an England divided between Saxon and Dane and pro- and anti-monastic factions, only a strong monarch could expect a long reign. Three years after their father's death, Edward at sixteen and Ethelred at thirteen were a natural focus for the rival groups.

Perhaps Ethelred's supporters made a suitable occasion for ambush, or perhaps the young king was headstrong and played into their hands. What happened was that Edward visited his stepmother, Queen Aelfrith, and his young stepbrother, both of whom were at Corfe. From here on the details are confused. It seems that the young king rode alone into the courtyard and was given the customary wine-cup in greeting. A press of retainers surged forward, one stumbling against him and catching at his free hand while driving a dagger into his body. As Edward fell forward, his horse either bolted or was driven away, dragging the young man's body by the stirrup for a considerable distance. When the beast was caught, the king's face was battered beyond recognition, and England had a new ruler, Ethelred.

A curious aspect of this barbarous episode is that Edward's body was buried with great haste in an obscure grave (possibly a nearby well), and was not discovered until several months later, when a curious glow arising from the spot led to investigation and the discovery of the corpse. There was a ceremonial state interment at Shaftesbury Abbey, and almost immediately miracles began to occur at Edward's tomb. Whether the miracles were authentic, or whether they were a political ploy by Edward's vengeful followers, they were an embarrassment to Ethelred. People began to refer to the dead king as 'the Martyr', and somewhat unfairly – for he had been only thirteen at the time of the regicide – Ethelred was thought to be an accomplice in the crime. Ethelred's nickname, the Unraed, meant literally 'he of no counsel'. History and contempt have converted it into 'the Unready', for he proved an unlucky king and was unable to control the ravaging Danes.

As for the haunting of Corfe, local people report that spectral figures have been seen in the castle, moving about in the ruins. These may not belong to the time of King Edward the Martyr, for King John once starved twenty-two prisoners to death in the dungeons there, and in the Civil Wars a prolonged siege of the Royalist forces by the Parliamentary army involved considerable losses on both sides. The shadows of the past may belong to any one of these three stages of drama, and no witness has so far been close enough to the phantoms to identify them.

More certain identity has been attached to one of the many ghosts of beautiful, ancient Glamis, ancestral castle of Queen Elizabeth the Queen Mother, whose family still lives there. Malcolm II, 'honoured among all men in Western Europe', according to the *Irish Annals*, reigned for twenty-nine years with a combination of diplomacy, deviousness and ruthlessness. However, he appears to have been one of the first of the early Scottish kings to impose a sense of order on his unruly subjects, though he sowed the seed of further dissension by marrying his daughters to the secular Abbot of Dunkeld; to the Norseman, Sigurd, the Christian Earl of Orkney; and to Finlech, the Mormaer or Steward of Moray. It was this last daughter who would have a son immortalized by Shakespeare as Macbeth, but long before Macbeth became Thane of Fyfe and Glamis his grandfather died in the castle. Some believe Malcolm II perished of wounds received at the battle of Hunter's Hill, others that he was murdered at Glamis by a group of his nobles. As they fled across a frozen loch, the ice gave way and every man was drowned; 'the righteous judgement of God' was how men interpreted the disaster.

As for Malcolm, centuries later a greater castle was built on the site and, on the spot where the King had died, a dull bloodstain appeared on the floor and could not be eradicated. Eventually, the stigma was covered by an oaken floor, and it has not reappeared. It may still lie beneath the boards, hidden but not removed.

Glamis has many ghosts. It is probably the most haunted castle in Britain. Since it is also one of the oldest, it has had time to accumulate its psychic records. We shall examine some of these as they occur in this ghostly royal history.

CHAPTER TWO

The Eleventh and Twelfth Centuries

Once William the Bastard, William of Normandy, exchanged those titles for Conqueror and King of England, it was apparent to the Saxons that life would never be the same again. This was no piecemeal conquest imposed by warbands of Norsemen, no gradual settlement by land-hungry Danes, but wholesale invasion and occupation on a scale not seen since Roman times. The country was no longer Saxon England (formerly Celtic Britain), but Norman England (formerly belonging to the Saxons). The Norman war-lords owned both land and Saxons. They built castles on the former and reduced the latter to a serfdom which was almost slavery. The face of land and people had changed drastically and irrevocably.

Now, nearly a thousand years after the brutality of the Conquest, the only trace of our Saxon ancestors lies in the language, a few place names, a church tower or two and in the occasional round blond heads which pepper the population. The Norman castles, by contrast, are everywhere. They lie about the landscape in various stages of decrepitude, some concealed under turf-clad mounds, others with walls and a few floors intact. All are too large to be erased from the landscape, and too formidable to be forgotten or ignored.

Skipsea Castle is in Eastern Yorkshire, lying between Bridlington and Hornsea. All that remains of its former magnificence is a hump of turf-disguised stones which barely suggest the baronial castle built by Drogo de Bevere after the Conquest.

De Bevere, a Flemish knight in the pay of William of

Normandy, showed particular courage during the battle of Senlac (later to become known as Hastings), and was rewarded with the lands of Holderness on the coast of East Yorkshire. Drogo appears to have been a brutal and avaricious overlord, whose greed for property even extended to the seizure of the sacrosanct church lands. He did not earn much love or respect from his Saxon underlings either, for he treated the defeated race as serfs and enforced his power ruthlessly. Had the new King even been aware of his vassal's activities, it is unlikely he would have raised any objection. These were the kind of men William needed, 'strong' individuals whose exercise of power would not be too much concerned with chivalry and principle.

William was sufficiently appreciative of de Bevere's efforts to give him as well his own niece in marriage. Almost certainly the girl had no say in the transaction. Female members of a ruling family were political pawns, who would be used as bargaining pieces or handed out as reward at the king's pleasure. In this case the victim's name is not even remembered; only the fact that her uncouth bridegroom took her to his new castle of Skipsea, where he proceeded to demonstrate the vast difference in their backgrounds and status. She was the lady of royal line (recent though that royalty was), gently reared and with a gloss of education, and he was the rough soldier-adventurer, without polish or aspiration other than to satisfy his appetites and his greed for power. Once the novelty of a royal bride evaporated, he treated her with great cruelty and eventually killed her by poisoning. He then seems to have come to his senses briefly, and realized that the woman he had murdered was niece to his overlord and king. De Bevere decided to make himself scarce before William could learn the truth. He stood to lose his lands and power but also, if he remained in England, his life.

He was not without guile, this soldier of fortune. He rode to London and presented himself before the king, saying that he wished to take his wife to his lands in Flanders for a while.

According to some reports, he even had the affrontery to persuade William to advance him money for the journey. No doubt the king regarded him by now as a relative who could be trusted, as well as a powerful baron who should be placated. Whatever the reasoning, de Bevere was suitably financed and took the first available passage to the Continent. Only just in time, as it happened, for the news from Skipsea arrived hard on the heels of his departure, and William's fury was considerable. The king sent a search party after the villain, but he had vanished and was not heard of again.

His wife, however, was. Over the succeeding centuries she has continued to appear around Skipsea Castle and its environs, a glimmering figure in white, neither speaking nor giving any sign of awareness of those she encounters.

There have been at least two recorded sightings of the white princess in modern times. The first was at the end of the nineteenth century when a horseman riding from Bridlington to Hornsea began to descend a hill just south of Skipsea. He saw ahead of him a young woman dressed in white. She moved a little way before him, on his left-hand side, keeping to the verge between hedge and road. He does not seem to have doubted her reality, but assumed she was a local girl who had been visiting a house he had noticed on the hilltop behind them. At one point, he looked around to see if anyone was at the house door waving her farewell, but the door was shut and the scene empty of watchers.

Something about the girl struck him as being refined and of good breeding; he was curious to know who she was and what she was doing walking alone, apparently impervious to the fact that she was being followed. The traveller and his horse were now twenty-five yards or so behind her, but, as the hill was no more than a hundred and fifty yards long, he was easily able to keep her in clear view. At its foot a small stream ran, crossed by a bridge. He expected that she would hesitate and he would catch her up before the crossing, but, even as he watched her, expecting her to turn right on to the bridge, the girl vanished.

When he reached home, he could not forget that he had actually been *watching* her when she became invisible. Such things do not happen, particularly in daylight and when the thought of ghosts has not even crossed your mind. The traveller believed in apparitions from that moment.

A farm labourer had an equally startling experience on his way from Skipsea to Bridlington two hours before sunrise. He was riding at a canter along Skipsea Lane, leaning forward with his head down, when the animal bolted off the road so suddenly that he was almost thrown. When he managed to rein in, he saw 'a fine lady, dressed in white, with something like a black veil over her head, standing close by'. He was thoroughly frightened, and on the return journey he was careful to find a group of people returning to Bridlington so that he might not have to pass the haunted place alone.

Curiously, both accounts stress the 'refinement' and 'fineness' of the ghost, and both observers saw her as a woman in white. Most ghosts *do* appear without colour – either as white, black or grey figures, or sometimes in a combination of monochromes. An apparition in colour is comparatively rare, and it may be that the reproduction of colour requires more energy than is available to the phantom. The possible methods of colour reproduction are discussed in a later chapter, for hauntings appear to operate in more than one way, although in all some form of external energy seems to be necessary to produce the effect which brings them to the notice of the living.

As far as I know, there have been no recent sightings of 'the fine lady' of Skipsea, generally assumed to be the Conqueror's ill-fated niece. However, since both the accounts quoted fall within the last century, this haunting must have been continuing for at least eight hundred years; an unusually long period for any 'place' haunting. As we have seen, there are older psychic records in existence, and Romans still occasionally appear to observers in the twentieth century. Many of these hauntings relating to distant historical events may be less concerned with ghosts than with timeslips, though it is sometimes difficult to know one from the other. The mechanism for both may be similar, and only the fact that timeslips appear to have a closer connection with the observer (in that the observer often actually takes part in the action he is seeing) makes the distinction between them plain.

William the Conqueror died in France in 1087, and was succeeded not by his rightful heir, Robert Curthose ('short hose', implying that Robert was a short man), but by the favourite third son, William, known as Rufus because of his weatherbeaten complexion. Rufus seems to have inherited his father's firmness and brutality and to have developed an aptitude for plundering the Christian church which made him unpopular with the clergy. The barons didn't much like him either, and in 1088 a body of them staged a rebellion in favour of his elder brother, Robert, but to no avail. Rufus apparently had a stammer as well as a slippery attitude to principles. 'Who,' he said, 'can be expected to keep *all* his promises?'

There was also a waiter-in-the-wings, the youngest son of the Conqueror, Prince Henry, whose hopes of eventually reaching the throne were threatened when Robert Curthose married Sybil, an heiress of the Italian branch of the Normans. Any heir of Robert's would be a contender for the crown after William Rufus's death. Unless, of course, that death should come speedily.

In the year of Robert's marriage, AD 1100, William had an unpleasant dream, in which he was 'let blood' by a surgeon and the stream of it reached to heaven, obscuring the light of day. He awoke heavy with premonition, a state not helped by an equally portentous dream which had occurred to a certain foreign monk which seemed, as much as his own, to prophesy Rufus's death.

It was the second of August and, although Rufus had

intended to go out to hunt in the New Forest near Brockenhurst, he delayed for several hours. The party was a small one and included one of the king's intimates, Walter Tyrell. The quarry were red stag, wild boar and fallow deer to be hunted with the brach, a type of foxhound, and the wolfhound or alan. What happened in the forest glade is not clear. William of Malmesbury says that only Tyrell remained with the king, and that after the latter had shot and wounded a stag and was running in pursuit of it, Tyrell aimed at another which his arrow grazed before glancing off and into the body of the king. William Rufus, speechless, broke off the arrow's shaft, but fell forward on to the wound, thereby contributing to his own speedy death. Tyrell, not unnaturally, decided to put distance between himself and the event and, leaping on his horse, escaped at full gallop.

The Malmesbury monk suggests that several supporters connived in his flight: 'Some began to fortify their dwellings, others to plunder, and the rest went to look for a new king.' A charcoal-burner, one Purkiss, found the king's body and took it into Winchester on a rough cart. Young Prince Henry, who had been a member of the fatal hunting-party, also rode straight to Winchester – but in his case to secure the royal treasure. Three days later he was crowned at Westminster, neatly sidestepping the claims of his brother Robert, who had been Rufus's nominated heir. The Normans were perhaps short on principle but they were long on pragmatism.

In the glade where Rufus died a stone monument was erected: the Rufus Stone, near Stoney Cross off the A31. It is said that on the anniversary of his death (which may be either 22 July or 2 August, according to whether one uses the Julian or the Gregorian calendar) the ghost of the Red King appears and follows the route of the cart on which his corpse was borne, a trail marked in his own blood.

Another, less likely, tale survives that a pond at Castle Malwood, a royal hunting lodge nearby, had been used by Tyrell to wash his hands after the killing, and that to this day it turns red in remembrance of the deed. However, unless Tyrell actually touched the corpse, it is difficult to see how he could have bloodied his hands.

Was Rufus killed accidentally, deliberately murdered, politically assassinated or ritually sacrificed, as Margaret Mitchell once suggested? Political assassination seems much the most likely. Henry's response to the killing was too smooth and immediate; Tyrell's flight so easy and safeguarded. And the fact that Tyrell's in-laws later received high honours from the new king is possibly too significant to be overlooked. In any case, Rufus's elder brother Richard had earlier died of a hunting accident in the same forest, so the precedent was there and could have supplied a conveniently plausible method of removing the main obstacle to Henry's ambitions.

I have heard of no one who has seen the ghost of William Rufus in recent years, and it is likely that the continued belief in its haunting is based on tradition rather than experience. The drama which sparked it is eight hundred and eighty-four years old, and one suspects that the original glade, which might have retained an impression of the event, has changed a great deal since then.

Henry I, the opportunist brother of William Rufus, occupied the English throne for thirty-five years, but his only male legitimate heir, Prince William, had been drowned in the loss of the White Ship (as much an innovation in its day as the *Titanic*), and his only daughter Matilda was now the rightful heiress to the throne. Matilda had formerly been married to the Holy Roman Emperor, but was widowed early and forced into a second diplomatic marriage by her father – this time to the fourteen-year-old Geoffrey, Count of Anjou. Matilda, although insulted by her union with a lowly count, produced a male heir, who would later become Henry II.

Many turbulent years of conflict would be lived through in England before Henry came into his birthright, however, for Matilda's claim to the crown was hotly contested by her cousin Stephen, who managed to forestall her with a coronation ceremony and thus became, by another piece of mediaeval manipulation, king in name if not in undisputed fact, from 1135–54. When Stephen died, however, his recognition of young Henry as his successor was honoured. By this time Henry's father, Geoffrey, Count of Anjou, had also died, and he found himself the ruler of a powerful 'empire' which stretched from the Tweed in the North to the Spanish border. Henry had augmented this realm by marrying Eleanor, heiress of the Aquitaine duchy, which brought added territory and power to the Anglo-Norman kingdom he ruled.

All this, however, was in the future. Henry II's childhood had been chronically disturbed by the warfare between Matilda, his mother, and his uncle Stephen, and he had been moved from place to place to keep him safe from capture. Although one might expect that any echoes of this powerful and turbulent monarch would relate to his adult life – his quarrels with his wife and with Thomas à Becket were notorious even in his own lifetime – the psychic echoes we have are of Henry's boyhood. They were reported by Christina Hole, who had the account from a Somerset resident.

The incident happened to a woman staying with friends near Cadbury Fort – the same camp associated with Arthur and his hunting party. She was out alone one day, and during her walk saw a particularly old and beautiful house standing in a nearby field. She remembered having passed that way on an earlier occasion, but had no recollection of having seen the house. She noticed it particularly because a man and a young boy stood outside it, and both were dressed in a fashion belonging to an earlier century.

She was puzzled by their costume and unable to identify its period. The clothes of the boy seemed considerably richer than those of his adult companion, and she assumed from this that the child must hold the higher rank. While she was gazing at them in puzzlement, the figures vanished.

On her return home, she mentioned the house (though not

the figures) to her hostess, asking what the place was and describing its location. Although her friend's family had lived in the area for many generations, nothing was known of any house in the field described, and her hostess knew of no dwelling there within living memory. The visitor then told her experience in full, suggesting that some local legend might account for both house and figures. She again met with a blank response. As far as the neighbourhood knew, there was no story to account for what she had seen.

The mystified family then began to look through their own archives, and found that during the Matilda-Stephen wars of the twelfth century, young Prince Henry had been hidden in Somerset for his own safety, taking refuge in the home of a man loyal to Matilda's cause, whose house was near the old Cadbury Fort. In time the building was destroyed and its exact site forgotten – until the sensitivity of a twentieth-century observer rediscovered it. Christina Hole makes the point that the percipient was not particularly interested in the period she so unexpectedly encountered, and could therefore not be said deliberately to have 'conjured' or created a sighting related to it.

But perhaps the most interesting aspect of this experience is that it is less a haunting, less an encounter with ghosts, than a true timeslip. The observer saw not only the man and boy – presumably the little Prince Henry and his temporary guardian – but the house too. All three had ceased to exist as actualities many centuries earlier, yet they reappeared in what must have been their original position and site at a certain moment in time; and were 'picked up' by the visitor in a form which translated itself in her mind into a real house and actual people.

What happens in certain timeslips, and what seems to have occurred in this instance, is that the percipient (who may be compared to a television viewer) receives information regarding a particular incident: in this case the one-time state of the field when it was occupied by a house, at the precise moment when the little prince and his companion were outside it. This presupposes (a) that the moment which had thus registered on the surroundings had been an important one, probably involving some strong emotion on the part of the people participating and (b) that this emotion had caused an impression to be made on the materials of the surrounding area, possibly through the transmission of the electromagnetic waves constantly given out by all humans and indeed by all material objects.

A 'broadcast' of this nature, heightened by intense emotion, might have generated enough power to register in the area for an abnormally long period. For much of the time it would be inoperative, but certain physical conditions might be able to set it in motion. Light, temperature, humidity, etc., when they coincided, might have reproduced the exact conditions of the day on which the original event took place eight hundred years earlier. Yet before anything could be experienced in the present time, one further factor was necessary; the presence of a brain capable of receiving the transmission and translating it into visual terms. So time, place, conditions and appropriate receiver had to come together before anything paranormal could occur. And since this, I believe, is the way most parapsychological experiences occur, it is not surprising that the majority of people do not have them – or experience them only rarely. A further factor with the very ancient hauntings is that the power of the initial record appears to grow weaker with time, and eventually to die away. It is a scientific fact that electrical fields dwindle and fade over the years.

Although Henry II was a man of strong character and passions, and lived a life of perpetual conflict, there seems to be no other psychic record of his existence than the one near Cadbury. His queen, an equally positive character, with an absolute genius for trouble-making in her own family circle, also left a single imprint on the future.

Eleanor of Aquitaine was a woman of considerable beauty, intelligence and energy. Perhaps if Henry had granted her a little power or given her some modest job on which to exercise her talents, his domestic life might have been pleasanter and his paternal troubles fewer. However, this was not a time for women to have a say in government; they were regarded by monarchs as property, pawns and breeders of male heirs. Eleanor was not content with this and, lacking any other outlet, turned to mischief-making. There is no doubt that she encouraged her four sons to regard themselves as rivals to their father as well as to one another and, over the years, she encouraged each of them to revolt, without her husband being aware at first of the extent of her involvement.

When, in 1173, the young Prince Henry, heir to the throne, followed his mother's advice and headed a rebellion against the king, Eleanor was captured trying to escape in disguise into the domains of the French king. Henry II naturally took this as an admission of guilt, and confined his meddlesome queen under house arrest for the next sixteen years, an incarceration which, however luxurious (and English castles at this time were still cold and draughty), could not have compensated Eleanor for life at the heart of things, for a finger in the political and family pies.

During her imprisonment, the queen seems to have been moved occasionally, and local tradition has it that she was held for a period at Quarr Abbey on the Isle of Wight. No doubt the imprisonment was a lenient one – all that Henry intended was to keep her out of his way and out of touch with politics – and Eleanor, with her love of French traditions of romantic chivalry, no doubt set up a minor court of her own to echo the joyous one she had known in her youth in Aquitaine. Minstrelsy and courtly love would have been a part of it, though almost certainly her gaolers would have tried to prevent her sons' representatives seeking her out, for fear of further plotting. Whatever kind of court Eleanor kept, Quarr was noted for its New Year's Day celebrations, a Feast of

Fools, on which an Abbot of Misrule was appointed, and the monks assumed female dress and sang highly unsuitable songs. The event seems to have been a vague remembrance of Roman Saturnalia.

Island lore has it that Eleanor's favourite walk was through the Grove now named for her, and that when she died she was buried at Quarr in a solid gold coffin beneath the trees in the grove. The tomb's entrance was reputed to have a pair of golden gates magically sealed by a spell. Unfortunately for romance, when a tomb was found there in the nineteenth century and opened, the only gold found was the hair of its female occupant. And since Eleanor was a dark princess, was actually imprisoned at Old Sarum for most of her sixteen years' incarceration and was finally buried in France, she is not a likely candidate for the occupancy.

None of which prevents the tale being told of a royal ghost which has walked the grove for seven hundred years, wringing her hands and regretting her treachery to her husband. Eleanor was not given to such remorse in life, as far as we can tell, for although there appears to have been a bond between Henry and his queen, it was of the love/hate variety, a classic case of irresistible force meeting immovable object. Yet both were fiery, handsome, passionate people, restless with energy and ideas and filled with a desire to shape events (in Eleanor's case) and the great Norman kingdom he had inherited (in Henry's). Only Henry succeeded, but the success of his law-making and redrafting of feudal England to control his barons' power was marred at the end by his sons' final rebellion and treachery. When he died at the age of fifty-six in France, no one would have been surprised if his spirit had returned to the scenes he had known in his days of temporal power, but there is no psychic record of King Henry II's activities other than the youthful South Cadbury episode.

Much of Henry II's attempt to weld England into a strong kingdom would be eroded in the following two centuries. Not all, however; he had built well and with foresight.

CHAPTER THREE
The Thirteenth Century

It was A. A. Milne who stated in a children's poem that King John was a somewhat unlovable character. If history is to be believed this was not surprising, for John, youngest (and spoiled) child of Henry II and his tempestuous Queen Eleanor, seems to have been highly unstable. Although capable of decisiveness and firmness for short periods, he was subject to violent attacks of the famous Plantagenet temper, was extremely suspicious, jealous and apparently trusted nobody but his favourites. Even they walked a tightrope, in case their devious monarch was laying traps for them. The fact that John had a good share of Plantagenet ability makes his lack of self-discipline all the more regrettable. He could, when he exerted himself, show flashes of statesmanship. He added dockyard, walls and arsenal to the town of Portsmouth in support of the infant British navy; he also chose the site of a new port in the north-west, to be known as Liverpool, and granted it its charter. He was, when he managed to overcome his inertia, a reasonably good soldier, though without either the flair or the application of his father Henry, or elder brother, Richard Coeur de Lion.

John's major weakness was self-indulgence. When he wanted something, he saw no reason why he should not take it. Refusal on the part of the owner only incensed him and made him more determined. He was indeed not a good man but a sly and clever one. His personal fastidiousness was remarkable: he once took eight baths in six months. Yet he enjoyed watching victims under torture in squalid dungeons, and had without compunction starved to death the twenty-two

French prisoners in Corfe Castle. A man of contradictions, a paradoxical Plantagenet, whom very few of his subjects loved and a great many loathed and distrusted. In addition to his other attributes, John also seems to have been well endowed with Plantagenet sexuality.

To the east of the Surrey town of Guildford lies a miniature lake known to the local people as Silent Pool. It is a sizeable sheet of water, rather a large pond than a small lake, but in its quality of stillness resembles the strange meres which dog the legends of the Arthurian cycle and the Middle Ages. One reaches the pool from the busy A25 road to Dorking, but climb the path leading to the glade in which the water lies and the twentieth century might not exist. The place is secluded, uncannily still, dappled with deceptive light and shadow; secretive, a place of waiting.

Some eight centuries ago the area was doubtless heavily wooded, the type of terrain which would attract royal huntsmen no matter what their quarry. John, as it happened, had not yet ascended the throne of England, but was minding it during the absence of its rightful occupant, Richard, who was on crusade. The profligate prince, according to legend, had been enjoying himself up and down Surrey, and happened to arrive in the neighbourhood of Silent Pool at the moment when a local village beauty named Emma was about to bathe in it. Innocent she may have been, but foolish she certainly was when she decided to paddle minus her clothing. Prince John's spies alerted him to possible sport and he rode post-haste to the scene.

Emma clung, as she usually did, to the overhanging bough of a convenient tree, and repeatedly dipped in and out of the water, no doubt unaware of her danger. When the hunting party abruptly appeared on the bank and its royal leader plunged his horse into the pool towards the maiden, she relinquished her branch and waded into deeper water. To no avail. John rode after her. Emma, by now out of her depth in both senses and unable to swim, screamed loudly and went under. Her brother was within earshot and, recognizing his sister's voice, dived in to her rescue. But as he could not swim either, this was ill advised. Both young people drowned.

It is said that if you approach Silent Pool when the night is filled with moonlight you may see the ghost of lovely Emma as she dips in and out of the water. And as you leave the little glade you may hear her last dying shriek as the pool takes her.

A nicely romantic tale, if not very credible. Would any sensible village girl have been so naive? The Saxons knew the nature of their overlords very well.

The pool is, in fact, memorable for its older history. In the days before the Romans it seems to have been sacred to some water spirit. Later, pilgrims are said to have bought a mug of 'Roman water', perhaps for its healing or holy properties. Later still, the Christian church held a Palm Sunday fair, which was transferred to the neighbouring village of Albury in the nineteenth century.

The ghost story may be only a corruption of the distant and hazy memory of a Celtic water goddess, naiad or guardian spirit of the pool. The early Christian church was quick to translate its pagan rivals into some harmless form – a saint or innocent spirit – in order to neutralize the threat. Is spectral Emma a racial memory of this kind? It is possible; King John, in any case, made a handy scapegoat. There seem to have been no sightings in this area for many years.

A far more potent and equally ancient haunting concerns the castle of Barnwell in Northamptonshire. Both the castle and the manor house across a stretch of smooth lawns are owned by the Duke of Gloucester, cousin of Queen Elizabeth II. The castle is ruined now, though its remains are considerable and impressive, and its atmosphere is a strange blend of the serene and the disturbing.

I was introduced to it in 1973 when doing research for *Haunted East Anglia*. In the course of those researches I met a local historian named Tom Litchfield, who farmed on the

Barnwell estate and whose interest in the castle had drawn my attention to its existence and strange story.

The castle was completed in 1264 by a Norman magnate, Reginald Le Moine, and is notable for its massive, three-bastioned gatehouse, an unusual feature since most castle builders confined themselves to two bastions, one either side of the entrance gateway. In Barnwell's case, most of the gateway is intact, and its three bastions appear almost as rugged and threatening as they must have been in the days of their building. The local villagers do not regard them with affection, for over the years many unnerving occurrences have taken place in the castle's neighbourhood, and in particular in the area around the south side of the ruins.

Several times in recent years, people walking nearby have experienced a sound 'like a rushing wind' out of the otherwise still night, leaving an equal calm in its wake. In one case the village postmaster, giving his dog a late night outing, went in search of the animal, which had run off towards the castle. The man was approaching the southern wall when he experienced a noise and a sensation like a wind rushing by. 'At the same time my dog raced past me towards the road, her hair standing up. She was waiting and trembling on the doorstep of the post office when I got home.' On another occasion a policeman on patrol in the area encountered the inexplicable wind. It was either this or another patrolling constable in about the year 1934 who had said (reported to me by Tom Litchfield), 'There is one place in the old castle where I wouldn't go for all the tea in China'. His reference was to the building's north-east tower.

I have discussed fully in *Haunted East Anglia* the details of the three séances held in September and November 1948 by Tom Litchfield and a friend of his who possessed some psychic ability. Both men were curious about the Barnwell castle stories. What they hoped to discover from the ouija activities I do not know, but they could hardly have expected the grimly macabre results they achieved.

In the first séance the men apparently contacted a thirteenth-century chatelaine of the castle, Marie, wife of Berengarius Le Moine, son of the original builder. According to this contact, the woman had been kept prisoner by being walled up in the castle while it was still in the building. In a question and answer session 'Marie' had said that her life had been ruined, and in answer to Litchfield's further questioning as to 'her' meaning replied:

A. Heathen rule enforcing a brutish captivity.
Q. Who imprisoned you?
A. Secret. I can never betray my soul's secret.

'She' added that the death had been a terrible one.

Subsequently researches by Mr Litchfield revealed that one of the Le Moine wives had certainly been named Marie. There is also a local legend (though with no historical basis) that Berengarius Le Moine walled up a woman alive into Barnwell castle. According to records of the area, a certain Marie Le Moine died in 1245.

The two experimenters progressed to their second séance, which was even odder than the first. The castle's builder Reginald Le Moine announced himself (referring to himself as 'the left bastion') and then his son and successor, Berengarius, took up the thread. In answer to Litchfield's question about what was hidden in the left bastion, the reply was

A. The horrid remnants of suppression which befell an honest lord. William forced my reason.
Q. Who is William?
A. We call him covert in Ramsey.

This response was believed to refer to Abbot William of Ramsey or Godmanchester, to whom Berengarius Le Moine was forced to cede the castle and lands in 1276. The abbot had a local reputation for secretiveness and guile, particularly in relation to financial dealings. The details of the transactions between the two men are not known, but the lands on which the castle were built appear originally to have belonged to Godmanchester Abbey. Was Le Moine in the abbot's debt? Had Le Moine seized church lands unlawfully? And what kind of spiritual or political pressure was brought to bear on him strong enough to force the handing over of his new great castle and the land on which it stood? 'William forced my reason' said Berengarius Le Moine, apparently in excuse for 'the horrid remnants of suppression' which existed in the castle's left bastion. How and why did William of Godmanchester force his reason? By demanding as early as 1245 that the sacrilegious castle be handed over? Marie Le Moine died in that year so, if she were 'suppressed' as a result of her husband's disturbed state of mind, what was the reason? Did she support the abbot in his claim for restitution, perhaps, and had her furious husband retaliated by shutting her up both vocally and physically? The 'honest lord' appears as confused in his reply to Tom Litchfield as he had been in real life.

The affair was strange enough at this stage, but with the third and final séance it became odder still. This was held in the north-east tower of Barnwell Castle on the night of 9 November 1948. The time was about 9.00 p.m. In one part of this tower, a chunk of fallen masonry forms a flat, table-like area, and it was here the two enquirers set out their ouija symbols. They placed a storm lantern to one side for illumination, though it served as much to cast shadows as light. The fragments of an alcove above their heads, the remains of the tower's one-time Upper Chamber, were shiftingly visible. The session was brief and horrifying.

Q. I wish to ask further questions. Are you willing?
A. Yes. The soul ascends to realms immortal but the flesh to worms most vile.
Q. Who is speaking?
A. I am the second bastion, Berengarius Le Moine.

Q. What have you to say?
A. I will fire to warn you.

Then, at once, in the tower, above their heads, came the loud crack of a pistol shot, or of a whip. The men raised their heads in alarm, and saw or thought they saw the upper part of a man's body in the inner doorway to the courtyard. It was dressed in the garb of a monk. The investigators left the scene in great haste.

Tom Litchfield was first and foremost an historian. He was not content to leave the matter there, though his friend, living seven miles away, was discouraged from proceeding by one remarkable fact. In the early hours of the morning following that last grim séance, he heard in his bedroom an exact replication of the whipcrack they had both heard earlier.

Tom uncovered the sequel to this disquieting series of events. In the Church of All Saints at Sawtrey, ten miles from Barnwell, the Le Moine family is commemorated by a brass tablet. Above the inscription is an insignia in the form of the upper torso of a monk, holding a whip in his hands. What is the significance of this? Did the Abbot of Godmanchester or Ramsey, by applying the whip of church discipline to the Le Moines, alter their history in a way which needed commemoration? A kind of unearthly reminder to eschew the sins of sacrilege and pride? Or was the materialization of monk and whipcrack during the ouija session merely intended to identify the speaker beyond doubt as a member of the Le Moine family, whose insignia it was?

Marie Le Moine had referred to her 'soul's secret', and did not name her murderer, though it seems clear she was killed by being walled into a dungeon in the castle building. But a dungeon has never been found at Barnwell, although all Norman castles of this period possessed one. In addition, there are the repeated references to the left-hand bastion, the significance of which is not clear. The wall of the far left bastion is abnormally thick and although it has a slit window on the outside this cannot be seen from within. Ten or twelve feet of space are unaccounted for in the width of the outer wall. It is significant that the rushing wind experienced by local people has invariably occurred near the gatehouse.

The curious factors in this bizarre haunting seem to point to the murder of Marie Le Moine by her husband, Berengarius, for reasons not known, but possibly connected with the possession of the castle land by the Abbot of Ramsey. Lacking further evidence, we can only guess at the rest of the story. The additional thickness of the wall in the far-left tower probably conceals a small room, and that room may hold the remains of a chest and of Marie Le Moine herself. Only excavation will prove the truth or falsehood of this surmise, and the present owner, the Duke of Gloucester, is unlikely to undertake it. Nor would I if I were Barnwell's owner.

Barnwell, for all its beauty (and it is a village of remarkable charm), retains an unusually strong historical atmosphere, a feeling of inhabiting both past and present. The strange magic of the castle seems to embrace the royal manor house opposite and the village itself. Whether the present inhabitants of the manor are aware of the secret of their thirteenth-century neighbour, I do not know. I believe that Princess Alice, the Dowager Duchess of Gloucester, knows the story, although she has not mentioned it in her delightful *Memoirs*.

As for the Le Moines – Reginald, Berengarius and Marie – if it were indeed they whom Tom Litchfield and his friend reached in their ouija sessions, how is it possible that they should still be concerned seven hundred years later with the castle they built in Barnwell? Perhaps it is less the castle which holds their attention than the crime committed there. If this is so and Berengarius and Marie survive in some form, they have apparently not yet overcome the spiritual damage inflicted at that time. Guilt and horror imprison them still in a past which (supposing one believes in survivals) they should long since have outgrown. This type of perpetuation can happen in the ordinary course of incarnate life. Can it also occur in the long reaches of life after death, when the energy or spirit is free of its body?

From my own researches and those of greater renown, it seems that the past, present and future divisions of chronological time have almost no relevance in the post-death state. There is little distinction between them. Individuals appear to exist in states of being and states of awareness rather than states of time. In order to make any progress in spiritual terms, it is necessary to resolve, then leave behind the mistakes of the last earthly life. If this cannot be done, the entity stays frozen in the particular time and place of earthly disaster. It must have been thus with the Le Moines of Barnwell.

To end this chapter, here is an account which is not tragic, unless one regards all death as tragic, which I do not.

Jedburgh Castle is about the first major monument to greet the eye if you have come into Scotland over the Cheviots and driven into Jedburgh town in Roxburghshire. The present façade, however, is nineteenth century, built upon the foundations of the original twelfth-century structure.

In the first castle of Jedburgh Alexander III married Yolande, whose father was the Count of Dreux. Although it was not the king's first marriage, he had no surviving male heir, and it was this that prompted him to wed again. Alexander had lost two children already, and a third, Margaret, who had married King Erik II of Norway, died giving birth to her daughter Margaret, a child later to be known as The Maid of Norway.

In October 1285 the wedding feast for the king and the beautiful Yolande was celebrated, and Alexander must have been filled with hope. He was forty-five years old, had taken a new young bride, and could surely expect to father sons who would secure the shaky and turbulent throne of Scotland. The occasion was one of rejoicing; the food was plentiful, the golden beverages flowed freely, and mummers and tumblers performed in the hall of the castle for the guests' entertainment. Then the noise and music of the revels abruptly faded into silence as a tall, cowled figure appeared in a corner of the hall. Such was its power that those who were nearest shrank away, and all the watchers felt a thrill of apprehension. The figure wore a mask, which suggested Death, as its garments hinted at grave cerements. Who or what was it which appeared to threaten the King's happiness and hospitality? As they watched, mesmerized, as rabbits by a stoat, the figure glided through the crowd. Not one of that gathering of gilded courtiers dared touch him, but when at last they plucked up courage to seize the mummer and throw him out of the castle for the tastelessness of his joke, he disintegrated in their hands. They were left clutching empty air, with a feeling of utter dread. There was nothing inside the clothes and mask.

There was little doubt in anybody's mind that what they had seen was a harbinger of ill-luck if not of death. Five months later, Alexander, riding back from Edinburgh to Kinghorn on a night of wild storm, had his horse stumble under him and was thrown over a nearby cliff and killed. The eventuality the king had feared had occurred; he had died without male issue, and in the kingdom of Scotland there was another bloody struggle for the crown.

A tall, black figure, hooded or cowled, is an archetypal image of death, and invariably appears to the house or person threatened. What it is and what conjures it into being is impossible to say. It seems to arise from some deep awareness in the human race itself, and has certainly been recorded many times in the course of history. Such archetypal warnings have become part of our folklore, having their origins perhaps in some aspect of the pagan religions which Christianity supplanted. Thus, white doves or an owl perching on a house, a picture or a mirror falling inexplicably from a wall, a sudden exodus of rats from a ship about to leave port, a dog howling outside the house – all these seemed to presage death. Most terrifying of all was the tall, dark figure, cloaked and hooded, which manifested itself on certain occasions. We retain the memory of these beliefs even while we scoff at them. They have an ancient history and once had great power over the human imagination. The fact that they are now reduced to the level of superstitions has drawn some but not all of their sting. Some part of us retains the memory of dread and still shrinks a little from their contact.

CHAPTER FOUR

The Fourteenth Century

Once, in a privileged and unguarded moment, I asked an eminent lady about the ghosts which are said to haunt Windsor Castle. She denied that any such phenomena existed, 'Windsor Castle', she said firmly, 'is certainly *not* haunted.' She, if anyone, was in a position to know, but the tradition of ghosts at Windsor is a long one.

Who better to haunt those stately stones than he who was partly responsible for its design, William of Wykeham? He has been seen on a number of occasions on the Round Tower, surveying his handiwork as though he were well pleased with it. The building has already stood for six hundred years and is likely to stand for another thousand or more, so its architect has every reason to be proud. Perhaps these were his feelings when his part in the structure was done, and he climbed to the battlements to look around him. But it is not Windsor's ghosts which dominate the fourteenth century; it is the echoes of Edward II, his wife Isabella, daughter of Philip IV of France, and her lover, Roger Mortimer.

That century also saw Chaucer (humorist and storyteller, courtier and poet) writing *The Canterbury Tales*. In them he depicted a way of life whose bawdy wit, worldly cynicism and warm wisdom were a reflection of the growing nation. The English were becoming conscious of themselves as a unity rather than an amalgam of different races. The woollen industry was blossoming into a flourishing cloth trade which had already begun to spread across the country; the moral and religious life had not yet broken down into sectarianism, and this imposed a sense of fellowship upon lord and commoner alike. True, those who had been serfs were demanding some measure of freedom, but this was a healthy sign, an indication that even the peasants were looking ahead and forming ambitions for the future. It was a symbol of growing national confidence. All would no doubt have been well had the infant England been sure in its leadership, but in Edward II they had an ineffectual young man living in the shadow of a great father.

Edward's hopeful beginnings (he had been created the first Prince of Wales after his father's subjugation of that country) soon became lost in a welter of opposition from the barons. There were signs of revolt at the end of Edward I's reign, for the magnates had grown tired of financing the king's interminable wars. Young Edward inherited an explosive situation and a hostility to the throne which his own behaviour did nothing to improve.

In spite of the young king's marriage to Isabella of Angoulême, he appears to have been a latent if not a practising homosexual. His friendship with Piers Gaveston almost brought him to disaster. It had begun in boyhood, when Gaveston was chosen as his companion. Edward's mother had died during his childhood and his dominating father was perpetually absent on military campaigns, so it was hardly surprising that the boys' relationship developed an unhealthy intensity.

Edward was always to be more at ease with commoners than with his own class, and in the case of his friendships he showed an extraordinary loyalty. The old king, well aware of his son's tendencies and fiercely critical, had banished Piers Gaveston, making Prince Edward swear that he would not recall his favourite without Parliament's consent – a consent not likely to be given.

No sooner was Edward I buried than his son recalled his bosom friend from exile and infuriated the barons by creating Piers Earl of Cornwall and giving him £50,000. Gaveston, though a skilled horseman and an expert performer in the tournament, seems to have had little idea of self-preservation. In the year of his reinstatement, he had the tactlessness to unhorse most of his noble opponents at the great Wallingford tournament and made matters worse by giving his enemies uncomplimentary nicknames – The Black Dog for the Earl of Warwick; the Old Hog for the Earl of Lancaster and so forth. Fury and resentment against the upstart grew after Edward's marriage to Isabella, for it became obvious that the beautiful young bride was to take second place in the king's affections to the beautiful young man.

Edward refused to bow to baronial pressure to exile Gaveston again, and seems to have delighted in annoying his nobles still further by extravagant gifts and gestures of affection to the favourite. In 1312 the barons rebelled and the king and Gaveston fled in different directions. Gaveston hid in Scarborough Castle, but was winkled out by the barons and taken to Deddington Castle, Oxfordshire, for summary execution. After this personal blow, Edward appears to have come to an uneasy truce with the barons, though it was not long before he found another close companion, Henry Despencer, who was no more to the nobles' taste than had been Gaveston.

The situation now began to alter. The chief opposition to Edward was led by the Earl of Lancaster and another powerful magnate, Sir Roger Mortimer. Since the latter was beginning to form a liaison with the isolated and neglected young Queen Isabella, Edward had good reason for speedy action. He assaulted and took Lancaster's castles at Kenilworth and Berkeley, and imprisoned Mortimer in the Tower of London. He completed his unexpected hat-trick by beating Lancaster in the open field at Boroughbridge and beheading the Old Hog in March 1322. He had avenged Piers Gaveston.

Edward's triumph was brief. Mortimer, aided by the Queen, escaped from the Tower and fled to France, where Isabella's brother, Charles IV, gave him sanctuary. The queen followed him, bringing with her her young son. King Edward, under pressure from the two Despencers, father and son, ordered the queen to return, but Isabella organized matters for herself by coming back with her lover, Mortimer, and landing in Suffolk with a few followers, their intention being to depose Edward.

Now the country decided its allegiance, for as support for Edward waned that for the queen's party grew. Edward and Hugh Despencer, attempting to fly England, were captured and handed over to the queen's followers. Despencer was hanged and the king imprisoned first in Kenilworth then successively in Corfe, Bristol and Berkeley Castles. By this time Edward no longer ruled. He had been deposed in January 1327, and replaced by his fourteen-year-old son, with the queen and Mortimer as regents.

Edward's fate was inevitable. As long as he lived he posed a threat to the new régime. At what point did Mortimer and his royal mistress decide that the king must die? At first he seems to have been treated with kindness, then as support grew for the ex-king and plots were made to rescue him, the regents saw the danger. At one point Edward's friends did succeed in freeing him from Berkeley, only to have him recaptured and once more incarcerated within its cold walls, this time with a sterner gaoler, Sir Thomas Gurney. By now Mortimer was alert to the threat, and sent instructions to Gurney that Edward was to be disposed of. The method of that murder was particularly repugnant. It was designed by someone with a devious mind, to leave no mark upon Edward's body which could lead to an accusation of murder against the king's enemies. Edward of Carnarvon died an excruciating death, during which his screams could be heard throughout the castle.

For years after his death these shrieks were heard at Berkeley, though they have not occurred within living memory and the dungeon walls may have relinquished whatever record they had of the murder. (It is known that the psychic record frequently present in an environment and whose replay constitutes some types of haunting fades in strength over a long period of time, eventually ceasing entirely.)

There are alternative stories regarding Edward's fate. Manuel Feschi, a Genoese priest who had worked in England, later wrote to Edward III that his father had escaped abroad, and was at that time living in Lombardy. This has never been proved, and it seems likely that the ex-king was murdered on Mortimer's instructions.

Whether or not Edward II actually haunted Berkeley, some characters in the drama certainly seem to have left a psychic echo in other areas. The young Edward III had watched with disquiet the increasing misuse of power by Roger Mortimer, and the queen's unwillingness or inability to check it. The news of his father's death must also have wounded him, leaving him with the desire to be revenged and to establish himself as absolute rather than puppet ruler.

Isabella and her lover were now living in Nottingham Castle, with a strong Welsh bodyguard, and such was the impregnability of the fortress that there was little chance of breaking into it by conventional means to drag out the guilty regent. However, the young king learned that a secret tunnel existed connecting the interior of the castle with a hostelry known as The Trip to Jerusalem, situated outside, and at the foot of the cliff on which the castle stood. One night a handful of the king's men crept through it and burst into the queen's chamber, arresting Mortimer before her eyes, though she pleaded with them in the language of her land and time 'Bel fitz, eiez pitié du gentil Mortimer!' Since 'fitz' is the Norman French for son, it seems that young Edward was with the storming party.

The queen's pleas had no effect, for Mortimer, having first been imprisoned in the dungeons below Nottingham Castle, was taken to London, convicted of murdering the king's father and hanged at Tyburn on 29 November 1330. Isabella was removed to Castle Rising in Norfolk and kept under house arrest there until her death twenty-eight years later. Some authorities refer to her confinement as imprisonment or enforced retirement, but it amounts to the same thing. She was segregated from all sources of power and out of reach of friendship; a bitter and lonely exile.

The Trip to Jerusalem still exists, its name commemorating its foundation in 1189 in a time of crusading fervour. Some of its underground cellars are carved out of the solid rock on which the castle stands, and from time to time the sound of a man's footsteps have been heard, restlessly tramping up and down, covering an apparently small space, then turning and repeating the process *ad infinitum*. An animal caged and waiting for an inevitable end, as Mortimer waited before Tyburn. The nearby dungeon is still known as Mortimer's Hole.

Marc Alexander in his excellent *Haunted Castles* recounts the experience of a group of American soldiers who, during World War II, visited The Trip to Jerusalem. They had left the bar and were on their way past the castle when somewhere above their heads they heard the frenzied voice of a woman screaming. They were unable to make head or tail of what was said, since the words seemed to be in a foreign language. Local people who were consulted were certain that it was Isabella's voice, the queen crying yet again 'Fair son, have pity on sweet Mortimer!'

Some say the ghost of the distraught queen may still be seen in the old corridors of Nottingham Castle, vainly seeking the lover locked away in his dungeon. If this still happens, it has its origin in an actual search made by the queen at the time of Mortimer's arrest. It is such frenzied actions which seem to impress themselves upon their surroundings.

Towards the end of her imprisonment in Castle Rising, Isabella's reason became unbalanced. This is not surprising considering that the castle is a forbidding building in the cold, flat landscape of north-west Norfolk. The wind howls dementedly around it in winter, and the queen, shut away from all contact with normal life, must have had little to occupy her time during the endless years of her incarceration. Long before her death in 1358 she became insane, and the echoes of her crazy laughter are sometimes heard in the castle ruins.

The She-wolf of France, as Isabella became known, is also said to haunt the churchyard of the Grey Friars in Newgate Street, London. Perhaps she was kept there during the time of Mortimer's trial. I do not know what form this haunting takes or if it still happens.

As for Piers Gaveston, whose friendship with the young Edward II had such fateful consequences, he is said to haunt the heights of Scarborough Castle, the last place he saw on earth.

Two points of interest arise out of this bizarre piece of history. The first is that Edward II's remains (if they were his; for another of the rumours surrounding the hideous screams in Berkeley is that they were those of a porter murdered by Edward when he escaped from the place) – that the king's remains were buried in Gloucester Cathedral, where in time his tomb became a place of holy pilgrimage. A more unlikely fate for the pleasure-loving Edward can hardly be imagined. Still, the church of the time found martyrs and the pilgrims they attracted profitable, and little was done to discourage the pilgrimages.

The second lies in the sentence heard by the wartime GIs as they passed beneath Nottingham Castle's walls. Foreign speech? If it were Isabella's desperate plea then it would have sounded so. But speech heard paranormally or psychically invariably sounds garbled, so that one is not sure whether one is hearing a foreign language or one's own with a degree of distortion. I have had several such experiences and have never been able to interpret what was spoken, although each time the rhythm of it has suggested that the language must be English.

A theory is that when the original words were 'recorded' by

the surroundings in which they were uttered x number of years ago, the sounds they made were of a certain frequency which the human brain could receive and identify. However, the 're-broadcasting agency' (i.e. the immediate surroundings) might have played them back later at a different frequency, thus making them unintelligible to the human brain. Had the words been taped when heard and then replayed at their original frequency, they would no doubt have made sense. (A case of this type is cited in my book *The Mask of Time.*) Certainly some recognizable form of recording and re-broadcasting seems to supply the mechanism for many forms of haunting.

From 1306–1329 Robert Bruce, descendant of the Anglo-Norman family of de Brus, was King of Scots, but he had not won that title easily or without bloodshed. He had for a while served the English crown in its Scottish struggles, and had even been appointed one of three joint Guardians of Scotland. However, his strong personal ambitions would not be satisfied by serving the English.

By 1306, Bruce's chief rival for the throne of Scotland was John Comyn the Red, and the two men mistrusted each other as only political rivals can. Bruce was thirty-one years old and the head of his family. Three times he had rebelled against the English king Edward I, and three times had been forced into humiliating submission and service. Red John Comyn had been a Guardian of Scotland with Bruce, but the two had quarrelled bitterly over some land, and Red Comyn had so far lost his temper as to seize Bruce by the throat. Neither forgave the other and hostility between them fermented.

Bruce appears to have been a devious man and perhaps deliberately plotted to remove this rival when the two next met. Curiously, Bruce chose a church for the rendezvous – that of the Minorite friars in Dumfries – and the idea was that there would be a council between himself and Comyn. Maybe the sacred nature of the place was intended as a reassurance to Bruce's rival; or maybe Bruce felt that he would be freer to act in such surroundings. Whatever the motive, the rival claimants met in February 1306, with disastrous results. Far from reaching agreement, the men quarrelled violently. Bruce drew a dagger and plunged it into Comyn's body, then rushed out of the building to tell his followers that he thought he had killed the Red Comyn. His friend Roger de Kirkpatrick was all for making sure, and ran back inside with some of Bruce's supporters. There seems to have been a skirmish en route, for Comyn's uncle was killed when he thrust his sword at Bruce (the armour the latter wore deflected the blow). Immediately afterwards the wounded Comyn was attacked where he lay and killed by the dirks of Kirkpatrick's followers. If the Minorite friars witnessed this bloody encounter, they probably had enough sense of self-preservation to pretend ignorance.

It is impossible to say whether or not this was a premeditated murder, though Bruce's immediate reaction suggests there was a plan. He ordered his followers to seize Dumfries Castle, then rode to Glasgow to seek absolution from Bishop Wishart – who, by the speed with which he gave it, showed calculated and cynical self-interest. Five weeks after murdering Comyn, Robert Bruce was crowned King of Scotland at Scone. His subsequent career was either brutal or glorious, depending on which side of the border you happened to live.

Only the site of the old friary of the Minorites is left, but there is still an echo of the past. It is said that both Bruce and Kirkpatrick haunt the area from time to time, no doubt reliving the events and furious sensations of that February morning in 1306. As I have said, it is such heightened emotions which record strongly enough on the surroundings to be retained for centuries. Hauntings, if they are genuine, might give us some knowledge of actual historical events.

Edward, Prince of Wales, eldest son of that renowned fighter Edward III of England, is better known to posterity by his nickname. At an early age he must have shown a liking for all-black armour, for it is as the Black Prince that every schoolchild recognizes him. He, too, was no mean warrior, and was renowned for his chivalry in battle.

England's policies were changing. After the Scottish wars of Edward I's time his grandson, Edward III, had been obliged to acknowledge Scottish independence under Bruce. He then turned his attention to France, where a failure in the male line of French kings had left what seemed to the young king an interesting vacuum. This, and the new development of the arrow as a powerful weapon of war, might have given him the confidence to tackle a long overseas adventure. It was to be very long indeed, lasting 115 years on and off.

It was inevitable that the Black Prince, brought up to knightly arts and warrior expectations should spend more and more time campaigning in France. He was to lead the vanguard at Crécy, and later developed a type of long-range guerilla raiding technique known as 'chevauchées' – *à cheval*, i.e. by cavalry.

Unfortunately we do not know what kind of king the Black Prince would have made, for he never reached the throne, but died at the early age of forty-six. However, he has left two records of himself. One is the inscrutable effigy on his tomb in Canterbury Cathedral. The other is his ghost at Hall Place, near Bexley, Kent, where he regularly stayed en route to and from the French wars. His phantom usually appears at dusk, generally clad in full armour. Often his appearances are accompanied by distant music played on mediaeval instruments. The manifestation is said to be an omen, either to the occupants of the house or to England itself. He was seen during World War I on three occasions, each time before a major British defeat. The members of the occupying family, too, can testify to the ill omen of his appearances.

The ghostly music is an interesting feature, as it may be a record of music played while the warrior prince was in residence during his lifetime. An echo of similar age occurs in

Fotheringhay church, Northamptonshire, where the sound of 'drums and trumpets' playing music of the fourteenth and fifteenth centuries has been heard from time to time. Fotheringhay has connections with the Hundred Years War, because the greater part of the church was built by Edmund Plantagenet, the fifth son of Edward III, and brother to the Black Prince. It is *his* son, Edmund de Langley, who is buried within the church, his body having been brought back there from the field of Agincourt.

Of that major prince of the fourteenth century, John of Gaunt, there is little psychic trace, though two buildings formerly owned by him are said to be haunted. The castle he built for himself at Bolingbroke in South Lincolnshire (and in which his son, the future Henry IV, was born), is now just a few turf-covered mounds which conceal the old walls. Here and there fragments of walls break through like rotten teeth from receding gums, and one catches a flying idea of the castle as it must have looked in its heyday – all bustle and colour as the great lord and his last lady (reputedly the one love of his life, Katherine Swynford) came down to it for a few days' peace.

In its less decrepit days, the castle was said to be haunted by the form of a hare, which local people asserted was the spirit of a witch imprisoned there. The Harleian Ms gives a lively description of the haunting:

> . . . . ye castle is haunted by a certain spirit in ye likenesse of a Hare, which at meetings of ye Auditors doeth usually run between their legs, and sometimes overthrows them, and so passes away. They have pursued it downe into ye Castle yard and seene it take in at a grate into a low cellar, and have followed it with a light, where notwithstanding that they did most narrowly observe it (and that there was no other passage out, but by ye doore or windowe, ye room being above all framed of stones within, not having ye least chink or crevice) yet they could never find it.

Christina Hole, who quotes this story in *Haunted England*, comments that dogs also often chased the elusive hare into the cellar, only to have it vanish under their paws. Invariably the baffled canines came out whining with terror.

This type of occurrence is more likely to relate to the ghost of an actual hare than to the spectre of a witch *turned into a spectral hare*, as interpreted by the Harleian Ms. Ghost animals are quite common, and if this one is associated at all with the unlucky witch, it may have been as an actual pet hare; or even of a wild hare which used the cellar as a bolt-hole to escape human or canine tormentors in its lifetime. Witch or hare, at least it had the sense to upset the pursuing Auditors (were they auditing accounts or merely listening in to local events?). A more intriguing ghost inhabits one, if not two, of John o' Gaunt's former houses in the South of England.

Wargrave is a charming village on the banks of the Thames in Berkshire and falls well within the area of Gaunt's enormous landholdings. The extent of these can be gauged by the number of inns named *The Red Lion*. A red lion was the Prince's symbol, and it was a mark of respect to name a hostelry in his honour.

Two large and beautiful cottages stand together in Wargrave, one known as Little Gaunt, the other as Gaunt Cottage. Local tradition has it that they were originally one, used by John of Gaunt when he was in the neighbourhood. The building had once been named Queen Emma's House, and one or two local families still call it so. Emma, daughter of Duke Richard I of Normandy and great-aunt of William the Conqueror, married successively Aethelred Unraed ('the Unready') and Cnut (or Canute), and held considerable power in England. Had she also owned a house in Wargrave, which would later belong to her distant descendant, Prince John of Gaunt? She seems to be the only Queen Emma in the history of the English monarchy and must therefore be a candidate for the original ownership.

But it was the owner of Gaunt Cottage who told me when I

visited in 1977 that both her home and its neighbour were haunted by a woman in white. She walks through from one building into the other as though they were still one property. The owner of Little Gaunt, however, who had occupied the cottage for twenty-four years, was certain there was not a ghost in her home. The accounts of the two neighbours conflicted. However, not everyone detects a ghost even when their own home is reputed to be haunted; or welcomes it when they do. The paranormal is intercepted only by a mind which can 'receive' and 'translate' the information available in an area. Many individuals have brains which operate against such activity; they do not experience so-called psychic events because of the way their brains function. This seems to be a physical fact and has nothing to do with scepticism, rational thinking or commonsense. We consider this aspect more fully later on.

After the death of the Black Prince, his son Richard became the heir of Edward III, and on the latter's death was crowned King Richard II. Although the new king was a man of culture who delighted in music, art and the literature of his time, he had come to the throne at the age of eleven after an isolated and lonely childhood. This was the time of the Renaissance, and the remarkable flowering of art and knowledge on the continent of Europe had begun to permeate Britain.

Unfortunately Richard was faced by a group of nobles with whom he had little in common; they in turn, men to whom combat meant more than culture, found him alien and unsatisfactory. It was the old story of barons versus monarch, and ended as unfortunately as had the power struggles between Edward II and his magnates; and as would the challenge of Parliament to Charles I. Richard was deposed and died a prisoner in Pontefract Castle. Although his body appeared unmarked after death, it was believed that he had been murdered on the orders of his usurping cousin, Henry Bolingbroke, the son of John of Gaunt. With the death of

Richard, the English Renaissance came to a premature end.

Although there is no ghost story associated with Pontefract Castle, the place of the king's imprisonment and death, a haunting exists for which Richard II may have been partly responsible.

The official version of the story of Herne the Hunter is that Herne was a keeper in Windsor Forest during Richard's reign and that, during the pursuit of a stag which turned at bay, the huntsman saved the king's life at the expense of his own. As the man lay dying, a stranger came out of the forest and offered to save him by magic. The king agreed, and the newcomer bound a pair of stag's horns on the head of the wounded man, and said that he would nurse the huntsman back to health. The king, grateful for his life, promised Herne that when he recovered he should be made head hunstman of the royal forest.

This promotion infuriated the remaining huntsmen, and as soon as they were out of sight of their monarch, they threatened Herne's magic healer with death if he did not undo his magic and dispose of his patient at once. The wise man resisted the blackmail, but promised that Herne would not be the hunt leader for long. There was some suggestion by the wizard that whoever damaged Herne would come under a curse, whose nature was not made plain. Herne eventually returned to duty but, strangely, had forgotten all his skills, so much so that the king dismissed him from his service. Whereupon the unhappy man hanged himself from a great oak tree in the Park. For centuries afterwards this was known as Herne's Oak, and Herne was said to appear beneath it, dressed in his hunting clothes – with a pair of great stag's antlers bound to his head.

On stormy nights, Herne can still occasionally be heard hunting the forest with his followers, the envious huntsmen on whom his curse fell.

There are several versions of the Herne hauntings, one being that the monarch concerned was Henry VIII rather than

Richard II; and that Herne had been a necromancer whose practices caused him to hang himself (or be hanged by someone else?) in the Great Park of Windsor. All the versions agree that from time to time the body of Herne was seen swinging from the oak's branches. Until, that is, 'his' tree was inadvertently cut down with other decayed trees in 1796 by order of George III. The king was extremely upset when he understood what had happened. It was by then a very ancient and decrepit oak, which implies that it was already a great age two hundred years previously.

Shakespeare's *The Merry Wives of Windsor* deals at length with the legend, which was obviously well known in his time.

The significance of the Herne story is that the strange apparition still appears. I was told by one of the eminent residents of Windsor Castle that the figure has been seen in this century. His appearance, like one or two other of the 'classical' ghosts, seems to be a harbinger of bad tidings for England. The Wild Hunt was heard in 1936 by two Eton schoolboys, who were dismayed to hear the baying of hounds and the sound of horses' hooves galloping towards them. More than dismayed when, with a draught of ice-cold air, many feet rushed past them. They *saw* nothing at all.

One final story seems to have its origins in the fourteenth century. It concerns that remarkable castle, once the centre of royal government, at Bamburgh on the Northumberland coast.

Anyone who has chanced accidentally on Bamburgh Castle is unlikely to forget it. It lies along the cliffs like a recumbent lion, its head reared to keep watch on the sea breaking at its feet. Bamburgh is actually built on the rocks which rim the shore of England's wild and beautiful north-east coast. At low tide, the sands stretch away from the castle's foot to the cold sea's edge and one can ride, drive or walk along them and look up at the fierce old building above. The sense of age and history are overpowering. So imposing is Bamburgh as a representative of the past, that it was used as scenic background in the film *Becket*.

Bamburgh effortlessly dwarfed the film, for it was the capital of such small kingdom of Britain as then existed; the kingdom of Bernicia, ruled by King Ida, AD 547–559. The place was named after Queen Bebba, who married Ida's grandson, Ethelfrith. Bebbanburgh became in time Bamburgh, and the castle has played an active part in British history almost without interruption since then. Legend has it that this was the original 'Joyous-Garde' owned by Lancelot of the Lake, Arthur's lieutenant. If Arthur were indeed a sixth-century ruler whose reign ended in 547 (see Chapter 1), Ida might have taken the castle on the death of Sir Lancelot; fanciful and totally unprovable but vastly attractive as a romantic notion.

Bamburgh has beauty, dignity and a suggestion of impregnability. When I visited it some years ago, I felt strongly that I had been there before, though I had not and I felt the same shock of delighted surprise experienced by most people. A more extraordinary feeling occurred when I entered the turret which houses a small picture gallery. Three portraits there struck me as being familiar. All were of the Forster family who had lived in and owned the castle in the eighteenth century; they were of a man, a woman and a young girl. I seemed to 'recognize' all three; the first two I felt I had known in real life, and I felt I had once been the third, the girl, at an earlier stage in time. It was, however, the face of the man which filled me with a sense of fear and dread, as though he had been responsible for a great personal unhappiness.

I learned that the couple had been uncle and aunt of the girl, Dorothy Forster; and that this girl had, at the age of twenty-one, married Nathaniel, Lord Crewe, Bishop of Durham, a man of seventy-one. Was this an arranged marriage? If so, by whom? By the girl's uncle, perhaps? And could this have been the cause of her unhappiness and fear? Certainly the portrait of the male Forster generated for me a shuddering sense of evil, and I was glad to leave the turret behind.

My mother's family were Border people, and would have known Bamburgh well, though there is no evidence of any connection with the Forsters. Dorothy haunts not Bamburgh, but *The Lord Crewe Arms* at Blanchland, and the identity of this ghost may have become confused with that of her niece, also a Dorothy.

Whatever the explanation for my personal unease in Bamburgh's gallery, the experience was less that of a haunting than a previous incarnation. Or did I merely pick up old intimations of mortality and unhappiness where they had once been experienced?

I have no direct evidence of the actual haunting of Bamburgh, though Joseph Braddock in *Haunted Houses* mentions a Miss Sylvia Calmady-Hamlyn whose relatives owned the castle in the late nineteenth century. Some time between 1898 and 1900, Miss Calmady-Hamlyn occupied rooms in the twelfth century keep, and both saw and heard a ghost in her bedroom. According to her account, the spectre appeared 'filmy grey'. He walked across the floor of the room, accompanied by the sound of 'clanking chains'. It was not until he left the room to walk along the passage and down the steps outside that she heard the even louder clank of his boots. The tradition of this ghost is that it is a knight in armour.The sound of 'clanking' is certainly compatible with the clattering of a man in plate-armour, or even in chain-mail, though the former is the more likely to produce the sound described by Miss Calmady-Hamlyn.

In its earlier days Bamburgh would have known armoured knights. The castle's towers were completed by Henry II in the second half of the twelfth century. Perhaps he and Becket did indeed ride to meet each other on those wide, chill sands between the towering castle and the bleak North Sea, as in the film. Historical truth is every bit as strange as filmed fiction.

CHAPTER FIVE

The Fifteenth Century

By the beginning of the fifteenth century, the House of Lancaster had taken over the throne of England. Richard II had been deposed ('persuaded' to renounce the throne) and had been replaced by his cousin, Henry of Bolingbroke, son of John of Gaunt, Duke of Lancaster. When this king, Henry IV, died, his son Henry Prince of Wales was twenty-six, and after a wild and turbulent youth faced the shock of sudden kingship with surprising maturity. Shakespeare's playboy Prince Hal grew overnight into the active warrior and diplomat history knows as Henry V.

England's old right to Aquitaine and comparatively recent claim to the entire French kingdom had fuelled the Hundred Years War, in spite of a temporary truce during the reign of Richard II. The young Henry V had no intention of renewing a truce which would have denied his right to the French crown, and in 1415 he led an expeditionary force across the Channel, settling down before Harfleur for a month-long siege. Shakespeare gives a splendid and probably highly flattering portrait of the young king in full spate before Harfleur.

> Once more unto the breach, dear friends, once more,
> Or close the wall up with our English dead!

and ends Hal's clarion call to death or glory with

> Follow your spirit; and upon this charge
> Cry 'God for Harry! England and Saint George!'

Marvellously stirring stuff, though it is unlikely the reality bore much resemblance to it. After a month of siege in high summer, the Harfleur garrison was depleted, but Henry's own forces were heavily reduced by dysentery. When the lateness of the season seemed to indicate a withdrawal to England, the king decided to march the 150 miles back to Calais rather than advance on Paris.

The French, however, had gathered a large force at Blanchetaque to deny the English a crossing of the Somme. Henry, aware of this, moved south and forded the river at Bethencourt, only to find the French again ahead of him, blocking the road to Calais at Agincourt. To fight or not to fight? The English, though heavily outnumbered, possessed one potent weapon: longbows and the men who handled them. The French, superior in numbers, had a major problem: dissension among their commanders. The result was a fierce and astonishing engagement with great carnage among the French troops, including several of its most prominent nobles. Of the English losses (light by comparison), the two most notable were Edward, Duke of York and Michael de la Pole, the Earl of Suffolk. The first had inherited royal blood, and descendants of the second would marry into it.

Edward's body was taken to the church at Fotheringhay in Northamptonshire, and interred there with splendid ceremonial music of drums and trumpets and pageantry befitting the death in battle of a grandson of Edward III. The church must have rocked to the sound and the small hamlet re-echoed to the high solemnity of the occasion. The country rejoiced in the victory at Agincourt. The royal family mourned the loss of one of its members.

How long do such echoes last? Edward's father had built Fotheringhay church and endowed the college attached to it. Now the son lies buried beneath the choir. Later Plantagenets would also find their tombs there. It is still a beautiful and infinitely graceful building, facing across the river the large grass mound which is the site of Fotheringhay Castle – a site historic in itself, since it housed Mary Queen of Scots in later times. The church has a lantern tower and many windows and, although I have not seen it at night, the effect of those lighted windows shining across the neighbouring water-meadows and quiet village can easily be imagined.

Some years ago two residents of the small town of Oundle – renowned now for its public school – set out to walk the few miles to Fotheringhay. It was an area Mr and Mrs John Priest loved and, since the day was hot and still, they were delighted by the thought of a riverside walk and a possible visit to the church. The village was silent, heavy with summer somnolence, and they were therefore astonished to hear the sound of music drifting from the church. It was not of the kind associated with a normal church service, so the Priests assumed that some concert was in progress, though both noticed the strange, almost barbaric quality of the sounds. As they opened the church door and tentatively entered, the music ceased and silence took absolute possession. The two sat quietly for a time in the empty church and then left, taking with them a vibrating memory – the sound of drums and trumpets.

Long afterwards, the Priests learnt that the ghostly music of Fotheringhay church has been heard many times. A local police sergeant was among the auditors of this echo from Agincourt. Police officers are not generally a suggestible or over-imaginative breed, and evidence from such a source deserves attention. Was it from Agincourt? It seems likely, for this had been an important period in the church's history, and the funeral of Edward of York would have been attended by great dignitaries, would have been celebrated by music, and would have generated great emotion and an impressive atmosphere. All these are factors which may have registered so strongly on the surroundings that their record remains active more than five hundred years later.

*

Forty-six years after the death of Prince Edward on the French battlefield, his grandson, another Edward (later to be Edward IV) finally reached the throne of England and became founder of the Royal House of York. He had had to fight his way to the crown through the rival claims of the Lancastrians and the defeat of Henry VI and his formidable queen, Margaret of Anjou.

Henry, gentle and ineffectual, had been deposed and imprisoned in 1465 in his royal Tower of London, and would die there by an unknown hand on 21 May. Later Tudor historians blamed this piece of infamy on Richard, Duke of Gloucester (Richard III), but it is highly unlikely that Gloucester was the murderer or had any connection with the deed. The ghost of King Henry is said to haunt the room where he was murdered, appearing each year on the anniversary of his death. But I know of no recent sightings of Henry VI in the Tower, so probably the record of that particular horror has now faded.

It is a curious fact about ghosts that in time they dwindle and eventually disappear. No haunting goes on for ever, it seems, though the length of time the psychic record lasts seems to depend on the type of haunting – i.e. whether the ghost is merely a mechanical record by the surroundings or whether it is a surviving and active entity which chooses to stay where it is, often in the last place it occupied before its earthly life ended.

Edward IV was a lively and amiable monarch, with face and figure handsome enough to turn the heads of half the kingdom's women. They certainly turned his, for he was a great womanizer, in addition to being a successful soldier and a competent administrator. When he did marry (and the event has always been regarded as a *mésalliance*), it was Elizabeth Woodville he chose, a beautiful widow whose partly noble blood seemed to Edward's family to be much inferior to their own. The marriage was kept secret for a while, but eventually acknowledged by the young king. This effectively established

Elizabeth as queen, and admitted her large and ambitious collection of relatives to the highest positions in the land. Edward, too, had relatives: two brothers, George Duke of Clarence, and Richard Duke of Gloucester, neither of whom regarded the Woodville faction with much favour. The animosity between the factions complicated the already tangled rivalry between York and Lancaster.

Elizabeth Woodville dutifully gave her husband three sons and six daughters, and it is the third of the princesses, Cicely, said to be the most beautiful of that family of lovely girls, whose echoes we shall hear later. However, before the Princess Cicely's story unfolded, a much greater drama was brewing around the life of Edward IV's younger brother, Richard of Gloucester.

Richard really became King by default. He was the youngest of the three Royal princes (George of Clarence, born between Edward IV and Richard, had been executed for treason prior to Edward's death, allegedly by being drowned in a butt of malmsey wine, which for a winebibber like Clarence was highly appropriate), and, apart from the two surviving young sons of Edward, was next in line to the throne. The elder of the little boys had been declared Edward V after his father's death, but before a coronation could take place enough doubt was cast on the children's legitimacy to cause Richard to set his nephews aside and assume the crown himself. Cynics say that the illegitimacy charge was convenient for Richard, but his supporters believe he had no choice but to take the throne.

What happened later is not clear. The boys were kept in the Tower, which was still at that time one of the royal homes, and for a while were often seen playing there. Then gradually their appearances became less frequent, until they were not seen at all. They disappeared from public view and from history. Richard was later blamed for their deaths though, if they were murdered, he need not have known until it had been accomplished. There were self-seekers at court who, to ingratiate themselves with the king, might have removed the competition of Edward's children. It is significant that about this time Richard quarrelled violently with a man whom he had trusted as a friend, the Duke of Buckingham, an intriguer who himself had distant claims to the throne. He was ambitious and unscrupulous; a combination of talents which might have caused him to take drastic action. Richard, on the other hand, had been devoted to his elder brother Edward, had served him faithfully for years and had been specifically appointed the boys' guardian by their father. Given Richard's temperament, it is unlikely he would have betrayed Edward's trust by killing his sons. The truth will probably never be known; what is agreed is the likely date of the little princes' deaths – 1483. They were not seen after October of that year.

There is an epilogue to this story. In 1674 Charles II ordered the demolition of buildings surrounding the White Tower, where the royal lodgings had been in Plantagenet times. When an outer staircase was demolished, workmen found a wooden chest buried ten feet beneath the bottom stair. It contained the skeletons of two children, the taller one placed on its back, the smaller of the two lying face downwards on top of it. The bones were interred in a white marble urn and placed in the Henry VII chapel of Westminster Abbey, with an inscription that these were the bones of the two princes who had been put to death in the Tower. There was no proof for this supposition.

That was not the end of it. In 1933, the container was opened and its contents examined. The conclusions of the learned experts was that the urn contained a mixture of human and animal bones, the latter thought to have been added by robbers bent on stealing the human relics (probably between 1674–78) and hoping to cover their loss; and that the human remains belonged to children of about twelve and ten respectively, whose sex could not be identified. In other words, they might or might not have been the bones of the little princes. As for the robbery, in 1728 the antiquary,

Thomas Hearne, discovered that some bones of the supposed Edward V and the Duke of York had been sent to the Ashmolean Museum in Oxford (by no less a person than Mr Ashmole himself) and had apparently never been returned to their source. This would account for the shortage of human bones when the urn was examined.

During the five hundred years since their deaths, the ghosts of the two boy princes are said to have been seen a number of times in the Bloody Tower, the possible site of their murder. One report has them pale and tragic in their long nightgowns, but the phantoms have never indicated who was their murderer. There have not been any reports of sightings in this century, so far as I know.

Richard III pinned all the hopes of his short reign on the likelihood of his young son (yet another Edward) succeeding him. The boy was not strong, however, and may have inherited from his mother Anne the consumption which killed her in March 1485. She was to survive her only child by a year, for on 9 April, 1484, at the home castle of Middleham, the ten-year-old Prince of Wales died after a short illness. The parents, staying in Nottingham Castle, had been unable to reach him before his death and were utterly distraught. They set off at once for the north, but could not arrive before the child's interment at Sherriff Hutton church in Yorkshire. This village housed one of the king's secondary castles, and seems to have been used almost as much as Middleham during his northern visits.

The boy's tomb must have been prepared very hastily and although it is not known whether the unhappy parents arrived before the small stone sarcophagus was closed it seems unlikely that they did. Their feelings on arrival must have been poignant indeed. Edward had been their only child and heir and much loved.

Sherriff Hutton church is not large, but it retains some unusual features. One is the great door, over half a foot thick, solid as a ship's side and iron-studded. This swings open and the visitor descends a few steps into the body of the church. Full view of the church nave and left-hand aisle is blocked by a pillar of colossal girth which dominates the entire west end of the nave.

When I visited this building some years ago, the summer evening was still bright with sunshine. The church stands at the end of a leafy lane, and the only human being in sight was a local man placidly mowing his lawn a hundred yards from the church gateway. I entered the building and looked around for Prince Edward's tomb, which I knew to be in the north aisle at its chancel end,but there was no way of seeing through a pillar several feet in circumference. Not until I rounded it did I glimpse the two tombs at the aisle's end: the furthermost was that of a crusader, and the small tomb I sought was immediately before it. Upon its lid was carved the effigy of the boy, his hands folded in prayer.

Time and circumstance had long since worn down the surface of the childish profile and prayerful hands, but when the parents came to the church the tomb was new, and as they stood beside it the material importance of their position was as nothing. They were not royal personages with power, but parents full of grief. How had they felt and expressed it, I wondered, under the eyes of their attendants? Or did they enter alone? My thoughts running along these lines, I stretched out a hand and laid it lightly on the cold, folded pair before me. It was as though I had set some apparatus in motion.

The huge entrance door behind me slowly swung open, and the sound of footsteps descended the shallow flight into the church. The steps paused, and I found myself irritated because of the interruption; some tourist, I assumed, had called before I had been able to aborb the church's atmosphere, the tomb's meaning. I resolved to stay a minute or so where I was in the hope that the visitor would do the same. Then, unexpectedly, I heard a single word called out; it seemed like a name, spoken two or three times, but its sound was so distorted I assumed it came from outside the building. A short silence followed, and I decided that I ought not to delay the visitor any longer. Then I heard the sound of footsteps crossing and recrossing the top of the nave, though whoever owned the feet was concealed by the massive pillar. A whole sentence was spoken in the same voice as before, though again the words were blurred and unclear.

I could no longer monopolize the church's main feature and moved back up the aisle, reaching the pillar and opening my mouth to apologize for delaying the newcomers. It stayed open with shock, for the space where I had imagined the visitors to be was empty; the great door was firmly shut. Apart from myself, the entire building was empty. My hair prickled alarmingly on my head, but I reasoned that there must be a logical cause for this odd occurrence. The church clock was an exceptionally large one for the building's size; its mechanism must be responsible for the sounds I had assumed to be footsteps. On my way out, I glanced at the clock face. Its hands pointed to ten past ten, its time when I had entered the building. My watch said 7.30 p.m. The clock was stopped.

But the voice I had heard – surely that was real? Someone outside perhaps? The man with the lawnmower? But there was nobody within 200 yards of the building, and the man and his mower were 50 yards beyond that, their sound muted from where I stood. In any case, he had no companion to talk to, for no one else was in sight. Whatever I had heard seemed to belong to some other time than that of the July evening.

Afterwards I recalled that nothing had happened until I placed my hand over those of the child's effigy. It was as though that simple gesture set a course of action in motion, over which I had no control. Was it, perhaps, a replication of an action performed centuries ago beside that very tomb, a gesture the mother herself might have made? The voice I heard had been female. Was it that of Anne, the queen? And were the footsteps hers, too? This was a totally unexpected and unsought incident. I was not – and this is a common remark of percipients after such encounters – thinking of the paranormal at the time.

After his queen's death in the Spring of 1485, Richard III appears to have lost interest in living. He had loved both wife and son and now he was alone, the last of the Plantagenet kings. He would die on Bosworth Field a few months later, almost throwing his life away in a last, reckless, death-or-glory charge down Ambien Hill. It was, perhaps, in his own mind a test of whether fate intended him or Henry Tudor (whose title to the throne was the slenderest of any) to rule England. Unfortunately, Richard had too often sided with the common people to endear himself to the barons. Enough nobles changed sides at Bosworth to put the Tudor on the throne. Richard was the last warrior king to die leading his troops into battle on English soil. His body was thrown ignominiously into the local river and what became of it is not known.

Of all the curious echoes of Richard Plantagenet, the strongest came to me several months after writing the above. A London woman, Ms Laura Dessau, wrote to tell me of a coach trip she had made several years ago to a village in Leicestershire. This was organized by a clergyman to enable a number of enthusiasts to visit a traction engine rally in the area, and the fact that the outing was to take place on 22 August probably had no significance for anyone save the Reverend Teddy Boston himself. He had been an active member of the Richard III Society for many years, and knew the date of the anniversary of Bosworth Field.

As the group arrived at its destination, one member (Laura Dessau) began to experience a strong sense of disorientation. The bright, warm sunshine of the day abruptly vanished, to be replaced by a heavy, overcast sky and a chilly wind. All around her great trees loomed and she experienced an extraordinary sense of compulsion, not to immerse herself in the rally but to get away from it. Indeed, it is doubtful if, in her state of mind, she even saw the rally. Her one desperate desire was to reach 'the hill'. 'You must let me have a horse,' she said urgently to her companions. 'I have to get to the hill. It's only a short ride. I must go.' She exhibited great distress, weeping and struggling frantically to climb through a nearby hedge in order to start her journey to 'the hill'. 'It's only a mile and a half,' she cried out to them, but her friends did not understand and forcibly restrained her, thinking she was ill or suffering from sunstroke.

But Miss Dessau could not feel the sun, for she was seeing grey skies and hearing the most appalling crashes, screams and groans, the sounds of heavily armoured men in combat. The din in her ears lasted for over two hours. At the end of that time she abruptly regained the present, to find herself wrapped in a jacket in blazing sunshine and surrounded by all the stalls and exhibits of the rally she had come to Leicestershire to see. The rally was winding up, its stalls disappearing. Ms Dessau's account concludes

> 'I should also point out that I had not known my destination and did not discover it until after this experience was over.
>
> Well of course the hill was the hill of the Battle of Bosworth, and it *was* 1½ miles from the field where the rally was being held. What is more, the battle was fought on that very date, in dark, chilly, unseasonable August weather, and lasted for about 2½ hours!
>
> I had correctly pointed out the route taken by King Richard and began to feel much distress when our coach did not take that road. I had also pointed out the route taken by his body after the battle, while in floods of tears, quite inexplicable to my companions.
>
> Some years later, I paid another visit to the site of this extraordinary experience and, apart from remembering the road taken by Richard to the battlefield, recognized nothing at all. It was totally unfamiliar.'

This encounter bears most of the marks of a classic timeslip. Its onset was sudden, the surroundings were changed at once from those of the present (trees, weather, etc.) and the percipient was totally divorced from the twentieth century of her companions by what she was experiencing.

An unusual feature is the length of time the experience lasted – upwards of two hours. A timeslip may extend from a few seconds to half-an-hour, but in my experience this is rarely exceeded. However, if Laura Dessau were 're-living' the Battle of Bosworth, the length of the experience might be expected to coincide with that of the original battle. I asked her whether or not she thought she had witnessed the decisive charge by Richard and his personal guard down Ambien Hill, but she had no recollection of having either heard or seen it. A strong pointer, this, in favour of authenticity, for had a lively imagination invented this time-dislocation, it would surely not have discarded the most dramatic and decisive event of the battle.

Timeslips are a well-authenticated phenomenon, but their mechanism is outside the scope of this work. I have, in any case, dealt with it at length in an earlier book.

Whatever happened to Laura Dessau on that hot August day appears to have related to a time much earlier than the twentieth century. What she described fitted perfectly the events of 22 August 1485, when the English crown passed from an old dynasty to a new. Did she take on the personality and experience of someone who had fought in or witnessed the battle? Had she herself, in a male *persona* actually been in the battle, to be reincarnated five centuries later as Laura Dessau? Was she picking up from the surroundings a lived-through experience of 1485, with all its stress and emotion? Emotion, as we have seen, is a basic ingredient, a motivating power, in most encounters of a parapsychological nature.

So, not so much the ghost of King Richard, as the ghost of the battle which deposed and killed him.

*

Henry Tudor (the seventh Henry) took as his queen Princess Elizabeth of York, eldest daughter of Edward IV and Elizabeth Woodville. There were no little princes now to stand between him and the crown, and his marriage to their sister would unite the rival roses of Lancaster and York. The House of Plantagenet ended, the House of Tudor began.

A few Plantagenets still littered the scene, however, among them the Princess Cicely, second daughter of Edward IV; and Margaret Pole, Countess of Salisbury, surviving daughter of that same George, Duke of Clarence, who found his end in the butt of malmsey.

Henry Tudor could not allow royal Plantagenets complete freedom without some threat to himself, but Cicely was now his sister-in-law and it was expedient to marry her to his kinsman, John, Lord Wells. When this man died ten years later, the Princess Cicely was either allowed to choose her own husband or, more likely, was married by the King's direction. She wed a commoner named Kyme or Keen, whose first name seems also to have been obscure, being variously quoted as John, Thomas or Richard. They retired to the Isle of Wight, where they lived in quietness, and she, who had seen the great and dangerous dealings of court, who had been called the loveliest of the bevy of Edward IV's beautiful daughters, died in obscurity before she was forty in a house whose site is now occupied by Great East Standen Manor.

She died on a day in August, and it is said that the monks of nearby Quarr Abbey stole her treasure. According to local legend and a member of the household of Great East Standen (its present version was built in 1737), an invisible female presence occasionally comes through an attic room and seats herself upon the end of a bed. The bed's occupant sees nothing, but merely feels the pressure of a human weight at its foot. The woman who has had this experience, a Mrs Rene Cooper, vouches for its authenticity, and believes that her psychic intruder is the Princess Cicely.

We saw in Chapter 2 that another royal legend exists on the Isle of Wight – that of Eleanor of Aquitaine, said to have been laid in a golden coffin by the monks of Quarr, with whom she had spent some of her weary years of captivity. We have also seen that Queen Eleanor did no such thing, but lived and died on the mainland. However, the tradition of a resident royal lady at Quarr remains, and when the abbey yielded up an old tomb in Victorian times, its occupant turned out to be a golden-haired woman. Queen Eleanor was dark as a raven, but Edward IV's loveliest daughter was golden-haired, like all his children. Was it she the monks had tended? And is it the Princess Cicely not Eleanor who walks through the Grove there wringing her hands? Only those who see her could know; and she has not appeared at Quarr recently.

Margaret Plantagenet, Countess of Salisbury and niece of Richard III, had led a curious and threatened life. On Henry VII's instruction, her brother, the young Earl of Warwick, had been forcibly removed from the line of succession in 1499 by the headsman's axe. But Margaret survived into the next reign and century and became a friend of Queen Catherine of Aragon, and in time friend and guide to the queen's little daughter, the young Princess Mary.

Lady Salisbury's devotion to the princess, her young kinswoman, was to cause her great hardship and heartache for, as Henry VIII discarded her Spanish mother, married Anne Boleyn and fathered the Princess Elizabeth, Mary fell into disgrace, was treated as a bastard and deprived of her household and friends. It is not clear how far Henry VIII's decision to remove his relatives was influenced by the fact that Lady Salisbury was one of the last of the living Plantagenets. Her son, Cardinal Pole, had strongly opposed the king's abandonment of Catherine of Aragon, and Henry was not likely to forgive this defiance. The Poles, therefore, were suspect on two counts: their Catholic sympathies and their Plantagenet blood. It was not long before the paranoiac Henry found grounds to imprison the countess in the Tower, together with her two sons, Montague and Geoffrey, and her nephew, Exeter. Threatened with torture, Geoffrey Pole broke down and incriminated his family, accusing them of treason by conspiracy with the King's Catholic enemies. In any case they had been suspected of planning to marry the Catholic Reginald Pole to the Catholic Princess Mary, thus providing a ready focus for plotters against the king's life and dynasty. Montague and Exeter were beheaded, and Margaret, the old Countess of Salisbury, was under sentence of death. She died by the executioner's axe 'in a corner of the Tower', but not willingly or easily. The year was 1539. Royal to the end and proud Plantagenet to the last, she refused to kneel before the executioner or to place her noble head upon the block. She evaded the man, who pursued her round the scaffold, swinging his axe at her in an attempt to carry out his task. She died violently and bloodily of multiple axe wounds.

From time to time since then the shadow of an axe has been seen passing over Tower Green before falling in clear definition, aloft and motionless, on the White Tower wall. But this area, the site of Lady Salisbury's death and several others, was turfed over in Victorian times, and there is no reason to suppose the ghostly axe-shadow relates to one death rather than another.

A spectral procession which has been seen in the Chapel Royal, and of which a queenly personage is a focal point, may relate either to Anne Boleyn or to Lady Salisbury. The chief figure resembles portraits of Anne, but the procession seems to have occurred on the anniversary of the Countess of Salisbury's execution.

Who is to tell in this castle of blood and terror which phantoms belong to which victims? The stones must be saturated in the vibrations of ancient horror. Hardly surprising that those scenes should occasionally be replayed for the benefit of sensitive onlookers and listeners.

Only I fancy that such replays do not work in quite this way.

They are not 'for the benefit' of anyone. What seems to happen is that either the constant repetition of one set of actions – say the processions of monks and nuns attending regular services at fixed times – or the intense emotion generated by another (which may involve love, hate, jealousy, anger, or terror; and may arise from battle, quarrels, violent death by murder, suicide or accident) will cause an increase in human electrical activity in the surrounding area. Human beings share the atomic nature of all matter on earth, and atoms, whether singly or collectively, generate electricity which gives rise to an electromagnetic (EM) field around its source. Humans are thus electrical animals, and the electricity discharged from brain, heart, skin and tissues is scientifically measurable. Electroencephalograms (EEGs) and electrocardiograms (ECGs) are in common medical use.

The electromagnetic field surrounding each human body varies according to the state of health and emotions of its owner. In times of stress, the electrical output seems to be stimulated in some way, and it is possible that this may result in an impression on the surrounding area by the electromagnetic waves. As far as I know, however, no human EM field has been measured under extreme stress conditions for comparison with the same field in its normal, unstressed state. Until this takes place, this theory remains a theory. Were it proved, it would account for a number of psychic experiences, both of the haunting and the retrocognitive timeslip type.

CHAPTER SIX

The Sixteenth Century, Part I

Henry VIII came to the English throne in 1509 and was to sit on it in splendour for thirty-eight years; a span which must have been something of a shock to a country accustomed to frequent changes of sovereign.

Henry had not expected to wear the crown. His brother, Arthur, was heir to their father Henry VII, he who had almost accidentally conquered at Bosworth. The young Prince Arthur, betrothed and then married to Catherine, a princess of Aragon, lived only until he was eighteen and then died, possibly of consumption, though it is more likely the cause was a virulent form of influenza – the dreaded 'sweating sickness' which was rife in England that year. Catherine, thus widowed almost before she was married, must have hoped for a speedy return to her sunny homeland, but was never to see Spain again.

For a while after his own Queen's death, Henry VII thought of marrying her (a parsimonious monarch, he was reluctant to hand back Catherine's dowry), but the idea met with opposition from the princess's mother, Isabella of Spain, and was quietly shelved. Eventually the parents on both sides agreed that the widowed girl should be betrothed to the new Prince of Wales, Henry, a strapping and handsome lad of fifteen. Catherine of Aragon's fate was fixed, her life's course decided. She had, as was usual at the time, no say in it whatever.

Henry became the eighth king of his name in 1509. He was just eighteen, and six years younger than his queen, but the fact that there was love between them, and that Henry regarded his new wife with blind youthful adulation, seemed to promise well for their life together and for the new reign. Catherine felt no less affection for her husband. At this time the young king was more like a young god, standing well over six feet, broad-shouldered and with the physique of a healthy athlete. His complexion was fresh and glowing with much exercise – until late in life he possessed vibrant energy – and his red-gold colouring and ready smile endeared him to all who saw him. He was intellectually bright and had the veneer of culture indispensable for a Renaissance prince. And so it began; a reign which promised a golden age and which would deteriorate into almost a reign of terror.

The problem with Henry was that he inherited the best of the Plantagenet physical characteristics (he bore a strong resemblance to his maternal grandfather, Edward IV) and the worst of their psychological qualities. He was wilful, vindictive and possessed of an ungovernable temper, besides being paranoically suspicious and egocentric. The considerable inherited charm could not balance such grave character defects. He would end his life less loved than dreaded.

Of his two surviving sisters, Henry preferred the younger, Mary, after whom he named his splendid warship, the *Mary Rose*. However, as he began to exercise political power in the courts of Europe, the young king realized what valuable bargaining properties he possessed in his sisters. He promptly married the elder to James IV of Scotland. He hoped this would guarantee Scottish good behaviour for his lifetime; a hope not to be fulfilled, since it ended, as we have seen, on the field of Flodden. He proposed to marry Mary to the young Charles of Ghent, although he knew her heart was set on his friend Charles Brandon, Duke of Suffolk. However Mary was destined for higher things, for when the widowed old King of France, Louis XII (a very dilapidated fifty-two) showed an interest in her, Henry promptly forced his passionate, pretty little sister into the marriage. Not surprisingly, she agreed only with reluctance, and made Henry promise that when

Louis died, she could marry 'as me liketh for to do'. With that promise in mind, Princess Mary shortly became Queen Marie of France.

What with the roistering, the late nights and the unaccustomed exercise, the decrepit Louis ('an ancient man, infirm and sickly') was hastened to his end. He had been accustomed to a quiet life and although his Frenchman's spirit was willing to enter into the young girl's world of late dancing, early morning hunting, and meals at all hours, his tired flesh was not. He collapsed and even his admiration for the bride young enough to be his grand-daughter could not stave off the inevitable. By December's end he was dead.

A time of acute anxiety began for Mary. Although she had Henry's promise that she might choose her next husband, she feared this had only been an expedient to silence her complaints. Even while the thought was going through her mind, Henry's council was debating whether to bequeath her to the next King of France, the young and enterprising Francis I, or to one of the Austrian heirs. Francis was already undertaking a little courtship on his own account, peering into Mary's bedroom to watch her in bed; an activity she found both repellent and disconcerting. Now Henry made a surprising error or a deliberate calculation; he sent Charles Brandon to Paris to bring Mary back to England. The unhappy girl could hardly have expected so good a stroke of luck. She immediately set about persuading the Duke of Suffolk to marry her, clinging to him like a desperate child, and giving him a 'now or never' ultimatum. Suffolk, bearing in mind his master's temper and temperament, was not anxious to cross Henry. 'The queen', he wrote to Wolsey, Henry's chief minister, 'would never let me be in rest till I had granted her to be married; and so to be plain with you, I have married her heartily, and have lain with her, insomuch as I fear me lest she be with child.' He continued, 'I was lyke to be ondon if the matter schold coume to the knollag of the Kyng me master.'

It had already come to the king's knowledge and Henry was

severely displeased. The only way Suffolk could escape royal wrath, according to Wolsey, was by offering to repay all Mary's dowry, plus a good deal more. Suffolk obliged for the sake of reinstatement. The newly-married pair were, however, banished from court, and settled down at Suffolk's country home, Westhorpe Hall, near Bury St Edmunds. During this period of the king's disfavour, two persons stood as friends to Charles and Mary – Thomas Wolsey and the Queen of England, Catherine, both of whom had interceded for them in case it should occur to Henry to remove their heads.

After their retirement to Westhorpe, Mary at least came less to court, attending pageants and ceremonial occasions, but otherwise staying at home rearing her children and planning a new elaborate garden in the French style. Hunting and picnics appear to have been her favourite pastimes, though financial difficulties – most of Mary's French revenue found its way into her brother's treasury – often forced the Suffolks to pay long 'visits' to other noble houses. In later years Mary travelled less and less, though Brandon did not follow her example. On one of his visits *à seul* he met the young and lovely Lady Catherine Willoughby, who would be his next wife. One wonders, in view of Brandon's increasing absence from home, if the marriage to Mary had lost its charm. A rhyme said to have been written by the Duke in the early days of his life with the princess, may point to a possible source of unease.

> Cloth of gold, do not despise,
> Though thou be matched with cloth of frize,
> Cloth of frize, be not too bold,
> Though thou be matched with cloth of gold.

Did she ultimately despise him? Had his vanity made him too bold in ordering her life, the life of a royal princess and former queen? We cannot know. But all utterances are possible clues to states of mind and certainly towards her life's end Mary saw much less of her husband, whether through indifference or because he had formed another attachment, it is impossible to tell. Mary, Duchess of Suffolk, died on Midsummer Day, 1533, of 'a pain in the side' (appendicitis?), and was buried in St Edmundsbury Abbey at a ceremony attended neither by her husband nor by the Earl of Lincoln, her eldest son.

Nowadays all that remains of the original Westhorpe Hall are the three-arched bridge over the western end of the moat, a flint wall and a block of masonry, part of a mediaeval building on the same site, and a shield in terracotta bearing the Brandon arms, placed over the doorway of the much smaller house built following the Hall's demolition in the mid-eighteenth century. Brandon surrendered the manor to the crown in 1538 and from the following year it formed part of the dowry of Anne of Cleves. Since then it has changed hands many times, and is now the property of Mr and Mrs E. J. Barker of Westhorpe Lodge, Westhorpe.

The Lodge itself was originally known as Westhorpe Manor, being contemporary with the great Hall. On the day I visited the parish – picturesque still, but containing only 180 people, much shrunken from its Tudor days – the sun shone clear and silvery after very early Spring rain. The old church of St Margaret's, large, beautiful, sadly dilapidated, must many times have seen the former queen, her husband and her children, though Mary's remains now rest in St Mary's Church, Bury St Edmunds, where they were removed after the Dissolution of that abbey.

Mrs Ella Barker showed me around the Lodge, a place of serene beauty which time and good owners have treated lovingly. The house is large by modern standards and still retains much of its Tudor past, though there have been a few additions.

There is a local legend of traffic between the Great Hall

and this, the smaller Manor House, reaching back four or five centuries. When the Hall was ruthlessly demolished in the eighteenth century (vandalized would be a better term for what occurred, since the building was practically flattened and furniture and contents were smashed by heedless workmen), that contact seems to have ended, and the tradition of connection by subterranean passage between the buildings cannot now be proven. Such traditions abound all over these islands; their very romance keeps them alive. And yet . . . perhaps some tenuous connection exists still.

Some years ago, in the month of May, Mrs Barker had a curious encounter. She woke during the night, was unable to sleep and left her room to visit the nearby bathroom. This meant passing the head of a broad flight of stairs which at one point bend in a right-angled landing beneath a tall window. As she passed along the corridor, she noticed a wide band of moonlight streaming in, illuminating the entire landing and the stairhead, both of which were as empty as one would expect in the small hours of the morning. On her return from the bathroom the solid figure of a woman stood on the little landing. She was wearing a long full-skirted white dress, but had no head-covering. Indeed, Mrs Barker particularly noted the figure's beautiful golden curls as the moonlight caught them. The other fact which struck her was that the woman was in some distress; she was wringing her hands and showing every sign of anxiety.

For a moment, the two seem to have regarded each other, then Mrs Barker, who felt that the lady's unhappiness might be caused by recent repair works taking place at the Hall, attempted to soothe her visitor. Sensing that what stood before her was not flesh and blood, though not attempting to identify the apparition, she assured it that if the repairs were troubling her, she might rest easy for they were almost completed. The visitor did not appear to register the words and after two or three minutes gradually faded into the air.

Mrs Barker told her husband of this curious experience,

but he was sceptical. There was no thought in the percipient's mind at this stage that she might have witnessed Mary. Not until some time later did she recall a portrait seen at Woburn Abbey of Mary Tudor, sister of Henry VIII, and realize that it and the apparition were identical. Mrs Barker assured me that at no time during the encounter did she feel surprise or fear, merely pity for the figure's distress.

Afterwards, she and I inspected the Hall itself or at least the eighteenth-century building which incorporates a fragment of the original Great Hall of Westhorpe. It is handsome still, with a deep though variable atmosphere inside it; by which I mean that the 'feeling', the 'sensation' each room generates and with which it affects a sensitive beholder, differs from area to area. The large, black-beamed screened room on the ground floor almost seems to be still inhabited – and by ancient rather than modern presences, though I had the impression that there had once been the activity and bustle of servants' quarters. Another beamed room at the top of the house has recently been discovered, and this too had the air of some secret, distant life. Not difficult to imagine ghosts here, if one felt so inclined, but we saw and heard nothing. Only the air in the rooms seemed full of information.

The Barkers bought the Hall in the sixties from a family composed of two brothers and two sisters, all elderly and all living in the house. Each had had the experience of firmly shutting doors before retiring yet finding them standing open in the morning.

Recent signs of Mary Rose Tudor have been absent. The Hall is now let to an organization which is converting it to a rest home, and the alterations are well in hand. Whether these activities will affect its resident echoes is impossible to say. Often wholesale repairs will end a haunting of long-standing. Conversely, such alterations may start up a haunting where none has been before. Possible explanations for such wayward functioning are offered in a later chapter.

*

If Henry VIII's younger sister haunts her former earthly home, it is surprising that his elder sister, Margaret, did not follow suit, because her marriage to the gallant young James IV of Scotland ended tragically in widowhood. But she had the Tudor/Plantagenet lusts in her, and soon consoled herself with a second husband. However, she appears to have cared for the gallant James, an attractive and lovable man by all accounts. Two interesting versions are given of the appearance of an apparition to him in the early years of the sixteenth century.

The court at this period in Scottish history spent much of its time at Linlithgow Palace. Princess Margaret had arrived as a bride of fifteen and spent much of the rest of her time there as queen. Although a marriage tie now existed between the houses of Stuart and Tudor, this did not guarantee peace between the two brothers-in-law or between the realms of England and Scotland. In 1512, Henry VIII joined the Holy League set up by the Pope and the Emperor Maximilian against France, and the French immediately appealed to their old allies, the Scots, for help. France and Scotland were as old in alliance as England and Scotland and England and France were in enmity. So although the Pope threatened to excommunicate James if he took up arms against England, further appeals from the French, a touching small gift of a turquoise ring from the French queen and a letter which called James her champion, persuaded that chivalrous monarch to march against his brother-in-law's armies. It was an ill-advised expedition, and Queen Margaret must have felt much apprehension; a husband on one side and a brother on the other. One version of events during the run-up to the clash of interests suggests that she tried to influence her husband's conduct.

The official, authenticated version of what occurred is that James was kneeling in prayer in the church at Linlithgow (quoted variously as either St James's or St Michael's) when the figure of an old man appeared before him. The apparition (for this is what the watchers took it to be) warned him that he would be defeated and killed on the field of Flodden, which indeed he was in 1513, to the great grief of the Scottish nation. In the several accounts of this visitation, there is no suggestion that the warning was from a living individual; it was conveyed to the king paranormally via the apparition of the old man. However, another version states that the queen's fear for her husband's life prompted her to arrange for an 'apparition' of the Apostle John to appear to the king while he prayed, warning him against his intended invasion of England. Whichever account is the truth, King James ignored the warning and marched into England at the head of the most brilliant army Scotland had ever raised.

The combatants met in a wild corner of the north-eastern Cheviots on the three hills of Flodden. James seems to have made several tactical errors in his furious battle with the English, though no doubt the traditional difficulty of controlling and deploying Highland troops, who were apt to be carried away by the thrill of the chase and plunder, contributed to the disaster. The flower of the Scottish army was scythed down, and James himself lay dead on the field, pierced by many arrows, his neck severed. It was a gallant but useless death.

For long years afterwards the Scots remembered and suffered from the massacre on Flodden Field. Even today it echoes in the familiar lament.

> We'll hear nae mair lilting at our ewe-milking;
> Women and bairns are heartless and wae;
> Sighing and moaning on ilka green loaning –
> The Flowers of the Forest are a' wede awae.

It would have been better for Scotland had her king heeded his ghostly messenger, whether he was genuine or staged by the queen. In any case, such warning apparitions are not uncommon, though their source is uncertain.

James IV left behind a baby son who would become James V, and eventually the father of Mary Queen of Scots.

The bloodthirsty nature of Scottish politics until comparatively modern times has something extraordinary in it. It is as though the factions of Scots society trusted only one method to resolve political and personal problems – killing. Often the murders were dignified by such terms as 'execution', 'combat', 'a just vengeance' and so on, but the taking of life remained a traditional and simple remedy for arguments, feuds, rivalries and frustration with one's fellow men. Perhaps this summary recourse to weapons arose from the difficulty the Scots found in keeping their tempers, or from a lack of fluency in argument and faith in the logical processes of law; or perhaps, in the earlier days, from the mere inability of law to offer any processes at all. However it was, for many centuries sudden dire death remained the easiest way, in the Scottish view, to solve insoluble problems.

James V was barely two years old when his father was carried from the field of Flodden. His mother, Margaret, preferred marriage to a widow's bed, and speedily wed Archibald Douglas, the sixth Earl of Angus. The infant James grew up disliking not only his stepfather but the whole Douglas clan, an emotion fomented into hatred by the estrangement between his mother and stepfather, and by the fact that the latter held him, James the king, captive on the Castle rock of Edinburgh. It is not known how the young king escaped from imprisonment, but perhaps this was arranged by his mother – now divorced from Angus – for in July 1528 both were together in Stirling, Margaret planning her third marriage. As a loyalist army gathered around the sixteen-year-old James, Angus retired to his castle at Tantallon, held out there for three weeks and then surrendered. He escaped into England while he was able, but forfeited all his estates.

The king had inherited a lawless land, where clan power decided who survived and who ruled. James V proved a match for his subjects. His ruthlessness in disposing of his enemies by just or unjust means secured his throne. Some of his activities were certainly prompted by malice and vengefulness. Janet Douglas, a sister of his hated stepfather, had married into the Lyon family of Glamis. When her husband died, she married Archibald Campbell of Skipnish, but James arrested both, together with the Lady of Glamis's young son, and confined all three in Edinburgh Castle. Campbell, attempting to escape, fell to his death. Janet Douglas, widowed a second time, had a harsher fate in store. She was kept in a gloomy dungeon until her sight was almost gone, then being convicted of witchcraft and attempting to poison the king, was sentenced to be burnt alive.

The sentence was duly carried out on Edinburgh's Castle Hill on 17 July 1537, 'with great commiseration of the people'. Janet was a woman 'of singular beauty' and in the prime of her life. Public opinion was impressed by her great courage and acknowledged that her offence was less likely to be witchcraft than the intense hatred the king bore for her family. James, as it happened, had occupied Glamis during its mistress's imprisonment and had appropriated to himself most of its costly furnishings. The young Lord of Glamis was saved from his mother's fate, but kept a prisoner until the death of James V released and restored him to his lands and (largely denuded) house.

Something of this incredible suffering seems to remain at Glamis, for from time to time the figure of a woman is seen floating above the Clock Tower, surrounded by a glowing aura of light. Local people believe the figure to be that of Janet Douglas. An uncanny knocking sound has also been heard in one part of the castle, and a Victorian guest at Glamis caused consternation to her hosts when she reported hearing what she took to be the sound of scaffolding being erected, at the unlikely hour of four o'clock in the morning. Perhaps it was the timing of this sound which gave rise to the idea that it was the noise of Janet Douglas's scaffold a-building. The theory has no foundation in fact, because the scaffold was erected in Edinburgh.

We shall return later to the much haunted Royal Castle of Glamis.

It was once a popular belief that haunting its earthly habitat was the sign of an unquiet spirit. If this were so, then Henry VIII should certainly appear in a good many places, for his dealings with his contemporaries were both cruel and treacherous; he had, in addition, a great deal of blood on his hands if not upon his conscience. Yet the only record of Henry's haunting is at Windsor Castle, where the sound of agonized groans and slow, dragging footsteps are occasionally heard in the cloisters near the Deanery. Henry's dropsical leg later in life caused him considerable pain. One can only assume that when he could no longer hunt and ride because of it, he used the cloisters for what little exercise he could take. His regular, laboured passage up and down this area might have imprinted itself upon the surroundings, giving rise to a pattern haunting whose strength is not yet exhausted.

The only report I know of a sighting of this ghost is quoted in Peter Underwood's *This Haunted Isle*, where the figure of Henry is said to have appeared to two soldiers in 1977. The figure faded into the wall as they watched. This may not even relate to the cloisters haunting, as Underwood refers to the Castle battlements as its background.

Interestingly, there is a tradition that Henry himself once saw the spectral Herne the Hunter while out riding in Windsor Great Park, and Anthony Hippisley-Coxe's *Haunted Britain* carries an illustration of the event by George Cruikshank. I have found no other reference, but presumably Cruikshank knew of it.

If Henry VIII haunts little on his own account, his earthly activities were responsible for several hauntings by others. His first queen, Catherine of Aragon, originally loved and respected by Henry, gradually fell from favour as the years passed and she failed to produce a surviving heir. It is difficult for us half a millenium later to understand what the lack of a male heir meant to a Renaissance ruler. Daughters were of little value to a reigning monarch save as political pawns. The possibility of a queen *regnant* was not seriously considered. A son and only a son would succeed.

Having failed to beget a legitimate heir, Henry began to think of appointing one of his bastards as his successor, the six-year-old Henry Fitzroy, son of Elizabeth Blount. He created the child Duke of Richmond and loaded him with various honours as an earnest of his intentions. This aroused Queen Catherine's indignation, though the only result of her outburst was to make Cardinal Wolsey persuade Henry to dismiss most of her trusted servants. The simple fact was that Catherine, now forty-one, was beyond childbearing, and only one child of her many births and miscarriages had survived infancy, the Princess Mary.

Thus began Henry's long, long struggle to free himself of his legal wife while Catherine sought to prevent him and secure the succession for her daughter. The conflict was to involve not only the policies and religion of England but the politics of Europe. If Henry's motive was to ensure a legitimate heir, his final motivation was the desire to possess a woman whom he had determined should bear that son. He had met Anne Boleyn, the black-eyed, black-haired daughter of his friend Thomas Boleyn, and the younger sister of his former mistress, Mary Boleyn.

By July 1533, on her husband's order, Catherine had been removed with her household to the episcopal palace at Buckden, on the edge of the desolate fens in Huntingdonshire, where Henry hoped she would be out of the public eye and away from the sympathy of the common people, who still regarded her as their queen. At first she was well treated apart from occasional harrassment from Henry's officials who doled out her meagre allowance. The place was pleasant enough in summer, but in winter it was prey to the sword-sharp east winds and the heavy, unhealthy mists from the nearby fens. Maybe Henry hoped she would die of its climate, but Catherine did not oblige. She spent her time in prayer and the injustice of her lot endeared her to the folk of Buckden.

Long before this, Wolsey, having failed to persuade Pope Clement VII to annul Henry's marriage, found the vultures gathering for his own ruin. When the king deprived him of the Great Seal, he knew himself finally broken. One of his servants, a certain Thomas Cromwell, wept openly, less for his master than for himself, because his own potential fortunes were in eclipse. He resolved to ride to London to offer his services to the king in the hope of gaining some personal advantage. Wolsey, headed for the Tower, cheated Henry by dying before he reached it. At the last he summed up his failure: 'If I had served God as diligently as I have done the king, He would not have given me over in my grey hairs.'

All this while Anne Boleyn had kept her royal lover at bay, refusing to echo the folly of her elder sister and become his mistress, believing that if she held aloof long enough he would make her his queen. However, she must have judged that after six years of waiting Henry's patience would give out, for by September 1532 she agreed to his importuning. Now openly his mistress, she relied only on his promise to make her his wife. Within a short time, the Black Crow (or the Great Whore as she came to be known by the common people) was expecting a child. The king's marriage now had to be annulled or repudiated and the need was urgent. Henry took the law into his own hands. Cromwell forced Parliament to declare the marriage to Catherine null and void, and the king wed his dark paramour. Three months later Anne gave birth to the heir for which her husband had sacrificed his rightful queen and his country's professed religion. Unfortunately for Anne, the child was a daughter, whom she named Elizabeth. The king was filled with anger and disappointment; in his disenchantment he began to turn his attention elsewhere. He needed a son and another change of partner.

Curiously, both the old queen and the young queen died in the same year, Catherine at Kimbolton Castle on 7 January 1536, and Anne in the Tower on 19 May.

Catherine's ex-husband, on hearing of his first wife's death, dressed himself in a brilliant yellow suit, topped with a white feather in his yellow cap, and said, 'God be praised, the old harridan is dead, now there is no fear of war.' (He had dreaded retribution by Spain.) The ex-queen's body, when opened for embalming by the Kimbolton chandler, was found to be perfect, save that the heart was black and had a growth attached to it. This was enough to start a rumour that Catherine had been poisoned, but since her maids had shared their mistress's food and survived poisoning seems unlikely. Inevitably, the initiator of any poison plot was deemed to be the new queen.

If Anne did desire her predecessor's death, her reaction on hearing of it was odd. 'I am her death, as she is mine,' she said. And so it proved; once Catherine had gone, there was no need for Henry to cling to her supplanter. And the king had already met his next queen and was making plans. Jane Seymour, small, pretty and pliant, waited in the wings.

The ubiquitous Thomas Cromwell, who had assisted Anne to the throne, organized her destruction. And it was Archbishop Cranmer, whom Anne had sponsored, who declared her marriage to the king invalid and her daughter a bastard. Anne was accused of adultery with four men in addition to incest with her brother; and of treason and plotting the death of her sovereign. She denied all the charges, but the result was the same. She was condemned to execution, by the sword rather than the axe in deference to her noble connections. The five men accused with her died before her and she, expecting death on 18 May, had to wait a further twenty-four hours for the arrival of the expert swordsman from Calais who would deprive her of life. 'I heard say the executioner is very good, and I have only a little neck,' she said, and laughed. Later she chatted and joked and called herself Anne sans-tête, as though life would go on for many years yet, and all was still to win, but on the morning of the nineteenth, with the mating birds of May in full song, she walked to the low platform on the small green within the Tower. And died. Elizabeth, her daughter, was not quite three years old.

These events are the stuff of drama, and both Anne and Catherine were strong characters – Catherine, a 'good' woman, pious and high-principled; Anne, wilful, bold, passionate, who vowed to the end her fidelity to the king and innocence of the charges against her. The emotions each experienced in the last moments of life may have been recorded in the place which housed her.

Buckden Palace in Northamptonshire, which held Queen Catherine for a year, is now owned, appropriately, by a Spanish monastic order, the Claretian Missionaries. It is they who have restored the building as nearly as possible to its original state. When I visited it, the monks had no knowledge of any haunting, though there is a strong local tradition that Catherine of Aragon has been seen in the little room behind the chapel. The room is cold, it is true, but so are other rooms in this old building.

Kimbolton, too, is said to be haunted, though the haunting is less likely to be by Catherine's restless spirit than that of a baby believed to have been flung from the battlements. However, local people do believe the queen to haunt the room she used in the castle – the Queen's Chamber – to which her fear of murder by poisoning effectively confined her. Enough of the prisoner's potent personality may remain in this area to give power to the tale.

Traces of Anne Boleyn are stronger, for the beautiful, unpopular Black Crow is said to haunt several places. One such appearance has been on the Thames, a replay of the queen's last boat journey from Greenwich Palace to the

Tower, when her barge breasted the grey waves towards the bitter end. There is also a persistent legend that she haunts Blickling Hall in Norfolk, which was once the home of members of the Boleyn family, though its owner was her uncle not her father. The queen is said to ride up the drive to the Hall once a year in a carriage drawn by a headless coachman, Anne bearing her own head upon her knees. This speaks more of legend than fact, for there is no reason why coachmen and horses should be headless merely because their passenger was. A legend just as fanciful is that Anne's father, Sir Thomas Boleyn, drives every year through the Norfolk countryside and over twelve bridges (or forty, according to some versions). Another says that when news reached Blickling of Anne's death and that of her brother, Lord Rochfort, four headless horses were seen bolting across the country nearby, with a headless man being dragged behind them. The whole equipage was pursued by shrieking demons.

A highly-coloured tale of this type probably reflects local shock at the time of the event. Local expectation, too, for surely any man who could volunteer, as Sir Thomas Boleyn did, to sit on the jury which would try his daughter, is an unnatural parent, a creature of evil. Boleyn, as it happened, was only a weak man who was so afraid of his king and for his own life that he was willing to betray anybody if it guaranteed him safety. The legend of his fearful ghostly journey was the countryman's way of expressing revulsion; though there may originally have been some unusual sighting which sparked the report.

The method of Anne Boleyn's death must have sent shock waves all around the country, because ghost stories concerning her come from many different venues. She has been seen at Bollin Hall in Cheshire, which claims to have been her birthplace; is said to have appeared at Salle Church, Norfolk, and there is a tradition that after her death her body was moved from its resting-place in the St. Peter-ad-Vincula chapel and brought to Salle, there to be laid anonymously under a black marble slab. However, when this slab was lifted some years ago, no bones were found beneath it.

If Anne Boleyn haunts anywhere, the Tower must be the surest candidate. The spectral procession referred to in the previous chapter as possibly concerning the Countess of Salisbury may equally well relate to Anne Boleyn. The officer who witnessed it was going the rounds one night when he noticed a light in the chapel. On questioning the sentry on duty, he discovered that such a light was often seen, 'and stranger things'. The officer climbed a ladder and looked in at one of the windows. What he saw was a procession of men and women pacing up and down; they were led by a woman whose face and garments strongly resembled those in portraits he had seen of Anne Boleyn. After some minutes the scene and the light vanished, leaving the chapel in darkness.

Another candidate for Anne's ghost was seen (again by a sentry) near the White Tower in 1864. The man was surprised to see a woman in white approaching him shortly after midnight, and issued the usual challenge. He received no reply, but she continued to approach and he could hear the tapping of her heels on the ground. Then the figure moved into a patch of moonlight and the sentry was horrified to see that it was headless. Not surprisingly, he fainted, and was later court-martialled for being asleep or drunk on guard duty. However, when the man related his experience, with the support of two other witnesses, he was acquitted. The story of the haunting was well known to Tower personnel, and the phantom has always been assumed to be that of Queen Anne. Occasionally only the sound of footfalls is heard, going towards the White Tower.

In spite of rumours that Anne Boleyn was born at Blickling, her actual place of birth seems to have been Hever Castle in Kent. The daughter of 'a mere knight' as Wolsey was later disparagingly to call Sir Thomas Boleyn, she did not come to Henry VIII's court until she was fifteen, having by that time spent four years at the sophisticated French court with her elder sister, Mary, both ladies of Queen Claude. Mary, lighter-minded than Anne and with less wisdom, had lost her reputation before she was seventeen, and on her return to England became the mistress of its monarch, being discarded six years later when she was pregnant with Henry's child and he was seeking a new lover.

Anne was dark, beautiful, passionate, lively and just coming into blossom. She met the young Percy, heir to the Earl of Northumberland, and the prairie-fire love affair which resulted was intended by both young people to lead to marriage. However, Wolsey and the king intervened and the boy and his noble father were ordered to find another alliance. Percy was forced into marriage with a daughter of the Earl of Shrewsbury and the young Anne Boleyn was left rebellious, angry and deeply hurt – a state not assuaged by being banished to the tedium of Kent and Hever. As it happened, her young lover had no happiness from his marriage. After two years his wife left him and, physically and psychologically ill, he had only his splendid inheritance to console him. Anne went for a time to Brussels to the court of Margaret of Austria before returning to Hever, where one of her neighbours was Sir Thomas Wyatt. He was unhappily married and fell in love with her; poet that he was, he wooed her in desperate, beautiful verse.

> They flee from me that sometime did me seek,
> With naked foot stalking within my chamber:
> Once have I seen them gentle, tame, and meek,
> That now are wild, and do not once remember
> That sometime they have put themselves in danger
> To take bread at my hand; and now they range,
> Busily seeking in continual change.
>
> Thanked be fortune, it hath been otherwise
> Twenty times better; but once especial –

In thin array: after a pleasant guise,
When her loose gown did from her shoulders fall,
And she me caught in her arms long and small,
And therewithal so sweetly did me kiss,
And softly said, 'Dear heart, how like you this?'

It was no dream; for I lay broad awaking:
But all is turn'd now, through my gentleness,
Into a bitter fashion of forsaking;
And I have leave to go of her goodness;
And she also to use new-fangledness.
But since that I unkindly so am served,
'How like you this?' – what hath she now deserved?

Anne was nineteen in 1526 when the king first seriously noticed her. The girl must have been of that kind from which all sexual enchantresses come; one who promised but did not give rewards; who aroused men's passions without much intention of fulfilling them; who, though willing to grant some physical favours where she loved, would probably remain spiritually *virgo intacta* all her life. She would therefore make devoted slaves of men or implacable enemies; and sometimes the one would ultimately become the other.

Henry, used to easy conquests, came up against a will as steely as his own. Anne had no intention of being as lightly won and cast aside as her sister Mary. And the king owed her something, for had he not wrecked her hopes and love for Percy? Henry was the grandson of that great lover and connoisseur of women, Edward IV, a man of sensuality and romantic passions. He wanted Anne for her youth and beauty, and because he felt himself approaching middle-age with a wife who could offer him nothing further.

Anne's price, however, was marriage. Her royal lover hardly believed his ears, but, his emotions being now heavily engaged, he found himself returning again and again to Hever, at first on the feeblest of excuses and then only to see her. Eventually, Henry offered to give up all other *amours* if Anne would consent to be his mistress. His mistress? She had no mind to fill the place left empty by her sister. And in any case, Henry would still be bound in marriage to the queen, so how could Anne be either cherished or safe in such circumstances? So the tragi-comic dance continued until the king tore himself free of Catherine and the old religion. Anne, having judged her resistance to a nicety, finally went to his bed on the strict understanding that she was to be his queen. Henry was still sufficiently in love to honour the arrangement; after all, Anne was to be the young mother of his many sons.

Looking at the painting of Anne Boleyn in the National Portrait Gallery, one sees in the intelligent pointed face, the watchful lively eyes, the likeness of her daughter Elizabeth. There is no hint of a tragic destiny here, but for all her canny waiting game, her lures and evasions, Thomas Boleyn's youngest daughter would live to be only twenty-nine.

Many a time at Hever she must have waited for the Royal rider to appear, galloping up the drive to the drawbridge, and must have waved to him from window or battlements. One record apparently exists of such an occasion, sent to me by a London correspondent, Miss Alexandra Cornish. The accompanying letter was interesting.

> In 1974 (it was late May or early June) my mother and I paid a visit to Hever Castle in Kent. We took the usual sightseeing trail around the Castle and grounds, we each had a camera – both of which were totally different in operation and film size. We stopped until it was almost closing time and decided to finish off the films by going around to a side garden where there is a lovely view of the Castle.
>
> In due course I had the films developed. The earlier photographs are quite unremarkable, then, as the sequence went on, I noticed that in both sets of pictures that around the ramparts there appeared to be a white mist

or haze. It moved gradually around the ramparts finally ending on the side facing the garden and was very 'thick' indeed, then – to my astonishment – I saw that on the ramparts there was a hazy incomplete figure of a woman, her hair pulled back into a bun, and apparently she is leaning sideways over the wall with her right arm raised in a wave to something or somebody approaching the main entrance at front. Naturally when we were there actually taking these photographs we saw nothing – if we had we would both have fallen in the moat for sure!

If you are wondering where the royal connection enters, well, I read that Anne Boleyn used to watch for Henry VIII who would ride over to the Castle from Penshurst, perhaps a tenuous connection, but I like to think that just maybe I have the only photograph of Anne Boleyn in existence!

The photograph to which Miss Cornish referred shows the misty shape of an upper female torso in one of the battlements' embrasures, its right arm raised as if in greeting, left arm apparently stretched behind as though holding the coping to steady itself. The 'bun' could as easily be part of the fashionable French bonnet of the time, an example of which Anne is wearing in the National Gallery portrait.

Did Miss Cornish and her mother unwittingly photograph a moment in Hever's history? Is it possible for such a moment to be engraved upon the surroundings, registered by them in such a manner that the imprint remains, an electromagnetic record held by stone and ancient brick? There are several cases of ghostly photography on record; cases too, it must be admitted, of photographic faking of psychic phenomena. However, this correspondent is a sincere and honest person who, like most of us, takes photographs only occasionally and for pleasure, and would no more think of faking a photograph – even if she had the technical knowledge to do so – than of boarding the next spacecraft for Venus. If one accepts that the photograph shows a figure on the battlements of Hever

Castle, that figure appears to be female and looking towards the Castle's entrance gate. It may also be said to be waving to some person or persons in its line of vision. Further than that one cannot go.

A tradition also exists that Anne's ghost crosses the bridge over the River Eden at Hever, although this haunting occurs only on Christmas Eve. She has in addition been rumoured to haunt Wicken in Cambridgeshire. A final echo of the Black Crow comes from an unlikely place: Moor Park Golf Club in Middlesex. Moor Park was the site of one of Wolsey's many stately residences, and it often welcomed the king and his current queen. Recently one of the Club's staff chanced to glance aside while walking up the stairs of the Club, and saw a figure in a long blue dress of historic style and pattern walking beside her. They kept pace, step by step, and the percipient appears to have found the experience highly unnerving. How the identification was made of the spectre as Anne Boleyn, I do not know, although there are references to Anne's appearing in other places dressed in a blue gown.

Of all Henry VIII's queens, Anne Boleyn seems to have left the strongest psychic impression upon her surroundings; perhaps because her guilt of the charges against her was unproven and probably fabricated. Few mnemonics remain of her now. Only sometimes on a summer's evening, if one goes through the great door of Blickling Hall, with the scent of roses filling the gardens and the space where once the moat ran, there is a sense of some other time and presence. And at the house's entrance one catches sight of a great bull's head carven in stone, a permanent reminder of the family who once lived here, and of the little sloe-eyed girl who visited and played beside the lake; Nan Bullen.

As for Wolsey, whose career became so involved with and dependent on Anne's, his spectre has been seen within recent years at the palace he created and ultimately gave to the monarch. Hampton Court, unfortunately for the cardinal, failed to buy him back into Henry's favour.

It was not until 1966 that anything was heard of Wolsey's paranormal appearance in his old palace. A performance of *Son et Lumière* was in progress at Hampton Court, and during one scene the figure of the cardinal was noticed under an archway. It was assumed that the figure was that of an actor waiting to make his entrance, until it was realized that there was no actor playing the part of Wolsey and, had there been, he would not have been where he was at that particular time in the performance. It was then assumed that what had appeared was a semblance of the actual Wolsey. Nothing has been seen of this apparition since, and why it should appear on only that one occasion is impossible to say.

Jane Seymour was four years younger than Anne, and just twenty-five when she attracted the wayward eye of her king. Her portrait says that she was precise, virtuous, moral and infinitely docile, having neither Anne's metal nor her passion. Henry found her a balm to his hurt pride (he had convinced himself that he had been deeply wronged) and increasingly sought her company. Chapuys, the friend of Catherine of Aragon, said 'nobody thinks she has much beauty,' and 'she is not very intelligent and is said to be rather haughty'. However, the young lady had gentleness and was prepared to regard her royal husband as the source of all wisdom, a state of affairs which suited Henry very well. He married her twelve days after Anne's execution.

Jane's early days of marriage were uneasy. She had been unwise enough to plead with Henry to forgive his daughter, the Princess Mary, for her refusal to acknowledge him as head of the English church, the title he had given himself after divorcing Mary's mother and breaking with the old faith. Jane, who had been Queen Catherine's lady-in-waiting before she was Queen Anne's, was fond of Mary, and not happy to see her shut away and degraded. However, bride or not, the king told her sharply to mind her own business. It needed Mary's submission to the king to restore her to favour – and to safety, for Anne's fate was still fresh in all their minds – and eventually she subdued her conscience and came to terms with the king, to Queen Jane's delight. Mary and her little sister Elizabeth (Ysabeau as Chapuys called her) were brought to Court and given places of honour. Yet Henry was deeply suspicious and never wholly convinced that he was not being plotted against, either by the Catholics or other malcontents.

During all that year Henry hoped the queen would become pregnant, but by September he told Chapuys that he was 'already old and doubted whether he would have children by the queen'. Yet it was for this very purpose that he had removed Anne Boleyn.

A month later, Henry had news of a rebellion in Lincolnshire. Sixteen thousand common people, peasants for the most part, rose against him to protest against his Dissolution of the monasteries. Henry was furious and wrote a vicious letter to the rebels, threatening to 'burn, spoil and destroy your goods, wives and children'. In vain Queen Jane pleaded for them. Henry roared at her to cease meddling and keep her views to herself. He had just informed the Lincolnshire men that they were presumptuous common folk of 'one of the most brute and beastly counties of the whole realm'. Nevertheless, the revolt spread to Yorkshire. The Pilgrimage of Grace was expressing in tangible form general grief at the loss of the religious orders and their public service. Inevitably, all ended in disaster. The leaders were executed in barely civilized fashion, the common folk barbarously; the royal despot felt marginally more secure and justified in his power; and his man-of-all-work, Thomas Cromwell, carried out any dirty commission given him.

The end of the rebellion brought good news to Henry. The queen was undoubtedly pregnant, and the heir this time would be legitimate, its parentage not in doubt. But plague was in the city and Jane, always fearful of the Black Death, was now doubly unnerved. She moved to Hampton Court's glowing buildings for her confinement, the King staying nearby. When the queen asked for Princess Mary's companionship, Mary arrived bringing with her the lively little Elizabeth, full of talk and questions and fascinated by her huge, glittering father. Henry, waiting anxiously to see if this last fathering were to be yet another girl, must have remembered his illegitimate boy, Richmond, who had died the previous year of tuberculosis. The son of his favourite sister, Mary Rose, was also dead now, of the sweating sickness. Only girls of the royal line were left, Mary Rose's elder daughter having given birth to yet another, Lady Jane Grey.

Queen Jane was thirty hours in labour, but she had a son. Born on the eve of St Edward's Day, he would be called Edward, after the saint and in memory of his father's grandfather, Edward IV of York, the burly optimist whom Henry resembled. England celebrated, rang bells, danced dances, lit beacons and bonfires, laughed, sang, felt waves of relief surging through it. The king would be satisfied at last; his succession was secure. There would be no more divorces, beheadings, womanizing. All now was well. The Princess Mary was to be the boy's godmother and appear in cloth-of-silver for his christening. The royal chapel at Hampton Court was decorated with costly materials, and a great procession of nobles, clergy and members of the Council attended. The two godfathers were Thomas Cranmer, Archbishop of Canterbury, and the Duke of Norfolk. The queen's imposing elder brother, Edward (Ned) Seymour, carried the small Princess Elizabeth in his arms.

Afterwards the new baby – a delicate, puny child, according to reports murmured *sotto-voce* between friends – was carried back to his parents in the room where he was born. But already Jane was feverish, her mind coming and going with the fluctuations of temperature and the disastrous consequences of her confinement. She lived on for ten more days and then slid quietly out of life, leaving Henry a widower for the third time. The king, officially mourning his 'poor, pretty little

Jane', announced that he was little disposed to marry again, though he was not averse to enquiring about the availability of the French king's daughter, Madeleine. But he had grown used to Jane; she was unobtrusive and companionable and he missed her. Of siblings who might have offered him comfort, he had little in common with his elder sister, Margaret of Scotland, and his favourite sister, Mary, had died two years earlier. Her widower, Charles Brandon, had immediately married a young girl, thus depriving his old friend and sovereign of any possible comfort from that source. Only his children remained, therefore, and he was quite fanatical about safeguarding the baby prince from any risk of poisoning.

It was three weeks after her death that Jane Seymour made her last journey from the chapel where she had lain at rest to Windsor for her burial. Already plans had been made to ask the French king for his daughter's hand, as soon as a decent interval had elapsed.

Some years ago I visited Wolfhall in Wiltshire, the ancient manor house on the outskirts of beautiful, mysterious Savernake Forest. This once belonged to the Seymours, and Henry had used the excuse of hunting to call upon young Jane. Local tradition still has it that the wedding took place in the original manor house, and that the nearby barn was the scene of a splendid reception for the wedding guests. Time has eaten away much of what then stood, and all that now remains is Wolfhall Farm, only parts of which are mediaeval. Neighbourhood views are that the place is strongly haunted, but when I talked to the occupants, their opinions were so diverse that the facts were hard to fathom. I had the impression that one or two of the inhabitants had experienced *something* which other members of the family would not countenance, and certainly not advertise.

Outside reports refer to an eighteen-year-old boy having been awakened by the movement of his bed as it was shunted about the room by someone unseen. Another youth once resident there is said to have seen an elderly bearded man in the building, though of what period is not known. Yet another bedroom has caused the family dog to show signs of extreme fear. It would seem that Wolfhall does indeed hold echoes of its past, though whether these are connected with the Seymours or later owners it is not possible to say.

Marwell Hall in Hampshire was also a home of the Seymour family and it too lays claim to being the venue of the famous marriage. The affair is said to have taken place in one of the upper rooms, and Jane is thought to haunt the house and possibly the avenue of yews outside it. A better authenticated haunting though is at Hampton Court, where Queen Jane has been seen (dressed in white, in true ghostly convention), carrying a candle and moving from the old Queen's Apartments, through the Silver Stick gallery and down the flight of stairs into the Clock Court. Was this a walk she made in life? And did it on one occasion have enough significance to generate a powerful emotion whose impact remained impressed in the area? The fluctuating chart of human emotions is quickly forgotten, often not outlasting its own day, and none can now know what this third queen felt. Perhaps the stones remember. . .

A slight echo of Queen Jane was raised by a postcard and letter I received recently. The card, in faded sepia, shows a stairway near the old Queen's Apartments at Hampton Court, and, superimposed upon it, the transparent figure of a woman, dressed more or less in Tudor costume and holding her hands to her head in a distraught fashion. The caption insists that the picture is of 'Queen Jane Seymour's Ghost, as seen nightly near the private stairway leading to apartments formerly occupied by her'. A nice piece of Edwardian imagination; although the woman's face does bear a resemblance to that of Holbein's Jane Seymour portrait, and the photographer must have taken some pains to get the rather impressive result; but no spectre posed for this picture.

*

Once Henry had recovered from his third widowing, he began to take an interest in European politics. There had been threats of treason to his person (largely imaginary) and rumours of war against his kingdom (largely home-created), but he did need a new European alliance. The small state of Cleves was beginning to consolidate and attract support under the leadership of its Protestant duke; and since Cleves was in a good buffer position between France and its German neighbours to the immediate north, Henry – or Thomas Cromwell on his behalf – saw advantages in cultivating the young Duke of Cleves. What better than to marry the young man's sister? Henry looked long and hard at Holbein's portrait of Anne of Cleves and was sufficiently reassured to proceed to the next stage. Cromwell duly arranged a betrothal between Protestant king and princess, and Henry congratulated himself upon his political wisdom.

When news came from Cleves that the proposed bride was attractive, the king looked forward ardently to meeting her. He gave orders for his palaces to be refurbished in her honour, while Cromwell laid on a fine reception. At thirty-four, Anne had not thought that she might achieve a king, and was excited and anxious to please. She had been brought up in a backwater, an old-fashioned court, strict in its etiquette, and provincial and unsophisticated in its manners. She was no beauty, being tall, thin, somewhat pockmarked 'and of very assured and resolute countenance'. She had little charm and was much under the influence of her mother. She spoke no language other than Low German. According to reports percolating back to Cromwell, she was overwhelmingly anxious to please; a quality which might be the only one Henry would find appealing.

This was not sufficiently in evidence to recommend her to the bridegroom at first sight. His hopes had been raised too high, and he was disappointed to find this rumoured beauty a raw-boned, swarthy lumpish woman, with uncouth manners and outmoded dress. Not Henry's idea of beauty at all.

Cromwell was uneasy when he saw that a mistake had been made, but they were now committed; the king would have to go ahead with his contract. 'There is no remedy,' complained Henry, 'but to put my neck in the noose.' Nevertheless, he looked for ways out of the marriage. If only it could be done without driving the Duke of Cleves into the arms of the French king or the Holy Roman Emperor, he would even now repudiate Anne. He postponed the wedding, to Anne's alarm. Even when it came to the ceremony, Henry procrastinated as long as he could before going to the chapel, and later that week it seemed doubtful whether consummation of the marriage had taken place. Perhaps it never did, but what the marriage did bring about was the culmination of Thomas Cromwell's work for the king. It made Henry the foremost Protestant ruler in Europe and isolated and partially immobilized the Catholic powers who opposed him.

All might have settled down had Thomas Cromwell not had bitter enemies in his own country. Stephen Gardiner, Bishop of Winchester, and Thomas Howard, Duke of Norfolk, resented Cromwell as an upstart with too much power. As long as he was the king's First Minister, there would be little chance of their own ambitions fruiting. Anne, the new queen, had been Cromwell's protégée. They could topple him only by supplanting her with a woman this lascivious king would desire, and for whom he would be grateful to them.

Norfolk was head of a very large family, and among his nieces was a young, lively girl, Catherine Howard, probably named for the king's first wife. The girl's mother had died young, and she had been reared by her grandmother, the old Duchess of Norfolk, who allowed her to run wild in the grounds of their country house in Horsham St. Faiths, Norfolk, and with other young folk of her own age. She grew into a warm, light-hearted sensual beauty, with the kind of fire that always dazzled Henry but which he neither understood nor could control. Catherine was a cousin of Anne Boleyn. She was also seven years younger than Henry's elder daughter, Mary, but once he had set his mind upon her, the difference in their ages ceased to exist for him. She was what he craved after these dreary months with his stolid *hausfrau*. Anne of Cleves had been forced on him by Cromwell, and he was determined to be free to take this vibrant girl in her place.

Henry's determination marked the end of Thomas Cromwell. So gross an error as the Cleves marriage was not forgiven. Once a minister had made a grave mistake he was not given the chance of a second. Cromwell was arrested at a meeting of the Privy Council and, although he raged against the injustice of it, he was shouted down (Traitor! Traitor!) by his erstwhile colleagues. Norfolk snatched the Order of St George from his neck and the furious Southampton tore off his Garter insignia. The Great Chamberlain of England was hustled through a back door into the boat which waited to take him to the Tower. His sovereign immediately seized his wealth. Cromwell, alone in his prison, had time to remember Queen Anne Boleyn and the five men he had so ruthlessly condemned with her. His own fate, he knew, would be as theirs. And so, since he could no longer afford arrogance, he wrote a grovelling letter to his monarch, to no avail. Norfolk, bent on seeing a second niece as queen and himself of yet greater consequence, fed Henry tales of Cromwell's treachery and greed. Ever morbidly suspicious and not at all eager to disgorge Cromwell's riches, the king listened.

In the meantime, the sovereign despatched the Lords Suffolk, Southampton and Wriothesley to visit Anne of Cleves at Richmond Palace. Thinking she was to go the way of other obstacles in her husband's path, Anne promptly fainted. Once revived, she was assured that if she agreed to a divorce, she would be treated with dignity and kindness. Anne had much sense and a realistic idea of self-preservation, and it worried her not at all that she was to be supplanted by another woman. Henry was doing the incredible and offering her a safe way out; it was hardly surprising that she leapt at the solution. She would have agreed to anything. A relieved monarch settled four thousand pounds annuity upon her, two great houses and their parks, and sundry bequests of jewellery. The marriage was declared null by the bishops and the newly entitled Madame de Cleves, 'sister of the king', retired to her stately houses, her head safely upon her shoulders. Cromwell's was removed on the morning of 28 July, with a single stroke of the axe.

There is no record, so far as I know, of Anne of Cleves haunting anywhere, either in her adopted country or elsewhere. She liked England well enough to remain in it, and at one time owned a house in Lewes, Sussex, known to this day as Anne of Cleves's House. In the local museum there is an ancient and unusual table generally referred to as 'the Knights' Table'. Its octagonal top is cut from a whole slab of marble, and the piece is enormously heavy. The wooden base has long since rotted away, and been replaced by four stone staddles on which the top is placed. The history of the table is extraordinary and is said to date from the twelfth century. It is, by tradition, haunted.

According to Stanley's *Historical Memorials of Canterbury*: 'Reginald Fitzurse, Hugh de Morville, William de Tracy and Richard de Bret slew Thomas à Becket on Tuesday, 29 December, 1170. On 31 December they rode to South Malling Deanery, near Lewes.' On entering the house they stripped off their armour and weapons and piled them on a heavy table which stood in the hall. Later, after they had eaten, they clustered round the great hearth fire. Then with a sudden abrupt movement the table appeared to jerk backwards throwing the whole pile of arms to the floor. The startled servants replaced the equipment and the knights turned away. But almost immediately there was a still louder crash as the table once more jerked and hurled the armaments even farther afield. There was consternation, as soldiers and servants searched under the heavy table to find the cause of the upheaval. Eventually one of the knights (according to Stanley) 'suggested that it was indignantly refusing to bear the sacrilegious burden of their Arms.'

This ancient piece of furniture would seem to have been an early form of the turning and jumping table so familiar in modern séances. And yet there is a difference, for the Knights' Table has been known to turn when no hand was near it, nor human energy-field to power it. For years it stood in Malling Deanery and occasionally on 29 December, the fatal anniversary, it has been said to whirl about and produce strange sounds.

On the day that Thomas Cromwell died at Tyburn, Henry, king of England, was twenty miles away at Oaklands, a private house, fastidiously donning the costume for his fifth wedding. He was congratulating himself on having discovered at last the perfect bride, the flawless girl, the rose without a thorn, the much desired and long-sought-for complement to the great king of a noble realm. Not for the first time, Henry was in love with the idea of love and of himself as lover. He was forty-nine, his youthful athlete's stature and hard body running to seed, fat and ulcerations of the leg, although his face remained unlined. This late harvest, a St Martin's Summer, filled him with renewed hope and vigour. He treated Catherine as though she were his most prized possession and caressed her openly, much as he would have stroked and fondled a rare jewel. He regarded himself as her protector as well as husband; she was petite, pretty, young and, according to reports, inexperienced. But reports lied. From early youth Catherine had mixed with young people of her own class whose preoccupation had been mainly with one another. Supposedly supervised by the old duchess, the Norfolk gentlewomen's dormitory was often invaded by young kinsmen and friends who stayed for late night feasts and lovemaking, while the old chaperone slept heavily upstairs. From the age of fourteen to eighteen, Catherine had had a passionate affair with Francis Derham, a distant poor relation of the Norfolks. Eventually the dormitory activities were discovered and banned, and Catherine was removed from the duchess's dubious care to that of the court.

The girl's mother had been a certain Jocosa Culpeper of Kent and a youth of Henry's bedchamber, Thomas Culpeper, may have been distantly related. Thomas seems to have been a highly personable young man, and a favourite with his master. He rapidly attracted the attention of Catherine, who might have seen him as a possible bed partner even while she was being courted by the king. But Henry had been assured not once but many times that his rose was lily-pure and he was most anxious to be convinced. For once he did not see what he did not wish to see; he saw only Catherine's warm-heartedness and generosity of feeling; the way she longed to share her sudden material good fortune with all her friends and relatives, even, to Henry's dismay (he was beginning to show signs of his father's parsimoniousness), to the extent of giving away several of his expensive gifts to her. The old Duchess of Norfolk, who had ridden with that earlier daughter of the Howards, Anne Boleyn, watched Catherine from a distance, muttering, 'She cannot die for what was done before'.

Looking now at the portrait of Henry as he was at the time of this fifth marriage (Holbein's chalk drawing in the Royal Print Cabinet, Munich), one sees a face of contradictions. The countenance is at once sensual and reserved, amiable yet suspicious. There is a craftiness about the eyes and a hard-lipped meanness about the tight little mouth. Above all, the impression is that of power, egoism and ruthlessness; and of a terrifying will. Such was the personality which had once been near-heroic; and such the physiognomy of the man who had once seemed to his people a young god. Henry, unaccountably, seems always to have held some core of self-doubt – perhaps of himself as king as much as of himself as man – and the fear could be resolved only by the violent removal of whoever caused it. If he had ever queried his own motives, he had long since ceased. A king has no need for self-questioning. Holbein's portrait is that of a dangerous man.

Catherine neither knew nor cared about this. She was deeply in love with Thomas Culpeper and sought opportunities to meet him secretly as often as possible. In this she was aided by Lady Rochford, the woman who had once been Anne Boleyn's sister-in-law and personal spy. That the queen and Culpeper were lovers there seems no doubt, for during the Progress of the king and queen to Lincoln and York that year the pair met many times alone, often staying together until the early hours of morning. Catherine, in an ill-advised note to Culpeper at one point, signed herself 'Yours as long as life endures'. She was young, and nothing in her experience could have prepared her for dealings with the type of man with whom she now shared marriage. She seems, also, to have had little idea of discretion, and her secret late night meetings with Culpeper were well known to several of her waiting-women.

The news of Catherine's previous amorous history (though not, at this stage, her affair with Culpeper) eventually reached the ears of Archbishop Cranmer, through John Lassells, a Puritan whose sister had been a nurse with the old Duchess of Norfolk during Catherine's liaison with Francis Derham. Lassells felt it his duty to pass the information to Cranmer, and the archbishop, who had neither the heart nor nerve to confront his royal master verbally with bad tidings, handed Henry a letter upon his return to Hampton Court after the northern Progress. At first Henry refused to believe it and sent for Cranmer to question him. For once the highly flexible archbishop did not budge and this caused the beginnings of doubt in the king's mind of his cherished rose's thornlessness. He dismissed the young queen's musicians and ordered her confined to her rooms as though she had been a recalcitrant child; or a prisoner. In the meantime he instituted enquiries among the queen's former associates and sent for Lassells and his sister.

During those early November days, when the air came dank and chill from the river and the blue wreaths of smoke rose from country cottage chimneys and the great hearths of Hampton Court, England's sovereign was in long, late-night conference with his ministers. They in turn interviewed all connected with the queen's life who might have information concerning her premarital guilt or innocence. One by one, Catherine's former friends collapsed under questioning, incriminating the queen ever more deeply.

Then the chief members of Henry's Council began on the young queen herself; first Norfolk as the girl's uncle and then the Archbishop of Canterbury. Cranmer had meant to warn her of the consequences of any misconduct, but by now the danger of her situation had dawned upon the nineteen-year-old girl and she was in terror. She poured out to him as to her confessor the full story of her premarital escapades. Culpeper's name was apparently not mentioned, and Cranmer appears not to have considered at this stage that the queen's married life might be involved. The story was told to the king by his councillors, and for a while he sat in absolute silence. Then he began to weep.

Had she been faithful in marriage, Catherine might still have escaped – suffered divorce perhaps, or banishment, in consideration of her unsuitability to mother royal children. But her servants talked. Culpeper's name was revealed, and before Catherine could warn him he was in the Tower. She was half-demented, refusing food and comfort and crying so desperately that her guardians removed any instrument which might lead her to suicide. The king sent his wife to Syon nunnery until he came to a decision, but he grieved over his lost hope and his betrayal. Her uncle, Norfolk, took pains to underline his own utter condemnation of the queen's character and morals. His family had supplied the king with two wives, both unsatisfactory, and his need to extricate himself was urgent.

By now, Henry had been so worked upon by those of his

council who wished to bring down the Howard faction, that he began to rage against Catherine and to threaten her with a fearful death. Yet even in the midst of this tirade, he broke down in tears of self-pity. His rose had been peerless and now had a worm at its heart. He would end his life as a comfortless old man who had hoped for a kind nurse and consort. Although Catherine, in her period of imprisonment at Hampton Court and later at Syon, had been in a state of near-hysteria, rebelling against the disaster she had brought upon herself, she had accepted death by the time she reached the block on Tower Green. 'I die a queen,' she cried, 'but I would rather die the wife of Culpeper.' Her lover had been executed at Tyburn two months earlier, in company with Francis Derham. Catherine was buried near the body of her kinswoman, Anne Boleyn.

There is no doubt that Catherine's state of mind in the last few weeks of her life was highly emotional and disturbed. She alternated between fear and frenetic hope, between distress for her lover and terror at what lay ahead of her. In addition, she had been made to feel the enormity of her wickedness in committing what in her family (the Howards never veered far from their private Catholicism no matter what they avowed politically) was regarded as mortal sin. Her mental state in the early days at Hampton Court must therefore have been tense, overwrought and desperate.

The story which has persisted over the centuries at Hampton is that Catherine, imprisoned by Henry's order in her rooms, managed to escape from her guards and run down the long gallery which backs the Royal Chapel. She must have known that Henry was attending service there and apparently had the intention of pleading with him. Had she been able to do so, she might have been reprieved. But the guards caught her and dragged her away screaming. Her husband stayed within his sanctuary, listening, doing nothing, thinking his own shadowed thoughts.

That there remain echoes in this area of the young woman's anguish seems certain. Many times over the intervening centuries, frantic shrieking has been heard in the Long Gallery. Occasionally a figure (of the traditional woman in white) has been seen in the neighbourhood of the Royal Chapel, and on one occasion an artist sketching the tapestries saw a disembodied hand appear in front of him. Not in the least discomposed, he sketched both hand and an unusual ring upon its index finger. Later the ring was seen to bear a strong resemblance to one worn by Queen Catherine during her lifetime. This story would have been more convincing had the *Daily Mail* reporter who quoted it named the artist; or given details of available proof that the ring had indeed belonged to Catherine Howard.

Speculation and flowery imaginings apart, there does seem to be some echo of the distant past in the Long Gallery. The sensation near the door of the Royal Chapel is not comfortable. When I visited it some years ago, I experienced a sensation of extreme coldness at the Gallery door leading to the chapel, and a feeling of utter misery and despair. So strong were these impressions that to move forward into the Chapel proper was the equivalent of forcing a physical barrier.

A correspondent, Mrs F. Kerridge of Towcester, writing to me in connection with time experiences, admitted that she had known Catherine's story and half-expected to find 'echoes' of it in the Long Gallery proper when she and her husband visited it. However, the Gallery had offered nothing untoward, and it was not until they reached the door leading to the antechamber of the Royal Pew (the Gallery and the Chapel Royal are separated by the Royal Pew enclosure in which the monarch could see and hear divine service without being observed by members of the main congregation) that Mrs Kerridge experienced a positive 'agony of distress'. The door into the Pew seemed to be its focal point. 'One went through a cloud – invisible but tangible to one's senses.' This correspondent thought the points of anguish (the 'cloud') had been dual, one at the door of the antechamber, the other in the Pew, with nothing between; by which I suppose her to mean that between the two points of sensation nothing at all was felt. The emotions of the listening Henry within the Pew, perhaps, and those of the frantic girl trying to break in?

Whatever occurred in that area between the time of Catherine's escape from her guards and her moment of recapture must have been emotionally high-key. Such stressful incidents do seem to have the ability to register on their surroundings and be retained by them. As I have said, the theory is that emotion – fear, hatred, love, pain, joy – results in a heightening of human ability to convey information by means of the electromagnetic field which arises from our own physical construction (see p.77).

Two further echoes of Catherine Howard's tragedy have come to my knowledge, though one is of an ambiguous nature. The first occurred to Mrs E. Hodgson of Mitcham, Surrey, who wrote

> My ghost story is one unidentified and unseen, but you may be interested, as it was encountered in the Chapel Royal at Hampton Court Palace.
>
> One summer afternoon some years ago, on the way to the Royal apartments, my sister saw a partly-opened door not noticed on previous visits, and we decided to look inside. We found ourselves standing in the gallery of the Chapel Royal, after walking down a few steps both stood, slightly in awe, absorbing the beauty around us.
>
> Suddenly I felt an intense chill in the air, as if surrounded by a wall of ice, in my mind I heard the command 'walk down and jump over the edge'. I realized that if I did so I would die, so remained quite still. Then I felt as if a hand was on my back pushing me forward, but on turning around saw nothing.
>
> Believing my life to be in danger I suggested that we

> leave, and was glad when my sister agreed at once. Outside the door she remarked, 'I was so glad when you said shall we go.' She then told me of her own experience which exactly matched mine. It was incredible, I feebly replied 'not you too', and we hastily rejoined the family.
>
> I have failed to find a written record of such an incident in the many books on Hampton Court. We are certain that our presence was resented by something or someone.

It is plain from Mrs Hodgson's letter that this was not their first visit to Hampton Court, and it is likely that both were aware of the haunting of the Long Gallery behind the Chapel. However, the experience they had seems to be unique, for as far as I know there is no other record of 'a will to suicide' in this area. If, as my correspondent suggests, 'something' was attempting to propel her over the edge of the upper tier, one is inclined to fruitless speculation on the source of the compulsion. Such urges are not uncommon, as anyone who has walked along a cliff edge or a castle battlement will confirm. The sense of an outside influence as agent is not usually felt, still less that of being forcibly propelled. Such physical propulsion is not unheard of in connection with hauntings, and indeed tactile hauntings, where the sense of being touched or pushed is engaged, have been recorded on many occasions.

If we suppose that Mrs Hodgson and her sister each experienced a compulsion and propulsion, what are we to conclude about its probable agency? What or who would have wished their deaths? Or, to look at it from another angle, who in that Chapel's history would have experienced a personal death wish or desired to destroy some other? Henry the king must be a likely candidate for either, though it is not likely the two sisters were the special targets of whatever force was operating. Rather that they were accidentally in the way of it, and therefore had the sensation willy-nilly. It is an interesting sidelight on the power of certain places to generate sensation, and it must be noted that the classical temperature fall took place for both women immediately prior to the experience.

The final account in this most ghost-productive period of British history, was told me by my friend, Renee Burgess, whose husband had been head of the Lighting Department at Anglia Television before his tragically early death. Earlier, Douglas had been employed by the BBC, and during his time with the Corporation worked on a programme concerning Hampton Court Palace. This entailed a good deal of photography in the Long Gallery, and at a certain point the crew decided to track the camera up to the closed door of the room where Catherine Howard had been held prisoner. In the manner of television men worldwide, they planned to add a bit of atmosphere by shining an eerie light on the scene, so that when the door of the room slowly opened (under the pressure of a flesh and blood cameraman-sized foot from within), viewers would be impressed. The arrangement had to function on cue, and the door's spectral opening had to coincide with the camera's arrival. It worked spectacularly well: the door creaked open of its own accord a few seconds before the door-opener could put toe to it. The team tried again, with the same result. And again. Each time the camera arrived within two feet of the door, the latter swung open of its own volition. After several minutes of these manoeuvres, the crew's teeth and knees were knocking loudly enough to have made Catherine's shrieks inaudible had she uttered them. Then someone tested the position of the camera, and it was found that when the machine was placed on certain floorboards, its weight caused the door to open spontaneously. 'At least,' said Renee, 'that's what they told themselves.'

However, from the total evidence available over many years, it seems that part of the Long Gallery, and in particular the entrance from it to the Royal Chapel, does hold some image, either audio, visual or other-sensory, which relates to the Catherine Howard/Henry VIII crisis.

CHAPTER SEVEN

The Sixteenth Century, Part II

After Henry VIII died in 1547, his son Edward reigned for a meagre six years. The young man died of tuberculosis in 1553, aged sixteen. He had no time to impress his personality, being under the influence of his uncle, Edward Seymour, Duke of Somerset and Lord Protector of England. Somerset fell to his rival for power, John Dudley, Duke of Northumberland, and was beheaded on Tower Hill on 22 January 1552. Northumberland took over the position of chief adviser to the young king. Unfortunately for the peace of the realm, he was a far from disinterested counsellor, and his hand contained a card which, if played wisely, might put his own son upon the throne, at least as a consort.

Henry VIII's younger sister, the Princess Mary Rose, had seen her daughter married to Henry Grey, Duke of Suffolk. One of the daughters of this marriage, Lady Jane Grey, was therefore cousin to Edward VI and in line of succession to the throne. It seemed a provident move to Northumberland to marry one of his sons (he chose his fourth son, Guildford Dudley) to the young girl with royal connections.

Jane Grey had a scholarly upbringing and a naturally academic bent, becoming proficient in Latin, French, Italian and Hebrew. She would much have preferred to remain a private person, pursuing her studies and following the Protestantism to which she was devoted. Whatever bargaining took place between her harsh parents and Northumberland, however, took no account of the girl's wishes. She was married to Guildford Dudley on 21 May 1553, much against her will. She was fifteen years old. Immediately afterwards, again without regard for her protests, Jane was transferred from the house of her parents to that of the Northumberlands, where she found both atmosphere and company so alien to her temperament that she fell into a deep depression and seems to have suffered a nervous breakdown.

By now Edward VI was coughing his life away, and since he too had been reared a staunch Protestant, he was vulnerable to Northumberland's reminders that his heir and sister, the Princess Mary, was a fanatical Catholic. Eventually, Edward succumbed to pressure and nominated Jane Grey as his successor rather than accept Mary as the next sovereign. He died on 6 July and Lady Jane was immediately publicly proclaimed queen at the Tower of London. The Princesses Mary and Elizabeth were both disinherited. But Mary's supporters were not idle. The princess had been summoned by Northumberland to attend her brother's sickbed, and she had already reached Hoddesdon in Hertfordshire. Elizabeth, similarly summoned, was cannier and pleaded illness to account for her absence. Doubtless Northumberland would have imprisoned both Edward's sisters had he laid hands on them, and their fate then would probably have been the block. As it happened, one of Mary's men reached her with news of Edward's death before she could continue to London, and she at once turned north and fled towards her Norfolk manor at Kenninghall. Although she was unaware of it, another of Northumberland's sons, Robert Dudley, was in hot pursuit of her with three hundred horsemen. Mary rested overnight at Sawston Hall in Cambridgeshire, home of the devout Catholic family of Huddleston, and then sped onwards. Dudley, arriving hard on her heels, burned Sawston to the ground in his frustration at losing the quarry.

Even now Mary was not aware that Jane had been proclaimed queen (Northumberland intended to keep the king's death secret until he had secured the two princesses and established his daughter-in-law). Mary therefore assumed that there was a temporary hitch, an optimistic attempt on the

1 Boudicca, the warrior queen of the Iceni, with her daughters. Her chariot is still occasionally seen emerging from the mists of Lincolnshire. *(City of Cardiff)*

2 Barnwell Castle, where, in the 13th century,
Marie le Moine may have been killed by being walled into one of the gate bastions. *(Jarrold Bros, Norwich)*

3 From time to time, the sound of a man's footsteps have been heard relentlessly tramping up and down the secret tunnel leading from this inn to Nottingham Castle. They are thought to be those of Roger Mortimer, lover of Queen Isabella, wife of Edward II.
(Forman Newspapers/T. Bailey)

4 Castle Rising, Norfolk, where Queen Isabella was imprisoned. She is said to have lost her reason here and her crazy laughter is sometimes heard echoing through the building. *(Eastern Daily Press)*

5 Fotheringhay Church, which still reverberates with the music accompanying the burial of Edward, Duke of York, after his death at Agincourt 500 years ago. *(Northamptonshire Evening Telegraph)*

6 Kimbolton Castle, said to be haunted by Catherine of Aragon, who died here in 1536. *(Jarrold Bros, Norwich)*

7 The only record of Henry VIII haunting anywhere is at Windsor Castle, where the sound of agonized groans and slow, dragging footsteps are occasionally heard. In later life Henry suffered from a painful dropsical leg. The portrait shows Henry when young. *(National Portrait Gallery)*

8 The ghost of Catherine Howard, Henry VIII's fifth wife, is said to haunt the Long Gallery at Hampton Court. Frantic shrieking has been heard in this area, and a disembodied hand sighted, possible echoes of the Queen's terror following her arrest. *(Hampton Court Palace)*

9 Both individual ghosts and the actual fighting armies have been seen on Culloden Moor, scene of the blood-thirsty battle between the Jacobite forces of Bonnie Prince Charlie and Cumberland's Army in 1740. *(National Trust for Scotland)*

10 Sawston Hall, where Mary Tudor (later to become Mary I) took refuge when pursued by Robert Dudley's troops. A Lady in Grey, thought to be Mary, haunts the Tapestry Room; knockings and movement have also been heard in the Panelled Room next door. *(Cambridge Evening News)*

11 George IV is said to haunt Brighton Pavilion's subterranean passage. The ghost of a dumpy, elderly woman, believed to be Martha Gunn, who bathed Prince George when he was a child, has also been seen in the State Rooms. *(Brighton Evening Argus)*

12 A ghost with an unusually round face and an unshaven appearance has been sighted on several occasions at Bolton Abbey. His long dark robes suggest a monkish origin. *(Telegraph and Argus Bradford)*

Dudleys' part to seize power. She had only to wait for her supporters to swarm to her standard and she would be secure. However, she was advised to cross into Suffolk and take refuge in the royal castle of Framlingham. More tidings reached her from London. Jane's proclamation as queen was being made all over the city, and notices branding the late king's sisters as illegitimate mushroomed at every door and crossroads. The proclamations were made to a resounding silence. The feeling in the country was for Mary, the eldest child of Henry VIII, the rightful heir; her small army at Framlingham grew rapidly. One by one the Lords of the Council began to slip away from London to join Mary's cause, and a few of them saw to it that she was proclaimed queen at Cheapside and St Paul's, the proclamation accompanied stylishly by two heralds and three trumpeters. Her subjects began to rejoice openly, and to celebrate in the streets of her capital. Queen Jane's short reign, the nine days' wonder, was over.

Jane had not wished to be queen. She was aware that Edward had first named not herself but 'male heirs of her body' as his successor. Whether Northumberland forged the nomination in Jane's favour or whether the dying king made the alteration is not certain. Now she found herself in the Tower, a prisoner, as was her husband, Guildford Dudley. On 14 November she was charged with treason and pleaded guilty. Although the death sentence was passed, it was expected that this would be waived and she would be allowed to retire into private life. And so she might have done had not her foolish father, still insatiable for power, joined in a further plot against Queen Mary. There would be no safety for the queen while her young rival lived and Mary at last accepted this. The death sentence on Jane Grey had to be carried out.

Jane watched her husband leave the Beauchamp Tower for the scaffold, and then 'hys body beying layde in a carre, and hys head in a cloth, did see his dead carcase taken out of the carre'. She died later in the day. Her father followed in

November of the same year. In the Beauchamp Tower there is an inscription on the stone wall of the great chamber. It says simply JANE, and is believed to have been carved by Guildford Dudley. It stands as a memorial to the end of a reckless gamble and overweening ambition.

Do any echoes remain of the tragic little Nine Days' Queen? Peter Underwood, among others, reports a sighting by a certain guardsman Johns on sentry duty at the Tower on 12 February, 1957. Hearing a loud sound from the Bell Tower, he glanced up and saw a white form, in the apparent likeness of Lady Jane Grey, standing on the battlements. The building where Jane was housed once stood nearby, and from it she watched her husband's last journey. No reason is given in the reports for the identification of the apparition as Lady Jane. But 12 February chanced to be the 403rd anniversary of her death. Anniversaries occasionally produce some psychic reminder of the event they commemorate.

Jane Grey is one of the sadder figures in English history. On the scaffold she told onlookers that she had never wished to be queen, and died 'a true Christian woman'. Blindfolded, she was unable to find the block, and said, 'Where is it? What shall I do?' Royal blood had proved no gift to this serious sixteen-year-old.

What of the man whose ambition instigated the tragedy – Henry Grey, Jane's father, the Duke of Suffolk? When his rising against Mary failed, and all hope of restoring his daughter to the throne was lost, he fled to his seat at Astley Castle in Warwickshire, where he went into hiding. However, his park-keeper betrayed him and he was returned to London and a final sojourn in the Tower. A fitting reward, perhaps, for one who had bought a pardon for himself by proclaiming Mary queen at the gates of that very Tower which then imprisoned his daughter. Suffolk's head, when it was found in 1849 in the church of the Holy Trinity in the Minories, still bore traces of red hair and beard; and the gashes which a blundering headsman had inflicted on his neck before finally decapitating him. Yet it is not the Tower which Suffolk haunts, but Astley Castle. His headless spectre has appeared there, though it has not been seen for many years. Northumberland, according to reports, occasionally haunts the Tower of London.

After this period of troubled uncertainty, the people of England might have expected a quiet and stable reign, but they were, as they had been for several centuries, out of luck. Mary, as devout a Catholic as her mother, was bent on restoring the old faith and thought the sacrifice of men's bodies to save their souls an act which must serve Christ. Protestant – heretic in her eyes – heads fell and people of both sexes were burned at the stake: a death of peculiar and barbaric horror. Ancient Cranmer, who had planted Anne Boleyn in her mother's place and then orchestrated Anne's death, was sent to join the bishops Latimer and Ridley in Oxford. The setts of stones in a street there still mark the sites of those funeral pyres. 'We shall this day light such a candle by God's grace in England, as I trust shall never be put out.' Thus Bishop Latimer to Ridley as the flames rose around them.

Mary, true daughter of Catherine of Aragon, had married into her mother's faith, by taking the secretive, pious and devious Philip of Spain as husband. Her English subjects viewed the marriage with a distaste which presently turned into hostility. Neither Mary's marriage nor her reign prospered. No matter how many Protestants were destroyed, much of the nation refused to abandon the Reformation her father and Cranmer had between them constructed. As for the vital succession which sovereign after sovereign had fought to secure, Mary, thinking herself pregnant, was appalled to find after ten or eleven months in waiting that she was not, and suffered not only national but international humiliation. Philip, an unloving husband to his loving middle-aged bride, presently returned to Spain to become Philip II. He stayed in Spain for nineteen months while Mary fretted, apparently forgotten. When he did return, it was only to persuade the English queen to involve her country in his war with France. Mary, still deeply in love, obliged, and money from her hard-pressed exchequer (*English* money, as her subjects reminded themselves) went towards Spanish support, and five thousand Englishmen went to stiffen and fight in the army of Spain.

After her husband's return to Spain (he spent only three and a half months in England on his second visit), Mary once more believed herself pregnant. She was forty-two, and although she immediately notified Philip that she was with child, he does not appear to have believed the news. His doubts were borne out by events, for the queen gradually lost health, fell into melancholy and by the end of October was adding a codicil to her will, revoking the clause which had referred to the hoped-for child. Although her sister Elizabeth was not specifically mentioned, it was made plain that the crown would go to her, the successor according to the law, and that Mary's 'most Dear Lord and Husband' should have no part in governing or ruling the realm. Her Council pressed her officially to nominate her sister as her successor, and eventually she acquiesced, sending a message accordingly to Elizabeth at Hatfield. The younger woman was asked to maintain the old religion and to pay the queen's debts on her accession. When Philip wrote to his wife suggesting that Elizabeth should first be given in marriage to a Spanish nobleman, he was too late. On 17 November 1558 Mary followed her custom of hearing early mass, and, even as she made the responses, left a world which had given her little but pain and which would not remember her kindly.

Elizabeth was Queen.

It might be thought that a life so stark with drama would have left several psychic imprints in the places where Mary had lived and moved, but the only known record of a haunting seems to come from the period when she herself was hunted and in danger.

Sawston Hall has been owned for many centuries by the Huddleston family. It is still in the possession of their descendants, and was, until the early 1970s, still lived in as a family home. The mansion is not the one which sheltered Mary as she fled from Robert Dudley's troops, for Dudley burned most of it to the ground. Mary, watching the conflagration from a distant hill, turned to Huddleston and said, 'Let it burn. When I am queen I will build you another and better one.' She carried out the promise, and the present Sawston was raised on the foundations of the old. It is a place of singular beauty and not a little mystery. Mary, an honest and faithful woman – qualities which should be remembered in her favour as counterweight to those which have earned her so much opprobrium – showed her gratitude to John Huddleston by knighting him and making him a captain of her husband's bodyguard.

It is several years since I visited Sawston, but I fell quite in love with it, felt as though I belonged there and could live there for ever. It was empty and echoing then, its furniture gone, and the place rented out for various social functions, yet its indefinable charm lay upon it like an old fragrance, and its great rooms and grand staircase flowed with the still-remembered movement of the past.

As the Huddleston family recall the story handed down to them through the generations, it was Andrew Huddleston, riding up with Mary from Hoddesdon to Norfolk and safety, who suggested that they should spend the night at his family home at Sawston. She, weary and glad to accept the suggestion, was warmly welcomed by John and Bridget Huddleston and given the best four-poster bed in a good bedroom. She had been asleep only a short while when her host awakened her with the news of Dudley's approach. According to family tradition, Mary escaped disguised as a milkmaid, riding pillion behind a manservant. But something of her sensations during her few hours at Sawston might have remained behind there, because sightings of a lady in grey haunting the Tapestry Room in which Mary slept have (inevitably) been attributed to the ghostly royal princess, while knockings and movements have been heard in the room next door, the Panelled Room.

Whether these occurrences still continue, I do not know, but certainly a few years ago, when the Tapestry Room was occupied by Tom Corbett, a clairvoyant, some strange incidents gave Corbett a restless night. Diana Norman, a journalist whose work on *The Stately Ghosts of England* had led to an investigative partnership with Tom Corbett, reports that both she and Corbett had the impression that they were followed up the main staircase when they retired to their rooms. Corbett actually heard footsteps, though his companion merely sensed 'a presence'. Both thought their sensations were due to the fact that a photographer colleague on their ghost hunt was immediately behind them. They were disconcerted to hear his voice calling up from the hall below to say he would join them when he had collected his camera gear. They were quite alone on the stairs. Corbett had a poor night's sleep, his rest being broken from 4.00 a.m. onwards by someone trying the latch of his door. His alarm clock, set to go off at seven, had shrilled at four, and aroused him to the extramural activities. The alarm sang out again at five o'clock, and almost immediately he heard someone walking around the Panelled Room next door. The performance was repeated at six, and Corbett had the impression that someone was checking his room. The clairvoyant was convinced that whatever had wakened him had been a night watchman, perhaps once employed to guard the house's security and now doing so *in perpetuo*.

Mrs Huddleston, though unable to throw more light on the watchman theory, told the investigators that a maidservant at Sawston in the last century had been setting the fire in the Tapestry Room when she heard three long knocks on the door. It opened and a grey shape floated past her across the room. The girl had been badly frightened. However, the family felt that no Grey Lady now haunted the place. So Mary, if it were indeed she, is probably no longer impressed upon the house she inhabited for so brief a time and in such stressful circumstances. Yet the testing and trying of the door still seems to be experienced from time to time, by persons sufficiently in tune with whatever operates to be able to translate its vibrations into sound.

When I visited Sawston, its employees told me of hearing ghostly female laughter from the upstairs rooms; and of spinet music floating enticingly down the stairs from an instrument vanished from the Hall these many centuries. Footsteps, too, are heard, and on one occasion a woman employee, carrying a bowl of flowers along the gallery in readiness for a forthcoming function, felt a hand placed on her shoulder. Thinking it might be her husband, since he was also in the building, she turned to greet him. However, she found herself alone; the gallery was unoccupied.

On yet another occasion when a film, *The Nightcomers* (another version of Henry James's *The Turn of the Screw*) was being made at Sawston, two security men heard the sound of music coming from the chapel. The building was not in use, and was deserted and silent. What had they heard? A long ago mass, perhaps? Was mass said for Mary when she was there? To make guesses on this subject, one would need to know whether or not the present chapel was part of pre-Tudor Sawston. Buildings are most likely to retain imprints of the action which occurred in them, although it is not unknown for events which took place in an earlier structure to continue to broadcast even when their original background has been destroyed or built over.

There is no doubt that Sawston contains numerous echoes of a variety of periods. Perhaps only the one relates to the time when Mary Tudor, Henry VIII's eldest child, sought and obtained sanctuary there. And yet . . . Dennis Bardens reports, though I do not know the source of his information, that during the evening of her visit to Sawston, Mary sat at the virginals, making music, and her apparition has been seen, smiling happily, as she plays. He also remarks on the fact that the music is heard from time to time. Virginals? Or spinet? A modern, unprofessional ear would have difficulty in detecting the difference.

On 17 November 1558, Elizabeth, daughter of Anne Boleyn, became queen of England. She was twenty-five, born under the sign of Virgo, which gave her an orderly mind, and was both gifted and intelligent. If we are to understand the enigmas of Elizabeth's mature character, we should first look at the influences of her childhood.

Her mother died when she was three, killed by her father's order and wish. She suffered a series of transient stepmothers and had very little stability, for she was frequently moved from one to another and from one cold house to the next. Her relationship with her father was equally unpredictable. Sometimes he appeared to love her, and sometimes to hate her. Being summoned to court to be near him was no guarantee of either his affection or her safety, for she was as likely to be rejected and dismissed with threatening words as to be promoted in his favour and kindness. The sun of Henry VIII's affection grew more fickle as he aged into chronic suspicion.

Apart from her father, there were the courtiers and political aspirants whose attitude towards this younger princess changed with the weather around the throne. Who was in the king's favour and who out, and for what reason, influenced unreasonably the attitudes of nobility and place-seekers to all three children of the king's body. Only the son, little Edward, grew up in family sunshine. The two girls would know only insecurity and anxiety until each in turn succeeded to the throne. Those twin emotions would be with them throughout their adult lives, manifesting in each according to her different temperament.

The primary course of Elizabeth's life – a steadfast refusal to marry – must have arisen from her experiences in early childhood or what she was later told about that period. Marriage for a woman, it seemed, could mean death at the hands of her husband; if not actual death, great jeopardy, which might be staved off only by utter subjection to the will of the man. Elizabeth's will was strong and her instincts for survival dominant. The princess was the product of her parents, both headstrong people. Anne Boleyn had been proud, jealous, ambitious for power, and with a mind of some subtlety. The king was devious, generous, mean, suspicious and possessed of an enormous ego. A streak of ruthlessness ran through him, as a vein of sexuality ran through both him and Anne. An interesting stockpot of heredity for the small red-gold child Chapuys had referred to as Ysabelle.

To look now at the portrait of Elizabeth at thirteen, painted by an unknown artist, is to see an unhappy child. The eyes are watchful, the mouth folded and secretive, the intelligent expression guarded. Then consider the portrait painted when she was in her forties. Assurance had replaced the wariness, but something circumspect remains. This is not a woman who will lightly commit herself to a course of action, preferring always to leave open a line of retreat. She has the look of a human being who will only feel safe in her own charge and never in the hands of another. But when all is said, such judgments are inevitably conditioned by hindsight.

Having intelligence from both parents, Elizabeth also had decided academic ability, perhaps exceeded in the royal circle only by that of Lady Jane Grey. Where she got her lively appreciation of the dramatic is not clear, but she seems to have possessed 'a sense of theatre' when no theatre in its later meaning existed. Her speeches were unashamedly emotional, patriotic and designed to charm her audience. Her feeling for visual splendour was highly developed and whether or not her magnificent jewels and costume in later life were inspired by vanity, they had an undoubted effect upon her subjects.

'Gloriana', 'The Fairy Queen', she seemed indeed. This was a woman who possessed abundantly the quality now known as charisma. This particular gift may be less an innate quality than the result of the suppression of certain elements in a strong and passionate personality. No matter what its source, it is an irradiation and Elizabeth Tudor used it skilfully in both her personal and public life.

The fact that she had been imprisoned in the Tower by Mary, who had suspected her of involvement with Wyatt's rebellion, made a lasting impression upon Elizabeth. She knew the terror of being abandoned to the prison walls, of passing under Traitor's Gate with no hope of coming out alive. She was always hesitant about signing death warrants, though, surprisingly, less scrupulous about condoning torture as a form of persuasion. However, the wholesale burnings of those with opposite religious views which had been the shame and scandal of Mary's reign were not indulged in by Elizabeth. She was a moderate in most of her policies, including religion, and seems to have blended a middle-of-the-road Protestantism with some slight feeling for Catholicism. What she would not tolerate was political disloyalty, and by this she meant disloyalty to the throne and to herself as its occupant.

The announcement of Mary's death and her accession was brought to her by a young horseman, who came clattering post-haste into the courtyard at Hatfield. He was that same Lord Robert Dudley who had pursued Mary to Sawston and then burned the place. Elizabeth had known him since childhood. Perhaps they had even occasionally shared birthday celebrations, for tradition has it that they were born at the same hour on the same day. Certainly they appeared to have an affinity of tastes and interests if not of character. They had also shared at least one peril: both had been imprisoned in the Tower at the same time, and each had known of the other's presence there, and had, according to gossip, contrived to meet. It is likely that the foundations of their long attachment were laid then, in spite of the fact that Dudley was already married to a Norfolk heiress, Amy Robsart.

Little is known of Amy, but apparently she had no education beyond that of a Norfolk squire's daughter. She was barely able to read and write, disliked domesticity, and seems to have been chiefly interested in luxurious clothes and the occasional attentions of her impoverished but noble husband. Robert had soon grown bored with his country girl, and although he kept her happy with small gifts and remembrances, he gave her less and less of his company. He liked the court and the excitement of nearness to the new queen; an excitement which was part sensual, part political, for he knew his attraction for Elizabeth, and the dormant ambitions of the Dudleys stirred in him. Sooner or later the queen must choose a husband. If he were near to her in position and in affection, why should she not look on him? The country had had enough of foreign consorts, and Mary's Spanish commitment had been bitterly resented by the people. So Robert, now Master of the Queen's Horse by royal appointment, danced attendance on his queen rather than his wife, and with proximity sovereign and subject grew nearer and dearer to each other. A fate not confined to queens and courtiers.

If Amy Dudley was the main obstacle to the marriage of the two lovers, there were others. Elizabeth's subjects expected her to marry a man worthy of the throne. The Dudleys, including Robert, they reasoned, had only recently been involved in treachery to that throne; they were parvenus, unscrupulous and without anything to offer in return for the power they sought. Robert Dudley was therefore not a fit partner or consort for their young sovereign, and England's welfare would be jeopardized should she choose so unwisely. Her counsellors, who considered Dudley vain, arrogant and self-seeking, did their best to distract Elizabeth's attention with offers from every eligible male in just about every royal house in Europe. The queen encouraged the suitors, flirted happily with them, then laughed and retreated; or prevaricated, half-promised – and retreated. She watched Dudley as he moved about her court with that ineffable and princely grace which even his detractors acknowledged. Watched him when he hunted, hawked, rode, or engaged in shooting matches, and betrayed, without caring who observed, her warm partiality for her Master of the Horse. She loaded him with every honour she could think of, and moved his suite of rooms from the damp ground floor of which he complained to a better suite next door to her own. Conveniently next door, as the gossips hastened to point out. Yet still her subjects were unsure whether they were lovers in fact as well as in spirit.

It was said that Elizabeth was sexually incapable, though for what reason was never made apparent. It was also said that she was a virgin by choice and intended to remain one. Indeed, she herself made similar remarks from time to time, though whether by way of explanation or as a dust-throwing exercise no one knew. What was known was the passionate and headstrong nature of both, the apparently strong attraction between them, and the uncaring disregard of gossip which Elizabeth showed. Her attitude seems to have been 'I am the queen and I can do as I please.' She was unmistakably Henry VIII's daughter. What would have pleased Dudley would have been marriage to the queen; what would have pleased her is harder to define. The illusion of marriage, perhaps, without its bonds and obligations; without its threats. She had no wish to share power, she also had no wish to lose her lover. Perhaps she oscillated between desiring and not desiring Dudley as a husband. Elizabeth was a chronic oscillator, and often turned the fact to superb advantage.

The future of Dudley lay not in indecision or compromise, but in marrying Elizabeth. If it were not for the fact that he was already married, he was convinced that future would be at Elizabeth's side. In Amy Robsart lay the obstacle to his life's success. How far the Queen's Horse Master was motivated by love and how much by self-interest it is impossible to say, but he set himself to win over some of his colleagues to regard him as their leader. There were many at court who, though having no liking for Robert Dudley, saw him as the only alternative to yet another foreign consort.

By the end of 1559, however, Robert felt it politic not to appear as an open candidate for the queen's hand, and he announced his strong support for Elizabeth's marriage to the son of the Holy Roman Emperor, the Archduke Charles. This piece of diplomatic backpedalling might have been suggested by Elizabeth herself though, when she eventually denied any intention of marrying the archduke, the manoeuvre rebounded on Dudley and cost him most of his newly-won popularity. His enemies – he had many – went so far as to plot his death, though nothing came of it. And so the triangle continued to hold: Elizabeth, Robert, Amy. No resolution would be possible unless one of the three died or surrendered all claim. Self-sacrifice does not appear to have been seriously considered by any of them. For some time it had been reported that Amy was suffering from cancer of the breast. However, she continued to enjoy reasonable health and there seemed no deterioration in her condition. Whatever ailed her, if anything did, it was likely to make too slow a progress to fit in with her husband's schemes.

In November of that year, the Spanish ambassador wrote to Philip II that he had heard from a trusted source how Lord Robert 'had sent to poison his wife', and that all the queen would do in the matter of her marriage 'is only keeping the country engaged with words until this wicked deed is consummated'. Whether or not this was just further malicious gossip aimed at Dudley's destruction, Amy Robsart was still alive by the end of the following March (1560). It was next rumoured that Robert intended to follow recent royal precedent and sue for divorce, though this, considering his position, would have been far less likely to succeed or to fit him to marry the queen of England. Nothing came of the rumour. It was succeeded by another: that the queen was carrying Dudley's child. This created even greater furore, for it affected the various foreign interests with matrimonial intentions. Cecil, Elizabeth's chief minister, despaired of what he described as 'her irregular conduct'. He seems to have entertained once more the idea of violently removing Dudley from the scene. He is reported to have told the Spanish ambassador that the lovers were again considering ways of getting rid of Amy Dudley, although the latter was continuing in good health and 'taking good care not to be poisoned'.

At the end of that week Robert Dudley's wife, living at Cumnor Place, where she had moved on her husband's instructions, was found dead at the foot of a flight of stairs, her neck broken. An inquest was held and it appeared that on the fateful evening Lady Dudley had given her servants leave to go to the nearby Abingdon Fair. She had remained in the house and was not seen alive again by the members of her household. The official verdict was accidental death, though rumours flew like rooks disturbed at feeding time. Amy had been murdered by assassins hired by her husband; Amy had committed suicide; vital evidence on the case had been suppressed, possibly through bribery by exalted sources. The gossip was exacerbated by reports that Lady Dudley's ghost had begun to appear on the stairs down which she fell. It was naturally assumed – and not only by Robert Dudley's enemies – that he'd had his wife murdered and arranged for an 'accidental' verdict to be brought in at the inquest. Heads were shaken and angry whispers exchanged throughout the country. If Amy's ghost had begun to haunt Cumnor, this must mean that she had been done to death. Dudley, though never tried for wife murder, was publicly regarded as guilty of it, both in his own country and abroad. His reputation never recovered from this blow, and thenceforth marriage with the queen was impossible.

Cumnor Place continued to be haunted by the spirit of the unfortunate Amy Robsart until the building was pulled down in 1810 by the then Earl of Abingdon. Although a later Cumnor Place arose, there are, as far as I know, no reports of its being haunted by Amy. However, the apparition was also said to appear in the park belonging to the old house, and twelve clergymen eventually combined efforts to lay it, banishing it to a pool which became known as Madam Dudley's Pond.

Cumnor is not the only place where Amy has been seen, for she appeared at Cornbury Park in Oxfordshire, and to Robert Dudley himself. It would seem that Amy made only one appearance at the end of Robert's life in 1588. He had by then been Earl of Leicester for twenty-two years. He had stayed at Cornbury on his way to Kenilworth and was hunting in Wychwood Forest when he came face to face with the apparition of his first wife. She warned him that he would be with her in ten days. On his return to the house from the hunt, he was taken suddenly ill and was dead within the time she had prophesied. The ghost of Amy Robsart has been seen a number of times since then in the park at Cornbury; to see it is thought to presage imminent death.

Looking back over four hundred years on the strange affair of Amy's death, it is still not possible to be sure what occurred. Dudley showed no grief for the sudden loss of his wife and little surprise. The queen also seemed to have been anticipating some such news, judging by a conversation the Spanish ambassador reported having with her. This occurred on the morning of Amy's death, 7 September, and took place on Elizabeth's return from hunting, that is, probably before 11.00 a.m. and certainly before news of the death at Cumnor could have reached the court. The Spaniard's report stated boldly, 'the queen told me, on her return from hunting, that Lord Robert's wife was dead, or nearly so, and begged me to say nothing about it'. How could Elizabeth have known the news before the event took place unless she had prior knowledge of plans for it? In that case she was an accessory before the fact and by implication a party to it.

Elizabeth, perhaps forced by public outcry, placed Dudley under arrest at Kew, although she released him as soon as the worst of the storm had blown over. But the affair of Amy

Dudley was never satisfactorily settled. There were those who believed she had committed suicide, though the extraordinary coincidence of her decision with the royal forecast of her death stuck in the public's throat. Perhaps most believed that Dudley had his wife killed and the queen just might have been a party to the murder. Whatever the truth, the affair continued to reverberate on and off for the next twenty years, and although Elizabeth never disowned Robert for long, she never agreed to marry him. More than once she accused him of overweening ambition and declared that she would have no master but herself.

Although in later years Elizabeth professed to despise her cousin, Mary Queen of Scots, for her hopeless and ill-judged emotional entanglements, it is interesting that she herself went a long way down Mary's road in her early years as queen. Darnley was murdered by Bothwell, probably with Mary's knowledge. How different was Elizabeth's part in the Dudley affair? Elizabeth's caution saved her from disaster, but it was a near thing.

The problem for Elizabeth, as it had been for her father, her brother and her sister, was that of the succession. If she did not marry, did not achieve a legitimate child, who would inherit the throne of England? The two nearest in line, though fairly remote, were the Queen of Scots, who was the grand-daughter of Henry VIII's elder sister, Margaret: and Lady Catherine Grey, sister of Lady Jane, who was the second grand-daughter of Henry's younger sister, Mary, Duchess of Suffolk. Ultimately Mary Stuart, already a widowed Queen of France, would be regarded as Elizabeth's successor. Mary apparently considered her cousin a bastard and a usurper of her rights to the English crown. Elizabeth, while understanding the apparent inevitability of Mary's succeeding her, felt nothing but hostility for the woman whose feminine charms earned her the love of men and the endearing nickname of 'Maybird'. Yet Elizabeth suggested the name of Dudley, her favourite, as a possible husband for Mary, Queen of Scots and late of France. Her reasoning was that, married to Dudley, Mary would have her Catholic influence negated, whereas left to her own choice she was likely to marry back into Catholicism and plunge England into the conflicts of Mary Tudor's time yet again.

The dilemma for Elizabeth was acute and subtle. One cannot believe that she seriously intended to let Dudley go to her rival (she had created him Earl of Leicester to enhance his suitability for a royal destiny). Perhaps she calculated correctly that Mary would never accept a commoner reputed to be the English queen's lover, for when the Scots queen remarked that her cousin of England expected her to marry her horse-master, Elizabeth gleefully repeated the comment to Leicester. In any case, Elizabeth suspected Mary of being interested in Henry Stewart, Lord Darnley, her cousin, an arrogant and vicious young man who frequented the English court. Time bore out the suspicion; the proposed marriage to Leicester did not proceed, and when Darnley went to Scotland, with Elizabeth's permission, the young Scottish queen fell deeply in love with him and put up the banns of their marriage. Elizabeth retaliated by refusing to recognize Mary as her heir unless the marriage was abandoned. Mary, naturally goaded to fury by this high-handed interference, went ahead and married Darnley. Which may have been precisely what her wily rival intended. Elizabeth knew Darnley's unreliable character and guessed that the Darnley marriage was likely to be Mary's undoing as a possible successor to the English throne. So it proved.

Mary, like several of her Stuart successors, seems to have possessed more charm and emotion than logic or commonsense. In marrying Darnley she was not only seriously antagonizing the woman whose throne she hoped to inherit, but arousing fierce opposition in her own country. Indeed a rebellion did break out, but Mary recalled James Bothwell from exile to deal with it. She rode with her troops, wearing a cap of steel and a mail shirt to show she was in earnest.

Gallant though this action appears, Mary's life was beginning to slide into the chaos which would culminate in Fotheringhay. She had unwisely shown favour to an Italian musician, David Riccio, and had made him her secretary and principal adviser. No doubt his Italian gallantry flattered her, or he might, like many of the men close to her, have fallen under her considerable spell. She seems to have been foolish and indiscreet in her friendship with the man, and as a result Darnley grew so jealous that he plotted his murder; a scheme which suited many of the Scots nobles, since they believed Riccio to be a papal agent.

Mary was now pregnant, a fact which had some influence on what her nobles decided to do about Riccio. The plotters apparently promised Darnley that if Mary died childless they would accept him as king in his own right. He appears to have taken the assurance with a naive trust that the promise would be carried out. How to dispose of the coming child (his own child, incidentally) and secure his wife's childlessness? What better way than to ensure that she miscarried? And how better to achieve the joint object of this and the removal of a rival than by murdering Riccio in front of the pregnant queen? It was an involved, cruel and brutal concept, and was carried out.

On 9 March 1566, towards evening, the queen was in her private room where she and Riccio were at supper. First Darnley looked in and abruptly retreated, to be followed by a group of nobles fully armed, who seized the Italian and dragged him from the queen's side, struggling and calling desperately to her to save his life. Mary must have run after them to the door, for Riccio's blood is said to have spattered her gown, as almost fifty dagger strokes felled the Italian. Darnley's dagger – though not used by him – was left in the corpse. Mary was immediately threatened by the murderers that if she attempted to speak to the city's people from the palace window she would be 'cut in collops'. She held her peace, though she must have been shocked and distraught. Her supporters, Bothwell, Atholl and Huntly, were hopelessly outnumbered and unable to reach her. She wept bitterly for her secretary and confidante, but vowed to her women that she would avenge him.

Darnley was killed less than a year later, when the house at Kirk o' Field where he lay sick was blown to pieces. His body and that of his servant were found in the grounds afterwards. Neither had died in the explosion; both had been strangled. Mary and Bothwell were jointly suspected of the crime. Mary's life from then on was a series of disasters, and these have left some psychic record in the places where they occurred. But what of the first, the precipitating event of her dark voyage – the murder of Riccio?

A senior member of the present royal family told me some years ago that 'the Riccio room', where the Italian was murdered, had 'a terrible atmosphere', and that as a child she had been very much afraid of Holyrood. It is understandable that a place where so much anguish and terror were generated should retain some imprint of those emotions; emotions whose echoes might be picked up by sensitive individuals years, even centuries, later and translated into the sensations felt by the original participants in the drama.

Mary Stuart's eventful life has left other echoes. She was deposed after her foolish marriage to Bothwell (who was widely believed to have murdered Darnley), taken prisoner, escaped and then fled over the border to the protection of her cousin, Elizabeth of England. The protection proved a delusion, because Elizabeth kept her prisoner in one place or another for nineteen years. As long as she lived, Mary would be a threat to the English queen and a possible claimant to her throne. As a Catholic, Mary also provided a focus for plots by those in England who wished to see the old religion restored. Elizabeth had the choice of either imprisoning Mary or executing her. She chose the former, though eventually, after a series of Catholic plots in which the Scots queen was implicated, she had no choice but to agree to her Council's demands and sign Mary's death warrant.

One of Mary's frequent changes of prison was to Bolton Castle in Yorkshire, and en route she apparently spent two nights with the Metcalfes at Nappa Hall. A visitor to Nappa in 1878 saw a tall woman crossing the hall. Thinking it was the farmer's wife, he ran after her and was about to touch her when she turned. He was astonished by the loveliness of her face. He also noticed her dress, which seemed to be made of black velvet. She looked at him briefly, then disappeared through a door which led to a stone spiral staircase in the west tower. The figure seemed to him to be that of Mary Queen of Scots, as her portraits show her.

Even before she reached England, one of Mary's many escapades had left a permanent impression. She is said to haunt Borthwick Castle in Midlothian, where she was imprisoned for a while after her marriage to Bothwell. The ghost is boyish in appearance, and said to be that of Mary dressed as a page, a disguise she adopted in order to escape from there.

Once over the Border, the refugee turned prisoner must have lived from month to month in the hope of escape and return to her lost kingdom. But the months turned into years and the hope dwindled. Her youth disappeared into middle age, and grey hairs and increasing hopelessness encroached. Her son, James VI of Scotland, had no desire to see her restored. He hoped, on Elizabeth's death, to unite the kingdoms of Scotland and England. The English queen had already half-acknowledged James as her heir.

Somehow, after all the Catholic plots in which Mary was known or suspected to be involved, Elizabeth had managed to avoid the issue of executing her; had always found excuses to postpone a trial and condemnation of her cousin. Mary's advisers and sympathizers were punished by death but Mary was merely moved to ever safer and more inaccessible prisons. In September 1586, she was taken to the Castle of

Fotheringhay in Northamptonshire, the Plantagenet fortress surrounded by marshes and circled by the wide slow rivers of Fenland. The winds blew flat and cold across the landscape that winter and Mary, looking out from the elevation of the castle mound, must have wondered what was left for her, and how much of life. There were villages nearby, Warmington and Barnwell, and the small town of Oundle. And there were some sympathizers with her cause. The family at Southwick Hall a few miles away were Catholic and very much aware of the sad royal lady who had suddenly appeared among them.

Southwick Hall now is a small, beautiful country mansion, a blend of mediaeval, Tudor and eighteenth-century architecture. It was built in the early fourteenth century by the Lynnes and Knyvets, from whom the present owners, named Capron, are descended. Capron was originally spelled 'de Caperun', one who came over with the Conqueror. There is a local tradition that Fotheringhay Castle and Southwick House are connected by an underground passage, and that the passageway conveyed traffic between the two Catholic households. Since Mary is likely to have been unable to attend mass in her prison, she may well have wished to join the family celebrating three miles away at Southwick.

The stone chapel at Southwick still stands and can have changed little from Elizabethan times. In the window niche, when I visited it some years ago, a marble table stood; it would have been the natural place for a small altar. The walls were panelled and hung with miniatures, and the atmosphere was one of waiting and of closeness to the past. I was acutely aware of the flight of stone steps which led to the rooms below; and the further flight ahead which descended again. There was a strong sensation of waiting for something. Or someone.

A member of the family stood with me at that time in the little room, and I asked Miss Capron if Mary had ever been seen in the place. She told me that on one occasion when she was in the chapel alone she heard the sound of footsteps approaching the room. She assumed they belonged to an intruder, and cautiously concealed herself behind a curtain to observe the prowler. What happened next came as a considerable shock to Elaine Capron. A tallish woman entered wearing a long dark dress with a raised collar pointed at the back. She was without any headdress. She walked to the altar and stood before it with hands clasped in front of her, remaining there unmoving for a few seconds before walking through the adjoining Priest's Room and descending the stone spiral staircase beyond. Miss Capron, with the briefest hesitation, hurried after her, only to find the turret stair empty and herself quite alone. The physical description of the dark lady fits Mary very well.

The story does not end there. A member of the family which owned Southwick, George Lynne, attended Mary's funeral, and a tradition persists in the family that he was given custody of her burial certificate, which he took back with him to Southwick Hall. The certificate has never been found and is thought to be hidden still somewhere in the Hall itself. Fact or romantic fiction? Impossible to tell. But as persistent legends of this kind frequently have a foundation in fact, it may be that somewhere in this old, lovely building lies a priceless historical treasure.

Mary lived at Fotheringhay from September 1586 to 8 February 1587. During 1586 her servants had discovered letters addressed to the queen hidden in a beer barrel. These apparently came from her supporters and talked (in code) of a plan to assassinate Queen Elizabeth and replace her with the Catholic Mary. What neither Mary nor her enthusiastic young plotters suspected was that every letter sent or received by her was read by Elizabeth's spies. The inevitable happened. Once the potential assassins were named, the cover was blown. The plotters were arrested and both they and their imprisoned queen accused. Elizabeth, who had on every previous occasion refused to order her cousin's execution, was now cornered. Mary had colluded in a plot to assassinate her and was as guilty as her supporters. The only way Elizabeth could be safe would be by Mary's death. After much prevarication, the English Queen finally signed the death warrant on 1 February 1587, and on the morning of 8 February the Queen of Scots descended into the great hall of Fotheringhay and was beheaded there.

What were Mary's thoughts when she came down the imposing oak staircase for the last time? There is a tradition that on that final descent, she forced her knuckles so hard into the banister rail that the crown insignia on her ring became impressed in the wood and remained there.

After her death, Fotheringhay Castle fell into decay. Her son, James, who had barely known and had not loved her, appeared undisturbed by his mother's fate. Now king of England, he ordered the demolition of the castle which had been her prison. Afterwards Fotheringhay became a mine for local gentry, farmers and builders – anyone who required stone or timber seems to have found it in the ruins of the old castle.

A local hostel in nearby Oundle, The Tabret, took its share of the loot, some of the panelling and part of the noble staircase from Fotheringhay being incorporated into the refurbished inn. Nowadays the hostel is known as The Talbot, and there is no doubt that some of its stones and wood are of great age. The fine staircase, though giving the impression of being seventeenth rather than sixteenth century, has one curious feature: it bears on one of the balusters at its head the minute but blurred imprint of a crown. Tourist fodder or actuality? None can know for certain. What is known is that the upper staircase and the two bedrooms at its head appear to be haunted. The figure of a woman has been seen in all three locations, on many occasions, usually by men. The figure's garments are consistent, being always a white dress, a grey shawl and a white cap. She stands either at the foot of the bed, gazing at its occupant, or on the upper staircase. Alterations to the building seem to exacerbate the haunting, and the spectre often appears at such times, and in February, the month of Mary's execution.

On one occasion a man occupying one of the affected rooms complained the next morning that he had been kept awake throughout the night by the sound of a woman sobbing. An employee I spoke to while researching the story, told me that when she herself slept in one of the haunted rooms, she had had an unnerving experience, having awakened to find someone holding her down forcibly to the bed. She had been quite unable to move, call out or switch on the light. A fairly recent sighting of the ghost occurred in the early seventies, when 'she' was seen by a male guest, though an even later report cites 'her' as having been observed crossing the inn yard just after dawn, the percipient here being one of the female staff.

The Fotheringhay staircase is thought in the locality to have been divided into two parts at the Castle's demolition; the lower portion being incorporated into the Manor House in the village of Warmington. This charming house's owner confirmed to me that a 'grey lady' had been seen upstairs, footsteps have been heard and doors have apparently opened of their own accord. But the ghostly figure favours the staircase.

Two staircases which may once have been one staircase. And two ghosts which may refer to only one haunter. Is it possible for a ghost to 'divide' itself and haunt two or more places at once? It would seem so, and the explanations may be twofold. If this type of apparition is merely an imprint of a personality which once suffered in the area then it will be the moment of suffering which is recorded, the emotion generated at a given time. On the other hand, if individual human consciousness does survive death, then there is nothing to say that it must do so in the whole form it occupied in one particular body during life. 'Spirit' would seem to imply energy, as 'body' seems to equal matter. Energy, according to physical laws, appears to be unlimited in form and able therefore to divide and subdivide itself, manifesting in more than one place at a time – and indeed several ghosts appear to do just this. However, in the case of the Fotheringhay associations, I believe the haunting is an imprint, an old recording of emotion experienced by a once-living human being. Whether that being was Mary the queen, or one of her ladies affected by the tragedy it is not possible to say. Local people naturally prefer to believe the apparition is that of Mary Stuart.

There is one final account of the haunting of The Talbot at Oundle, and this was sent me by a Scotswoman, Mrs L. G. Moffatt of St Andrews. In about 1974, Mr and Mrs Moffatt paid a visit to the south of England, and had hoped to make the long journey in one hop. However, by the time they reached Newark, both were travel-weary, and as night was drawing on they decided to find a suitable hotel and continue their journey in the morning. They travelled for some miles, but the only hotel they found with available accommodation was The Talbot at Oundle, Northamptonshire. They arrived just before midnight, having telephoned their requirements ahead, and were shown up two flights of stairs to a room at the top of the second flight; Mrs Moffatt believes it to have been numbered either one or two. I quote from Mrs Moffatt's letter:

> It was a comfortable place. The bed was large, the sort you had to climb into. However the room was deadly cold and I asked Peter to open the window and let the warm night air in. The panes were leaded and firmly stuck. Needless to say we had no bathroom and I left the room to find one. The landing and staircase were poorly lit, presumably because it was late and the hotel was closed for the night. Halfway down at a window stood an elderly lady in what looked like a mob cap and night attire. She was sort of moaning. I felt extreme unease and went back into our room and asked my husband to come on to the landing and

wait for me. He did, and saw the figure as well. She went down the stairs and disappeared through a door. Peter and I were whispering by this time, and not being able to see a bathroom I decided that *she* must have gone into one downstairs. I followed her into the same room but it was completely empty. The whole thing was uncomfortable and we spent an uneasy restless night.

It was not until four years later that a guest of the Moffatts, reading a library book on interesting old hostelries, discovered a photograph of the haunted staircase at The Talbot in Oundle. The Moffatts at once recognized it and were fascinated to read its history, which they had not known until that moment. Mrs Moffatt says that merely to recall her experience on the stairs recreates her feeling of intense unease. At the time the nature of that experience does not seem to have occurred to either of them, because on entering the hotel dining-room for breakfast the next morning they had at once looked round to see if their lady of the previous night were present. As, of course, she was not.

This account is valuable because of its detail, its corroboration of other, earlier sightings, and the fact that the percipients were in ignorance of either the ghost story or the history of The Talbot. The Moffatts were casual visitors, and left the place as unaware of the significance of their encounter as of the hotel's history or legend. In other words, they were not influenced by previous knowledge or expectations. Mrs Moffatt made one further point. The library book which told them The Talbot's history also said that Mary had received the news of her death sentence standing on the stair, or looking out of the window. Both staircase and the large landing windows came from Fotheringhay Castle, but it is not known whether it was here that the queen heard the fatal news. In any event it is the Moffatts' own experience which is interesting.

Some time after beginning work on this book, I received a

letter from Mrs Fay Scott of Edinburgh, who had an interesting story of Holyrood and its most famous inhabitant. At one time Mrs Scott and her husband lived on an island in Loch Lomond, reputed to have been part of Mary Queen of Scots's dowry on her marriage to Darnley. Mrs Scott had an interest in the queen, and had acquired a piece of tapestry worked by Mary during her imprisonment at Hardwick Hall in Derbyshire (the redoubtable Bess of Hardwick also loved tapestry work and must have shared numerous embroidery sessions with her royal prisoner). Mrs Scott's interest in the subject took her to the house of Lennoxlove in Haddington, near Edinburgh, the home of the Duke of Hamilton, Hereditary Keeper of Holyroodhouse. In conversation with the curator, she discovered that he had previously been head curator and guide at Holyrood Palace, having worked there for twenty-five years before semi-retirement. The curator, Mr A, mentioned that his son had died in a motor accident, and that in their grief the family arranged to hold a seance in their then home, one of the gatehouses of Holyrood. It was, said the curator, an extraordinary experience. First the participants saw the apparition of a man in sixteenth century dress, which announced, 'I am French and this is my home'. Later investigation showed that a man named French had been an official in the palace during Mary's reign. This appearance was followed by a more startling one. The figure of a tall woman dressed in black appeared, and spoke a few words in a soft voice marked by a strong French accent. Mr A was unable to understand what she said, but assumed she was Mary Queen of Scots. Mary, brought up from childhood in the French court, and for a short while Queen of France, retained traces of a French accent all her life.

Some time later, Mrs Scott raised the subject of this strange conversation with the present curators of Holyrood, more in the spirit of testing their reactions to the possible haunting of the Palace by Mary than of questioning Mr A's veracity. Their answer was that they were not at all surprised by the story, for at some time in Holyrood Palace they had *all* seen her.

It is an intriguing fact that almost all sightings of Mary of Scotland – whether or not the percipients recognize the ghost's identity at the time – refer to a tall woman dressed in black. Mary did wear colours in her youth, and she is once recorded as having charmed the Scots lairds by wishing she had been born a man. On this particular day she had worn dazzling silver and green.

If certain of the events in the life of Mary Queen of Scots are psychically recorded, what of those in the equally eventful, though less tragic life of her cousin, Queen Elizabeth? Considering that Elizabeth was a woman of exceptional personality and strength of character, these are surprisingly few.

Peter Underwood recounts one of her appearances, at Rufford Old Hall in Lancashire. The figure of a majestic woman was seen through a window by a man standing outside the building. He hurried into the Hall's dining-room and saw the figure of the queen, still fully visible, and still standing where he had first seen her. He moved quietly towards her, but although she seemed unaware of him, the figure began to blur as he approached and vanished entirely, leaving him in a state of bewilderment. The man was certain the apparition was of Queen Elizabeth I. Perhaps the most striking factor in this account is that the figure appeared in full colour; an unusual feature, since hauntings invariably seem to occur in the white/grey/black range. If, as seems likely, hauntings need to use energy in order to function at all (and it will be remembered that forms of energy such as heat, electricity and gas are often affected in the area of a haunting), perhaps the form of apparition using the *least* energy may be that without colour. In other words, to reproduce a coloured image may require the use of more local energy than is available; in which case an apparition is more likely to occur in colourless form.

Why should Elizabeth appear at Rufford? There is no record of any dramatic event happening to the queen here, which might have generated enough feeling to register itself upon the surroundings. The young Will Shakespeare is said to have played here once (and his ghost has been seen in the Hall) but this is unlikely to have been before the queen. Perhaps something occurred at Rufford which made the place special to her. There is no known evidence one way or the other.

When I visited Hatfield House – local inhabitants refer to this building as the Old Hall, for the present Hatfield House, completed by Lord Salisbury, descendant of Burghley, Elizabeth's Chief Minister, stands directly opposite – I was assured that the queen haunts the Hall and not the House. It was here that much of her young life was spent; here that Robert Dudley, galloping headlong to reach her, first gave her the news of her sister's death and her accession to the throne. Here, too, she had been courted by that headstrong gallant, Tom Seymour, brother of her stepmother, Jane; the sexual aspect of this courtship placed Seymour's presumptuous head upon the block and gravely endangered the adolescent princess's claim to the succession and even her life. So Hatfield Old Hall should certainly be impregnated with memories of Elizabeth, her thoughts and emotions, before she attained the throne and safety.

The officials at Hatfield House said they knew of no haunting in the old building opposite, but opinion among local residents was that Elizabeth had been seen more than once, looking out of one of its windows. Sometimes the stories of hauntings arise from a conviction that in certain places there *should* be, *must* be hauntings. Surmise and wishful thinking then combine to start a legend, which will grow with the telling; and repetition merely adds conviction and circumstantial detail. On the other hand, a long-standing, persistently and reliably attested story of a haunting often means that such an event did occur in the place concerned at some time in the past.

One such is the account of the ghost in the Queen's Library at Windsor Castle. This is a well-documented account of an incident in February 1897, when a young guardsman, Lieutenant Carr Glynn, was quietly reading. He heard the click of high-heeled shoes on the wooden floor and, glancing up, saw a woman in a black dress, wearing a black lace scarf over her head and shoulders, apparently making for the inner library. A few steps above this level a picture gallery had been built by Elizabeth I, though it has now been adapted for true library use and houses books. The woman in black walked past the young officer, paying no attention to him, went into the gallery then turned to the right where there had once been a flight of steps connecting it to a terrace below. The stately lady did not return, and Glynn, unaware of the former existence of the steps, could not imagine where she could be; he assumed she was at work in an inner room and would eventually emerge.

Nevertheless, when one of the Library officials entered, he questioned him, describing the woman he had seen and asking her identity. The startled attendant had seen no one enter, and was certain that Glynn was the only person using the place. When the guardsman insisted he had both seen and heard the visitor, the official finally went into the gallery, followed (we assume) by a highly curious and interested Lieutenant Glynn. No one was there; Glynn suggested that the woman might have left by a door in the corner. The only difficulty was that the corner did not have a door, though the attendant knew it had once had one, before the removal of the staircase to the terrace.

It seemed, then, that the lady in black had been following a path which she must have used many times in the past – across the library, up the steps into the gallery, through the door at the head of the stairs and on down the steps to the terrace itself. The fact that door and stairs were now non-existent made no difference to the progress. The woman had, of course, disappeared, having never existed save as a phantom, an imprint from the past. Later it was learnt that the same figure has been seen many times, by, among others, Queen Victoria's eldest daughter when she was a child.

This ghost, believed to be of Queen Elizabeth I, seems to be of the 'pattern-haunting' type. Some explanation must be given of what is meant by pattern-haunting. There seem to be two main types of haunting (though I dislike the term 'haunting' and prefer to regard events of this kind as a psychic recording). The two groups are (a) hauntings which are the result of similar past activities in the same area by living humans, continually repeated over a long period of time; and (b) motivated, individual activities which are rarely predictable and appear to denote the actions of a thinking individual, possibly indicating a surviving intelligence inhabiting the area it might have known in life.

The Library haunting by Elizabeth seems to come into the first category, because the queen must have taken that trip many, many times, during the course of her long life. These continually repeated events – always the same in detail – seem to imprint themselves upon the surroundings, and continue to replay long after the original participants have left the scene. Thus we hear of ghostly processions of monks and nuns continuing to attend a mass which disappeared, in buildings which also vanished, at the time of the Reformation. The music and chanting of services may continue to be heard long after the end of all religious practice in a building. Such patterns are not confined to churches and cathedrals. Any action repeated regularly and often may cause a psychic imprint on the surroundings which that environment may retain and replay at intervals. Such recordings may also take place of 'one-off' events, as described, though the record here seems to be created not by the 'grooving' of repetition, but by a 'burning-in' of fierce emotion. Imprints on surroundings seem to occur in both cases, though only that which registers a repetitive original event can truly be called a 'pattern-haunting'.

An interesting fact about this type of occurrence is that it takes no account of alterations which may have taken place since the original action. If a floor level has been lowered since the real-life performance of an event, a 'pattern' ghost will continue to walk at the old floor level, appearing to observers to be walking a foot or two above the present floor, a fact which can be highly disconcerting. In the case of the Queen Elizabeth spectre, the removal of the original door and stairs to 'her' terrace has made no difference to the route the ghost takes, for 'she' follows the path originally laid down and travelled by the living queen.

One might say that whichever part of the surroundings is holding the record of the original activity is acting as both slide or movie projector and tape recorder. It replays exactly what it has recorded, no more or less, and in the position where the original was recorded, no matter what has happened to the background since then.

Elizabeth's life was long by the standards of that age, and she died in her seventieth year. She had hunted, ridden and dressed as exotically as ever until nearly the end, but her world had changed and all but disappeared. Leicester, whom she had loved all her life, had married Lettice Knollys when he understood that he might not have the queen. Elizabeth had raged bitterly at that but eventually forgave him. And when her beloved Robert died suddenly in September 1588, she grieved deeply and for the most part silently. He had written to her shortly before he died, one of the many affectionate letters he had sent her through the years, and on hearing of his death she wrote on the back of it 'His last letter' and placed it in a drawer near her bedside. She had fifteen years of her life left to live.

In the winter of 1603 the cold was particularly bitter, though the queen refused to wrap in furs or abandon for warmer wear her gorgeous taffety and cloth of silver. However, she agreed to transfer from damp, chilly Whitehall to more congenial Richmond. But by then she had caught a chill and grew gradually worse. She sat on the cushions on the floor, reluctant to take to bed, and when her attendants remonstrated she made them pull her into a standing position. She remained there for thirteen hours, unmoving, impervious to pleas and protests, answering nothing and remaining upright only by force of will. At last she allowed them to lift her into bed and there she stayed, occasionally mildly delirious, but for the most part slowly drifting out of life. When her courtiers asked her to lift her hand if she agreed that James, King of Scotland, should succeed her, she slowly raised her hand.

While she lay waiting to die, a strange thing occurred. One of her ladies-in-waiting (reputed to be Lady Guildford), finding the queen sleeping, left the room to return to her own apartments. She had not gone more than a short way when she saw the queen approaching her down the corridor. Startled, she looked away for a second, and when she turned back, the figure had disappeared. She hurried back to the royal bedchamber, and found Elizabeth exactly as she had left her and still asleep. Now nearly four hundred years since the occurrence, it is said that she was seen more than once, walking with her firm, light stride through her rooms at Richmond, her spirit apparently travelling purposefully while her failing body lay in its bed. The phenomenon of astral travelling is often experienced in times of grave illness or after severe accidents, the spirit or energy or consciousness of an individual being able to divorce itself from the physical matter of the body and take independent action, without severing itself from the bodily substance it inhabits.

When Elizabeth finally died, asleep, her ghost haunted the gatehouse at Richmond for a while. Her ring was thrown down from there to the rider who would take the news to James VI in Scotland. At last he had become James I of England and the two countries a single political unit.

CHAPTER EIGHT

The Seventeenth Century

Elizabeth died on 24 March 1603. Ten days later, her cousin of Scotland, James VI, began his journey to claim his major estate, the realm of England.

James Stuart had some charm, a lively mind and an aptitude for business affairs. He also had a number of repellent personal habits, dribbling saliva when he ate or drank and wearing his clothes in a slovenly fashion. He was not fastidious about his personal hygiene or his speech, which tended towards multiple obscenities. Not addicted to washing, he usually rubbed only his fingertips with the damp end of a table napkin. He was learned, spoke with a rich Scottish accent, drank a great deal (though was rarely drunk), was incurably restless and an incorrigible buffoon. He was not, however a fool.

James had a strong conviction of the sanctity of kingship, which he was to pass on to his descendants, but he often undermined its dignity by ludicrous or vulgar behaviour. These traits did not prevent the English from giving him an enthusiastic reception on his arrival in London. He was the first male ruler they had had for fifty years, and the relief from petticoat government was welcomed by the royal counsellors. At least this must have been James's initial impression, but much of the warmth of his reception was due to gratitude for a genuine Protestant successor to Elizabeth. James had not done badly in his governance of Scotland. What he failed to realize was that England was not only much larger but also a quite different country.

Apart from James's obsession with the Divine Right of

Kings to govern without interference, he seems to have miscalculated totally the increasing strength of the English Parliament and to have misunderstood its function. The Members of the House were now demanding more power and responsibility for government while James had every intention of giving them less. Other sources of discontent were his initial severity towards Catholics, his personal extravagances (his impoverished upbringing led him to think of the English treasury as a bottomless gold mine), and his tendency to restrict honours to his personal circle, which contained a large number of Scotsmen. James was also, according to the court, a little too fond of the handsome young men he collected around him.

The plot which almost resulted in the blowing up of Parliament has become celebrated as the Gunpowder Plot, but it was not a single attempt to influence a new reign. Plots against the life of Elizabeth had been occurring regularly over the past twenty years and had as regularly been thwarted by the efficiency of her security service.

Elizabeth's policy had been to wrest political power from Spain and its ruler, Philip II, her erstwhile brother-in-law. To cover this particular motive (and Philip's, which was to defeat Elizabeth and extend his power into her territories), both sides pretended that religion was the issue – Catholic rule versus Protestant. So all the plots against Elizabeth, and against James when he ruled, were said to be fostered by Catholics to regain possession of the English throne. Mary Queen of Scots had died as a result of such a plot. English Catholics certainly wished to revert to the old days and were only too willing to work towards it by devising schemes against Protestant rule. The upshot of the manoeuvring in Elizabeth's reign had been war with Spain, producing the attempted invasion by a succession of Spanish Armadas.

After Elizabeth's death, the plots continued, but with a difference. The efficient spy service developed by Cecil now infiltrated the Catholic conspiracies at will, and used its insights to immobilize the plotters and use the information as anti-Catholic propaganda. When a certain Lord Monteagle sat down to supper in his house in Hoxton on 26 October 1605, he did so not only as a member of a Catholic circle which was planning to blow up the Parliament building, but almost certainly as a Government agent; a fact not, of course, known to his fellow conspirators. Monteagle had been wholeheartedly Catholic, but seems to have changed his coat on James's accession. During supper a letter was delivered to the Hoxton house, warning Monteagle that Parliament was to be punished . . . 'and yet they shall not sei who hurts them'; it advised him to absent himself from the place of danger. The letter was unsigned.

Other warnings had gone to certain Catholic Members of Parliament in an attempt to save their lives; these were assumed to have come from the conspirators. At the end of October, Monteagle had visited Richmond to discover if the young Prince of Wales would be present at Parliament's opening, and was told he would not. However, the conspirators understood the king would inaugurate the session which would bring about the Union of England and Scotland, and there was to be a Royal State Opening. They therefore expected to dispose of the Protestant sovereign and his co-religionists with one explosion. A highly economical scheme, but chancy. According to a letter from the Earl of Salisbury (Cecil) to Sir Charles Cornwallis on 5 November 1605, both the queen and the prince should have been at Westminster for the Opening; but this was probably Cecil painting the picture as black as possible for propaganda purposes. According to his letter, wood and coal had been planted in a nearby vault eighteen months before, and gunpowder had been brought in at intervals, until the conspirators had two hogsheads and thirty-two small barrels of the stuff, the whole being concealed under a pile of wood and faggots. The ringleader, according to Salisbury, was Guy Fawkes, a servant of one of the Percys of Northumberland, who was apprehended as he was preparing the bonfire which was to elevate the King and Commons.

This was the official story. From unofficial sources, it is obvious that Cecil not only knew of the plot from the beginning but probably inspired it through his agents. Some of the Catholics, restive against the régime, were foolishly incautious or extraordinarily naive in their militancy. Monteagle appears to have played the part of double agent, or Judas, depending on the viewpoint. The warning letter can have been no surprise to him, and his subsequent actions were remarkably co-ordinated for one who had just been shocked by a murderous conspiracy.

In the event, although the explosives were well concealed, Sir Thomas Knevett decided to clear the wood out of the vault. When he returned to do so, he found a man named 'Johnson' (Fawkes) just about to leave; Knevett arrested him on suspicion, which was confirmed when the pile of wood was examined. Fawkes was either tortured or tricked into confession, and although many of the conspirators planned to flee overseas when they knew they were discovered, they left it too late. Particularly savage torture was employed on Fawkes, and most of the prisoners suffered some form of the unspeakable cruelty then prevalent. In the end they died by beheading or by the triple method of being hanged, drawn and quartered.

It is little wonder that an event so emotionally fraught and shocking not only burned itself into our calendars, but left some psychic echo. There has long been a tradition of the haunting of Westminster Hall by a man in a black cloak and broad-brimmed hat. He is said to 'loiter' about and then disappear near the old Court of King's Bench, beneath which passages led to Guy Fawkes's cellar near the old House of Lords. The apparition is thought to be that of Fawkes, who was finally executed in 1606.

Not only the enemies of James I have left paranormal echoes. James's temperament was homosexual, and he was not the first monarch with such inclinations, as we have seen. There is little doubt that George Villiers, the first Duke of Buckingham (in the Villiers line), was a 'favourite' in this sense; he was certainly made much of by his sovereign, and gained considerable political power as a result. James called his friend 'Steenie' and doted on the handsome young man who, according to the enamoured king, resembled St Stephen.

The young man rose to great heights, although he did not possess enough intelligence or ability to sustain his offices honestly. The corruption and greed of his administration earned him public loathing, particularly as he promoted his relatives, several of even less ability than himself. The result was rising opposition in Parliament, both to Buckingham and to the king. But by now James, at forty-seven, was showing signs of senility. Buckingham, noting this and alert to his own interests, began to exert his influence on the young Prince Charles, who, after the premature death of Henry Prince of Wales, was next in the line of succession. Soon Buckingham could do no wrong in his eyes, and this increased the duke's unpopularity.

After the death of James I in March 1625, Buckingham and the new king involved the country in a series of minor wars on the Continent and a consequent heavy demand on the Treasury. This thoroughly alarmed Parliament, and there were several other causes of dissatisfaction, both to Parliament and the common people, in the policies of Buckingham and Charles. The hard-won rights of the people of England were being forcibly eroded. As Charles I's reign progressed, the struggle between King and Parliament split the country and brought the king to disaster.

Predictions of disaster for Buckingham were plentiful, though they were generally regarded as wishful thinking. One occurrence did not come into that category. One night in February 1628 an officer of the King's Wardrobe, stationed at Windsor Castle, was awakened abruptly from sleep to find his bed curtains drawn back, and 'a man of very venerable aspect' regarding him. The intruder asked the officer if he knew him; the officer believed he recognized the man from a parish where he had been at school. He replied that he thought the visitor must be Sir George Villiers. The apparition confirmed this, saying he wished the officer to take a message to his son, the Duke of Buckingham. The message was that if he did not 'somewhat to ingratiate himself to the people, or at least to abate the extreme malice they had against him, he would be suffered to live but a short time'.

The ghostly visitor vanished and the officer returned to sleep. On waking the next day, he was inclined to think he had dreamed the whole affair. The following night the ghost reappeared and put his request more strongly, saying that if the officer did not obey he should 'always be pursued by him'. By now the man was convinced he was experiencing a recurrent nightmare, and so took no action. On the third night the apparition came again, this time with 'a terrible countenance'. He bitterly reproached the officer for ignoring his request. The officer replied that it was difficult enough to get access to the duke without expecting him to believe such an extraordinary tale. The ghost, whom the officer had by now accepted as that of Sir George Villiers, gave him 'two or three particulars' which he was ordered not to mention to anyone save Buckingham.

The man carried out the instructions, managing to get an interview with the Duke through a friend at court, Sir Ralph Freeman. Afterwards the officer informed Freeman that the Duke had turned pale when told the 'particulars' entrusted to him. Buckingham swore the information was known only to himself and one other.

Afterwards Buckingham went hunting with his king, but his mind was obviously elsewhere. He left shortly afterwards to visit his mother, with whom he stayed several hours, conducting a conversation loud enough with excitement to be heard in the next room. The duke appeared deeply troubled and angry, a reaction he had never previously exhibited in dealings with his mother, for whom he had 'a profound reverence'. The lady herself was in tears and much disturbed. When, on 23 August, Buckingham was assassinated by a disaffected subaltern at Portsmouth, the news did not surprise his mother. She had been warned in advance by the victim himself.

Although this ghost was reported by only one person and for a single purpose, this does not invalidate it as a genuine apparition. What it cannot be called is a haunting, since that term more properly belongs to recurrent appearances over a period of time. However, it does seem to have been a genuine ghost, in that it falls into the 'surviving entity' type of apparition: that which appears to retain both will and decision-making abilities, suggesting a true survival of consciousness on the part of a once-living individual. This is no 'pattern' haunting, no 'recorded' ghost or action. Apparitions whose function is primarily to warn are not uncommon in the field of death-survival research. Spectres of the dead do frequently appear to the living; sometimes to warn, sometimes to bid farewell, and occasionally to pass on information vital to the recipient or to the dead person himself when alive. Sir George Villiers was a warning ghost whose warning was ignored.

Charles I, a man of integrity and gentle courtesy in private life, was much less scrupulous in public affairs. His reign coincided with a time of incipient change, with a Parliament beginning to see the rights of the gentry (and eventually of the common people) to be as important as those of the king. The mediaeval and Tudor idea of government was giving place to disturbing democratic tendencies.

Charles, for his part, wished to alleviate the lot of the poor, without understanding that this held no appeal for the gentry. The problem was that Parliament wished to govern the country for the benefit of its members (magnates and country landowners) and the king wished to govern according to his ideas of the duties of a monarch. The ideas, set on a collision course from the beginning, proved more incompatible as each side developed its own policies for governing, and for resistance to the alternative system.

The king had two strong ministers, whose views on government matched his own. Thomas Wentworth, Earl of Strafford, known as Black Tom, was held in awe if not fear by many of his contemporaries. He was a man of formidable character, fierce temper and dictatorial manner. He was also a man of loyalty and capable of deep affection and gratitude to his friends. He was efficient, energetic and fearless. Charles does not appear to have understood him or even to have liked him much. The second able man was William Laud, Archbishop of Canterbury, who matched Strafford for energy and shared the latter's ideas about a strong stable government under the authority of the crown. The two men were to be united by their despair at the behaviour and methods of the king they served and supported.

Unfortunately for his two servants, Charles was not an energetic man. He preferred hunting and contemplating his magnificent art collection to the hard business of administration, which required concentration and attention to detail. The king understood how he wanted to govern without realizing that it required a dedication of which he was incapable. For dedication he substituted stubbornness.

Strafford was Lord Deputy in Ireland from 1633–9, and had ruled as a tyrant a land lawless even by the English standards of the period. By this time Charles was in difficulties with the Scots, who had refused to accept the Anglican prayerbook Laud tried to impose upon them, and had issued a Covenant which was a direct challenge to their English monarch. The Scots had a good army; Charles could not match it and Parliament was unwilling to provide him with one. He saw only one way out of his dilemma, and sent for Thomas Wentworth, Earl of Strafford. He, if anyone, would be able to dominate Parliament and solve the insoluble.

However, the English gentry knew Black Tom's reputation

and were determined not to be stampeded into granting the king either an army or money to support it. Their leader, John Pym, was already in touch with the Scots, and when Strafford discovered this, he urged the king to dissolve Parliament and rule alone, saying that 'being reduced to extreme necessity . . . (he was) loosed and absolved from all rules of government'. Matters went rapidly downhill. The Scots defeated an English army at Newburn, and the king had to offer terms to them, guarantee to pay them £25,000 a month pending their claims for compensation, and summon another Parliament to raise the money. An ignominious end to Charles's challenge to parliamentary government.

Although the complaints about the king's governing style were many and various – so much so that the factions found it difficult to agree on any single course of action – there was one factor on which the opposition was united: Strafford. It was learnt that he was intending to bring in Irish mercenaries and possibly use force rather than the processes of law to carry out the king's policies. This finally crystallized hatred and fear of him into action. Pym launched a fierce verbal attack on Strafford in the Commons. Although Strafford was in the Lords at the time, he was warned and slipped away to consult the king before Pym laid his case for an impeachment before the Upper House. When Strafford returned to the Lords, he was arrested.

His trial opened on 22 March 1641, and for the next seven weeks the nation thought of little else. Although Pym and his colleagues had created a public picture of a domineering, traitorous tyrant, the man who stood arraigned in Westminster Hall was ageing, bent and sick; he aroused some sympathy. Moreover, he defended himself so well that the hatred began to wane and to be tinged by doubt. The charges were frail and difficult to substantiate, and the impeachment hearing was on the point of collapse when Pym arranged for a Bill of Attainder against Strafford to be put to the Commons. This was a more serious business, for it could declare by Act of Parliament that Strafford's death was necessary for the state's safety. Although there was doubt in some minds as to the justice of the proceedings, the Bill was passed on 21 April by a majority of a hundred and forty-five. King Charles immediately wrote to Strafford promising that he should not suffer in life, honour or fortune, for that, said the King, would be 'a very mean reward from a master to so faithful and able a servant'.

In the event it was the king himself who caused Strafford's case to fail. He intimated that under no circumstances would he consent to the Bill of Attainder, and it was suspected that he intended to connive in Strafford's escape from the Tower. By now the Lords, who might have saved Strafford by refusing to pass the Bill, were alienated and suspicious of Charles's motives. The clamour of a mob around the building where they sat placed additional pressure on them. If the king meant to rescue Strafford by refusing to consent to his death, then it did not matter if they themselves passed the Bill of Attainder. The king could always veto it.

Strafford foresaw what would happen and that if the King failed to veto his death, the royal honour would be destroyed in the eyes of his subjects. Whatever his faults, he had a deep loyalty to the sovereign he served, and sought to save Charles by publicly releasing him from his promise. Perhaps he also hoped that with the onus of condemning thrown back on the Lords, they would be unwilling to take it and would jettison the fatal Bill. But circumstances were against him. The Lords, hearing the mob outside yelling for 'justice', tamely voted the Bill through. It went before the king at Whitehall, and the rowdies moved their ground with it.

The King was not intimidated by mobs, and refused to go against his conscience. He consulted his religious counsellors, two of whom advised that he should follow his conscience and save Strafford; the third (a pro-parliamentarian), pointed out that he also had a duty to serve the needs of his people. If his conscience as a man and his conscience as a king were in conflict, his royal duty must prevail. With tears in his eyes, Charles finally gave his consent to the Bill of Attainder, and effectively signed Strafford's death warrant.

It was not only a gross personal betrayal, but was possibly the greatest political error of Charles's life. He had removed the one man who could have held the balance between Parliament and the crown. The King regretted what he had done, realizing too late that he should have stood fast by his conviction and his friend. He felt this guilt to the end of his life. Strafford was executed two days later, at noon on 12 May, and, in his final speech from the scaffold, spoke his purpose: 'In all the honour I had to serve His Majesty, I had not any intention in my heart but what did aim at the joint and individual prosperity of the king and his people . . .'

The two men, different in background, temperament and character, had been curiously united in purpose – to uphold the authority of the throne. This link perpetuated itself in a strange manner after Strafford's death.

The king's political defeat did nothing to help relations between himself and his Commons, and war between the two factions became inevitable. By 1645, Charles was with his army at Daventry in Northamptonshire, and chose as his headquarters The Wheatsheaf Inn in Sheep Street. The king had about 4,000 foot and an equal number of horse and intended to engage the parliamentary forces the following day. However, during the night Charles awoke abruptly from sleep to see an indistinct male figure standing near his bed. He recognized the Earl of Strafford. Aware that what he saw was no living being, the king cannot have been surprised that the spirit meant to communicate. In his *History of Naseby*, Mastin says that the ghost urged Charles to continue his march northwards and not to give battle, adding that the king would never conquer by force of arms.

Not unnaturally, Charles was much shaken by this event.

The visitation and its warning were repeated the next night. The king wanted to take the apparition's advice, but was fiercely opposed by several leaders of his army. The royalist forces remained and fought the catastrophic battle of Naseby on 14 June, when they were soundly beaten. The king lost all his guns, the entire infantry and most of his baggage train.

The room where the apparition appeared was later modernized and changed, but could be seen as late as the 1940s.

Many times during the rest of his life, King Charles referred to the pre-Naseby warning, saying he wished to God he had heeded it. Towards his own end, he remembered Strafford increasingly – not the spectral warning so much as his betrayal of his servant. If he suffered, were his trials not a just retribution for forsaking Strafford? When Charles went to the block, he died with dignity and courage. It was to create an image of martyrdom which would cast a very long shadow.

One would expect that Charles of all monarchs would leave behind some psychic echo, some paranormal impression of suffering and distress. There are a few isolated examples, but they throw little light on their assumed sources. An interesting feature of many hauntings with historical origins is that they do give information about the original action and the emotions connected with it.

Charles I's ghost is said to frequent the Canon's House at Windsor Castle. It has also appeared at Vernon House in Farnham, Surrey, where Charles was briefly held prisoner en route for London. A shadowy figure has been seen on the stairs in this building and is thought to have been that of the king, though since it was static, there is no certainty of identification with King Charles or his imprisonment there. He is also said to appear at Penkaet Castle in East Lothian, and at Marple Hall in Cheshire, but there seems no reason why he should haunt either building.

A more detailed haunting concerns Billingham Manor on the Isle of Wight. Charles I was held captive for a time at

Carisbrooke Castle and, according to local tradition, rode out to listen to a plan of escape suggested by the Manor's owners, the royalist Worsley family. Charles discarded the plan as impracticable, but some record of the event seems to have lingered in the house itself: in the 1920s, when Sir Shane Leslie and his family stayed at Billingham, they were disturbed by noises reminiscent of furniture moving, swords being drawn and the sound of a falling body; sounds which might have indicated some violence in the house's past history, though this is more likely to have concerned smuggling activities than the English Civil War.

On the night Shane Lewis was awakened by the inexplicable sounds, what was remarkable was that a sliding panel in the dining-room showed chinks of light around its outer edges. The intrepid Leslie pushed aside the panel and he and the little group around him were astonished to see, gazing at them, the disembodied head of the executed king. The apparition had been seen on two earlier occasions, each time fading slowly into nothingness. The islanders connected its appearance (as on this occasion) with the incidence of executions at the nearby Parkhurst Prison. Perhaps with the abolition of capital punishment, the phantom has ceased to appear; there have been no recent reports of it. The connection between apparition and executions does, in any case, smack less of paranormality than of sympathetic magic.

The most extraordinary experience connected with Charles I is reported by Jeffrey Iverson in *More Lives Than One*. Iverson, a television producer in South Wales, based his book on case histories of the respected hypnotherapist, Arnall Bloxham. One of Bloxham's subjects for hypnosis was a film cameraman named John Pike who was known to Iverson as an outstanding photographer and a reliable individual. Pike seems to have been sceptical on the subject of hypnotic regression, the field in which Bloxham was then working. The hypnotherapist, in regressing subjects to apparent earlier lives, had garnered some interesting results. When it came to

John Pike's turn, the cameraman was puzzled to see pictures and recall events completely strange to his twentieth century *persona*. He found himself to be a Kidderminster farmer, wealthy for the time; while under hypnosis, he described the clothes of the period and the coins he carried on him. He also spoke of riding to London in the year 1649 and how, seated on his horse sidesaddle (an unusual posture for a male rider), he watched over the heads of a great crowd of citizens and Roundhead soldiers the execution of King Charles I in Whitehall. John Pike remembered that as the axe rose and fell he could not bear to watch, but shuddered and turned away. Imagination or 'distant memory'? A recollection from the collective memory of the race itself or evidence of a former personal incarnation? I am inclined to the latter theory, for there are many similar incidents on record throughout the world.

But to have seen that memorable and dreadful regicide – would that not have left a mark upon every person there present – a mark so deep that it might be remembered through several lives and deaths by those who witnessed it? That is if you believe, as I do, in consciousness as an eternal continuum which survives bodily death.

There lives a man in Norfolk who owns the pair of shoes worn by the Stuart king on his last day on earth; shoes which took Charles of England to his final public rendezvous. What echoes should rest in them!

Here is a final psychic remnant of the high drama of the Civil Wars. One of the King's commanders at Naseby was his soldier nephew, Rupert of the Rhine, son of Charles's much loved sister, Elizabeth of Bohemia. Prince Rupert, a great cavalryman and an experienced soldier, had one fatal fault: impetuosity. This may occasionally seem a virtue, for leading a full-scale cavalry charge needs a spirit of reckless daring. Rupert developed this arm of warfare to an extraordinary degree. The prince has been blamed for failing to beat the parliamentary forces at the battle of Edgehill in 1642, but what happened was that once launched on the exhilarating downhill charge into the enemy's flank, he was unable to control his troops' headlong pursuit of the fleeing opposition. They chased the foe for several miles, leaving their own infantry unprotected and under attack by the opposing cavalry. When the Prince regained control of his chase-happy forces and returned to the scene of battle, it was too late to snatch the victory which should have been the king's.

For several weeks after Edgehill, the battle was said to be re-enacted as a psychic record. In the early hours of the morning country folk nearby would hear the sound of drums and the groans of the dying, the noise of cannon and horses neighing. The scene itself then materialized and the movement of armies and individuals could be seen. Eventually, the intensity of the parapsychological echo grew less and, as far as I know, this three-hundred-year-old event has not been replayed in recent times. However, Prince Rupert has occasionally been seen riding his white battle charger and accompanied by a pet dog. He is said to revisit the site of the charge which cost the Royalists victory and almost lost them the battle.

Such reports of battle hauntings occur all over England and at several sites on the Continent. Marston Moor and Culloden have both seen replays of their bloody struggles. Hand-to-hand fighting probably generated more terror and anguish than the sophisticated sudden-death technology which is man's modern method of killing *en masse*.

The wars ended, the king was dead, and his young heir had fled to impoverished safety on the Continent. The Commonwealth had imposed its own brand of rule and religion upon an England still licking its cuts and gashes. The Merrie Englande of Elizabeth had become a folk memory, as distant as the slopes of Parnassus or the magical isle of Shakespeare's *Tempest*. Life was grim, earnest, solemn and many activities were frowned on if not actually forbidden.

Then the Commonwealth became the Protectorate of Oliver Cromwell, and all chance of a revival of monarchy seemed at an end. One man ruled without a crown and without the actual titles of royalty. The young king was over the water, and a large number of English men and women wished he were at home.

After Cromwell's death, the *ad hoc*, improvised nature of Commonwealth and Protectorate offered little political foundation on which to build, and the alternative to continuing a confused state of government seemed to be the recall of the monarchy. So Charles, Prince of Wales, presently became Charles II, a cynical, charming, easy-going young man of thirty, wittier than his father and in some ways wiser. One thing he had learned from the miseries of his adolescence and youth: that very little on this earth was worth fighting and dying for; and that to oppose forces likely to defeat you was the act of a fool. He was not, therefore, a man of strong principles, but one who believed in expediency. Having lived so many years in poverty and depression, he would not jeopardize pleasures or possessions for the sake of principle. He bent to the wind of change as it blew, knowing that winds die down or alter direction. The essence of Charles II was perhaps captured in Lord Rochester's Epitaph:

> Here lies our sovereign lord the King
> Whose promise none relied on;
> He never said a foolish thing,
> Nor ever did a wise one.

Once he was safely on the restored throne of his father, Charles II began to indulge his taste for pleasure. There can have been few monarchs with a more highly developed sense of life's joys. Sensuous and sensual stimuli seem to have been essential to him; his Plantagenet ancestry had carried a strain of hedonism which surfaced every third or fourth generation, infiltrating in turn Tudors and Stuarts and producing many variations on the verb 'to indulge'. Charles II's variety was sensual and sexual. He had many mistresses and numerous offspring by them. However, by his legitimate wife, Catherine of Braganza, he had no child, so when he died his brother James would succeed him.

History has with reason recorded Charles as the Merry Monarch. As soon as he ascended the throne, back came all the old, enchanting pleasures banned by the killjoy Puritans of Commonwealth and Protectorate. Theatres re-opened, fairs reappeared, dancing, which had been frowned on as licentious, was welcomed back with delight, and the land began to ring again with music, song and laughter. And, of course, with debauchery, for the damming of the human instinct to joy and enjoy can only be temporary; and when the dam breaks, the huge tidal surge of pleasure will not necessarily stay within the bounds of propriety. It is unlikely anyone save the Puritans mourned the sudden flood of permissiveness. The king was come; long live the king!

And the king lived indeed. Tall, young, striking and with enough wit and charm to lure swallows out of the sky or ladies from their husbands, swarthy Charles established a court of sufficient splendour to compensate himself and his followers for their dismal, impoverished, war-ruined youth. He did not neglect work, and attended whatever meetings and committees required his presence, no matter how early in the day or how late he had revelled the night before. He had something of his father's reserve but overlaid by an ease of manner and affability which won hearts and confidences. But his ministers knew him well enough not to trust him too far.

Charles enjoyed stage performances; he gave Drury Lane theatre its Charter, and paid it frequent visits. In 1948 a man reported that on an afternoon that summer he 'saw' the king visiting the Theatre Royal accompanied by a crowd of courtiers. The company walked down the gangway at the side of the stalls, climbed on to the stage and mingled with the performers who were playing *Oklahoma*. In Restoration times it was still the custom for gallants of the court to seat themselves in boxes on the side of the stage or on the stage itself, so the sighting in 1948 might represent an occasion when the royal party had done precisely this, the king and his immediate attendants presumably occupying one of the boxes. It has not been recorded whether the members of the *Oklahoma* company were aware of the strangers in their midst.

Although Shakespeare's heroines were all portrayed by boy actors, as was the custom in Elizabeth's reign, Charles II had seen drama staged at the French court, where they were taken by women. He made his approval of the custom known and Drury Lane (the only playhouse in London immediately after the Restoration) now cast women in women's roles, and actresses began to learn their trade. There were many females in and around the theatre apart from actresses, since prostitutes regarded it as a profitable area for business. Most of Drury Lane's patrons were wealthy men-about-town or about the court, and although the audience also included wives or other women partners, this did not discourage the whores and their employers. Indeed, it had been traditional even in Elizabethan times for owners of theatres to be brothel proprietors as well. In addition to the professional vice-vendors, there was a large substratum of amateurs – women existing on the fringe of respectable society.

It is not certain which category Nell Gwynn came from, but tradition has it that she was an orange-seller in the theatre. She quickly forsook her fruit basket for the stage, and soon became a great favourite with audiences, including the king. Charles, who got along as splendidly with working people as with his own courtiers, seems to have had an especial affection for Mistress Eleanor Gwynn. She was his mistress for many years, and was remembered on his deathbed in the famous injunction 'Let not poor Nelly starve'; whether his successor carried out the instructions one cannot be sure.

Pepys, an ardent playgoer, particularly admired Nell Gwynn in Dryden's *The Mayden Queene*, and also notes her performance in *The Tempest* – 'Nell in her boy's clothes mighty pretty'. Presumably she was playing Miranda. He retained his liking for the king's 'witty, pretty Nelly' long after she had fallen from high estate and was nearing her life's end, on several occasions lending her a yacht (Pepys was Secretary for Admiralty Affairs). He also, it seems, kept a printed portrait of the actress, showing her clad only in a pair of angel's wings. What part she can have been playing boggles the mind.

Charles seems to have treated Nell Gwynn very well. She was a talented comedienne and no doubt amused the monarch rather than making demands on him. She had numerous rivals, for Charles was an incorrigible collector of women and rarely dismissed any from his service, merely adding new ones to his payroll. Nell seems frequently to have accompanied him on his expeditions to the country, and echoes of these visits remain in certain places.

One such is Pewsey, a straggling, pleasant village in Wiltshire. In Restoration times an inn known as The Phoenix stood in the village centre, and its name is preserved today in a hostelry on the opposite side of the road. Nell Gwynn is reported to have stayed at this inn while her royal lover was lodged at Fyfield Manor, a few miles distant. Naturally the ghost said to haunt the remains of the old Phoenix building (now part of a modern garage) is that of Nell. When I visited it, one of the two garage staff had heard noises in the old part of the building on numerous occasions, though he thought they might be caused by rats rather than the ghost of the actress. His colleague denied all knowledge of a spectre, so it may be that the first man was more reticent than if the experience had been shared.

Occasionally, Charles II would buy a house, discreetly placed, in which to establish one or other of his mistresses. The delectable small manor house of Salisbury Hall near St Albans is said to have belonged to Nell Gwynn, a present from the king. Here, she persuaded Charles to give a title to her child by him by dangling the boy over the moat and threatening to drop him in. Charles responded by begging her not to let go of 'the Duke of St. Albans'. Two of the later inhabitants of this house were the mother and stepfather of Sir Winston Churchill, and Antony Hippisley-Coxe reports that Lady Churchill's second husband, George Cornwallis-West, saw the figure of a woman in a blue fichu. He was strongly reminded of a former nursery-maid, but on his mentioning the matter to his mother, she pointed out the nursery-maid's known resemblance to portraits of Nell Gwynn. He assumed that it was Nell's ghost he had seen, and it is possible that she would leave behind some psychic trace of her life which might be detectable by later visitors.

During my research for this book, I received a letter from Mrs Noreen Lambert of Radlett, Hertfordshire, whose home is within walking distance of Salisbury Hall. She told me of a visit she and her family made to the place some thirty years ago, when it was unoccupied following de-requisitioning by the Royal Air Force. The Lamberts took their daughter of fourteen and their baby son with them, and were accompanied by a neighbour's daughter. They looked around the house, but all the party had what Mrs Lambert describes as 'a creepy feeling', and she had the sensation of being watched. The two girls, in particular, felt uneasy, and insisted on taking the baby's pushchair with them even up into the attics, rather than have to collect it again from the ground floor (the baby, I hasten to add, was going to accompany his parents).

The tour was not a comfortable one, for the two young girls were so terrified that they almost trod on the adults' heels in their determination not to be left behind. Both insisted that the building was haunted, though it does not seem that they had any evidence of this, other than the sensation of the house itself. Some time later the Hall was sold, and the Lamberts met the new owners. The subject of Salisbury Hall and its history was raised, and the new occupants agreed that the place was haunted. At the time, however, alteration work was still being carried out, and it was possible that the disturbance of the surroundings would result in the destruction of the haunting. This is common, and the reverse can also occur; that is, alterations to a house which has no history of haunting may set one in motion. The reason for this concerns our old friend, the tape-recorder principle. If a part of the environment – door, ceiling or floor – 'holds' information recorded by activity near it in the past, removing that 'recorder' will result in the haunting's destruction. By corollary, if the recorder has been hidden behind later accretions, as sometimes happens with fireplaces, for instance, removal of the later screen may uncover the feature which holds the information of past action, thus enabling it to 'broadcast' or play back the record. There are many instances of both kinds of activity in the long history of hauntings and, although no efforts have been made to prove the theory, the evidence seems to point to its truth.

Salisbury Hall had a reputation of being haunted until comparatively recent times. Whether it still is, only the present occupants know. When I called at the Hall, I was not able to sample its atmosphere, the tourist season had not yet opened, and the doors were firmly shut to visitors.

Charles II inherited his love of hunting from his father and grandfather, and purchased several hunting-lodges. One was the building now known as The Manor, Farnborough Place, Hampshire, though the original house's appearance was radically altered by Christopher Wren.

A curious incident occurred here shortly after World War II, when a returned soldier, Albert Bailey, became a founder member of a local Ghost Club. The Club seems to have been a part of the rush to establish new and essentially peacetime interests which swept the country in the post-war years. For some it was amateur dramatics or evening classes. In this corner of Hampshire it was a Ghost Club. The Manor was an obvious target for investigation. Part of its history was known, and there were rumours of a tunnel beneath it which led to the crypt of the nearby church. Generations of the Anglesey family were buried in the crypt and in discussion with the proprietor of the Manor (at the time functioning as a hotel) the question was raised of jewellery buried with the dead earls.

As a result, and against some local opposition, an expedition was set up to explore the tunnel. There was some ambiguity about its purpose and talk of presenting any treasure found to the nation, though Albert Bailey had reservations about giving away something the team did not own. None of which prevented the group from descending into the house's cellars, and locating and opening up the tunnel with crowbars and pickaxes, an operation which took the men four nights. This seems to have been undertaken lightheartedly, out of curiosity and a need for excitement.

Albert Bailey returned alone to the excavation the following day. He met the caretaker, who refused to go near the cellar, saying the whole place unnerved him, as he felt he was being watched. Young Bailey was made of tougher material, and went on down until he reached a spot where he encountered a most unpleasant feeling: 'I knew a fear I had never known before. I heard a whispering in my ear; only faintly, but it was there.' The voice seemed to be male and mocking. The air temperature dropped sharply, and the investigator shivered with cold. This was followed by the sound of harp music, apparently coming from a room immediately above the cellar's dankness. Then, again as though whispered in his ear, he heard the voice of a woman sounding 'slow, cultured and divinely pretty'. A strong scent of roses accompanied these words:

> Though I scorn to fawn or flatter
> My heart is ever true.
> All unconscious of the matter

You reject a prize.
Take me, try me.
As you are so
Faithful you will find me.

Voice and perfume died away and Albert Bailey was no longer afraid, but later the cellar workings were filled in and no further attempt was made at investigation.

One of the interesting features of this incident is that the experience had no visual elements and was purely auditory and olfactory. Bailey heard and smelled but did not see anything. Local theory was that Nell Gwynn once occupied this hunting-lodge with the king, though Albert Bailey was not willing to make guesses about his feminine whisperer. It was a fragile, romantic and unsubstantiated encounter, but the feature which makes it noteworthy are the words the young man heard. They are fairly certainly the words of a song, and have an authentic flavour of the seventeenth century. So far I have been unable to trace any such lyric, but apart from being a comedienne, Nell Gwynn was also a singer. Was this fragment ever part of her repertoire, one wonders? Not enough is known to answer that question, so the episode remains tantalizingly inconclusive.

Another of the 'hunting-lodge' stories relates to Salcey Forest in Northamptonshire. The lodge this time is Salcey Lawn, a large country house deep in the Forest. Nell Gwynn is supposed to have spent a good deal of time here (when did she ever find time to act, with so much gadding about the countryside? Or perhaps she gave up her career for her king?). The usual word-of-mouth tradition says that Charles discovered his mistress was meeting another man in the seclusion of Salcey, and had this interloper followed, murdered and buried in the Forest. At intervals since a tall man wrapped in dark cloak and hood has been seen striding through the woodlands. He has appeared many times over the years, but vanishes before he can be accosted.

In 1880 a Mr George Green, working as a groom at the stables of Salcey Lawn, saw the figure of a woman seated on a garden bench in an orchard. The figure was too shadowy to be actual and Green was certain he was not watching a living person. He and a colleague saw the figure on several subsequent occasions, and identified it (for what reason is not known) as that of Nell Gwynn. The male ghost is thought locally to be either that of a monk or of Nell's supposedly murdered lover. The sometime owners of Salcey Lawn thought they had seen the spectre of Charles II, but since the house was altered earlier this century no more sightings have been reported.

Accounts of this kind smack of fiction and the accretions of legend. One has to ask how characteristic it would have been of Charles II to have a rival murdered; and the answer is not very. He was a tolerant man, sexually sure of himself, and with enough humour to have found a more amusing way to dispose of competition.

One further echo of Mistress Gwynn is in Dean Street, London, in an old house reputed once to have been the actress's home. In recent times the top floor of this became a strip club known as The Gargoyle. J. A. Brooks in his *Ghosts of London* reports that a number of people over the years have sighted the figure of a woman wearing a high-waisted dress and a large hat covered with flowers. Her appearance has always been accompanied by an overpoweringly strong scent of gardenias, which has lingered in the area after the figure has disappeared. Brooks mentions that the ghost usually vanishes by way of the lift shaft. Nell's sense of comedy must still be active. The only false note in this account is that women's dress of the Restoration period was not highwaisted. The bodice generally came to a deep point below the waistline, though the generally low decolletage might have created a high-waisted impression in an observer.

Others of Charles's mistresses to leave psychic echoes are Barbara Palmer, Countess of Castlemaine and later Duchess of Cleveland, and Hortense Mancini, Duchess of Mazarin.

Palmer had been a famous beauty in her youth, but in old age grew enormously large with dropsy. She died in Walpole House, in Chiswick Mall. Her slow, heavy footsteps have occasionally sounded on the stairs there, and her swollen body has been seen in silhouette against the windows. Apparently she has also appeared in Chiswick House looking from one of the windows, though the house was not built until fifty years after her death. This does not destroy the validity of the sighting, because some buildings might have existed on the site prior to the erection of Chiswick House. If it were a place Lady Castlemaine frequented during her lifetime, there is no reason why her semblance should not appear there after death. What decides the location of a haunting is what happened there; what emotion or action there was, and how deeply both were impressed into their surroundings.

Hortense, Duchess of Mazarin and her close friend at Court, Madame de Beauclair, had made a pact that whichever should first die would appear to the other as a confirmation of survival. The duchess died first and for several years no message or apparition came to Madame de Beauclair, with the result that she disbelieved in her friend's survival. One evening a third friend (possibly the Duchess of Cleveland) received a message that Beauclair did not expect to survive the night and requesting her immediate presence at St James's Palace. With reluctance, this friend did as bidden, only to find Madame de Beauclair apparently perfectly healthy, but convinced of her impending death. She said that she had seen the Duchess of Mazarin, who had materialized in her room and announced that she, Beauclair, would die between the hours of twelve and one that night. Her companions tried to reason her out of the idea, but at the time foretold her face changed colour, she called out, 'O! I am sick at heart', and died within half-an-hour, apparently of a heart attack. This type of haunting belongs in the category of warning apparitions, which appear to have the power of decision and suggest that human consciousness may truly survive.

Are there any instances of Charles II appearing in spectral form? Two have come to my notice. One concerns a family named Bradshaw, living and farming at Southorpe in Cambridgeshire. The Bradshaws' home seems to have possessed a ghost. One bedroom was so strongly affected that all four of their children were afraid when sleeping in it, and the youngest persisted that *it* was behind the dressing-table, though he could not specify what 'it' was. Over the years, footsteps have been heard, doors have opened and small items of equipment have disappeared and reappeared. Such goings-on often support the presence of a poltergeist, which is *not* a ghost, but the presence of psychokinetic energy, thought to be 'thrown off' by a living agent, usually an adolescent child. The individual producing this energy is often unaware of it but seems to have some control over the way the energy behaves; a paradox not explicable any more than the phenomenon itself.

The Bradshaws refer to their ghost as Charlie, on account of a belief that King Charles II was chased along a nearby road by Roundheads, presumably in the long hide-and-seek after escaping from the Worcester battlefield. There is no reason, however, to suppose he was as far east as Cambridgeshire; if the Southorpe ghost is connected with a Stuart king, the Charles is more likely to be Charles I. On escaping from the siege of Oxford, Charles I made his way towards Lynn in Norfolk, intending to take ship from there either to Montrose's army in Scotland or to a foreign country. To reach Lynn, he probably skirted Cambridgeshire, arriving eventually at Downham Market. He was also negotiating with the Scottish army in England and, having failed to find a ship out of Lynn, the king accepted Scottish assurances of good faith and travelled north to join their forces at Southwell. In so doing the royal party crossed the Ouse at Southery Ferry traversed the Fens by way of Littleport, Ely and Earith. Of course, the Scots broke their agreement the following year and handed Charles to the parliamentary forces.

I think the Bradshaws' ghost is more likely to be connected with a former inhabitant of the house, rather than a fugitive king who might have taken cover in a neighbouring wood. It is the house and not the wood which is affected.

Another anecdote about Charles II relates to one of his interminable hunting-lodges. The original house is now a farmhouse, and when my correspondent, Mrs H. Charlton of Wimbledon, visited it several years ago, its kitchen still had the original huge fireplace and great meat hooks embedded in the ceiling. Mr and Mrs Charlton had a son intent on becoming a farmer. Having undergone his early training at Bicester, he moved on to the Burford farm. His parents were invited there to stay for a weekend, and it was on this visit that Mrs Charlton had an unusual encounter.

During the night she left the bedroom and, returning along the corridor, she sensed that something had suddenly 'appeared' in front of her. Although she could see nothing with the physical eye, she believed that what was there was a semblance of Charles II, 'and I knew', she said in her letter, 'that he was dressed in all his splendour'. She was not, and she ran back into the bedroom to tell her husband 'Charles is still here!' He thought she was being over-sensitive to the atmosphere, and did not attach any importance to the incident. As Mrs Charlton explained in a later letter, it was momentary, and her reason for flight had been less fear than the belief that she 'was not suitably dressed to meet a king'. Even now, Mrs Charlton does not know whether the house has ever been reputed to be haunted, but whenever she went into the corridor she had the sensation of a presence other than her own. She did not 'see' the king again.

The 'seeing' of an apparition while knowing that one is not seeing anything in the physical sense, is just one more puzzling aspect of a complicated mechanism. I have also had the experience of 'seeing' with some faculty which was not physical sight: an ability of 'second sight'. Information seems to be conveyed to the brain which results in a pictorial impression, but the information comes from some other faculty than the physical sense of seeing. This may also be an electromagnetic transmission. A television set receives electrical impulses which it transmutes into visual and audible patterns: pictures and sound. The mechanism is known as a scanner. Certain biologists think the human brain may possess a scanning mechanism of a similar kind. If this is so, the phenomenon of 'seeing' which we think of as psychic may be part of our natural brain function; one of which we have virtually no knowledge.

The last of the royal echoes from the seventeenth century is of Charles II's eldest and illegitimate son, James Scott, later the Duke of Monmouth. A young man of good looks and charm, Monmouth was the son of Lucy Walter, whom Charles had met when he was a young, neglected and homeless refugee prince in Holland. Lucy always insisted that there had been a form of marriage between them, and Charles, though annoyed by this challenge to the dynastic marriage he hoped to make, found it difficult to deny the charge. He wanted complete control of his son, and infuriating the discarded Lucy would have defeated his ends. Not until Lucy Walter died in 1658 did he feel free either to choose his future queen or to take charge of the boy.

Monmouth was the eldest of Charles's several bastards. When Queen Catherine of Braganza failed to produce a child, the old spectre of the succession reappeared. Who was to succeed Charles? Next in line was his brother James, Duke of York, but James was a convinced Catholic, and a popish ruler would not be tolerated by a people now far into Protestantism. A strong parliamentary movement arose to exclude James from the crown, and to support as an alternative the king's eldest son, Monmouth. His illegitimacy seems to have been less a disadvantage for kingship than the Catholicism of the king's brother.

There were others who put forward James's elder daughter, Mary, as the next heir to the throne. As a result, the succession became a tug-of-war between political parties, though Charles handled the situation skilfully enough to avert any chance of another civil war.

Charles and James did not get on, and the king showed increasing affection for his son, Monmouth, as time passed. However, when in February 1658 Charles suffered a massive stroke and lay dying, the brothers were apparently reconciled. After Charles's death, James acceded to the throne in an atmosphere of welcoming expectation; much to his surprise. The euphoria did not last long. On 11 June 1658, the Duke of Monmouth landed at Lyme Regis, gathered a small army around him, had himself proclaimed king at Taunton and Bridgwater and marched on Bath and Bristol. His efforts came to nothing and he retreated, but was caught by the king's troops at Sedgemoor. Monmouth was captured and executed, and his followers were tried and condemned by Judge Jeffreys at the Bloody Assizes. The Monmouth rebellion was over.

Sedgemoor is a flat, open plain, and where the King's Sedgemoor Drain crosses it a spectral group of soldiers has been seen, the remains of Monmouth's defeated army. On 3 July, the ghost of Monmouth himself occasionally appears, in the act of escaping from the battlefield; the moment presumably registered for posterity by the fear and despair he experienced at the time. In fact, although Monmouth fought bravely at the head of his infantry, he abandoned his men and took flight when he saw the battle was lost. He was hauled before his uncle, King James but there was no reconciliation and Monmouth went from the Tower to the block. Jack Ketch, the executioner, bungled his work, and took 'five chopps' to decapitate the handsome, reckless son of Charles II and Lucy Walter.

James II was deposed three years later, and the much-troubled succession passed to his daughter, Mary, and her husband William Prince of Orange.

CHAPTER NINE

The Eighteenth Century

James II inherited an advantageous political situation from his brother Charles, and squandered it by trying to impose Catholicism upon a reluctant country. James did not realize how far his countrymen had swung away from their old religion. The English regarded themselves as a Protestant nation, and were alarmed by any attempts to turn back the clock. Their zealous king began to give his co-religionists posts barred to them for years. When Catholics were also appointed to Privy Council, the army and the universities, apprehension spread; dismay grew when a son was born to James's young second wife, Mary of Modena. A Catholic Prince of Wales ended hope of a Protestant succession.

Apart from the nobility, where political power now lay, the people most affected were James's daughters by his Protestant first wife, Anne Hyde. The Princesses Mary and Anne had been next in line of succession to their father, and were brought up as Protestants. Many of the English governing class had expected Mary and her husband, William of Orange, to take the throne after James.

Few of the king's policies pleased his nobles, and finally seven leading statesmen invited James's son-in-law, William of Orange, to invade England. The astonishing thing was that William accepted without hesitation, and this normally cautious, methodical man landed his force at Torbay on 5 November 1688, having dodged an English fleet waiting to intercept him off the Essex coast. The country stood by, uncertain how to react; the last thing the English wanted was another civil war. The other surprising factor was that although Mary loved her father she threw her full support behind her husband. Intense religious loyalties often overrode allegiance to blood and kin.

Once William had landed, he proclaimed that he had come in order to call a 'free' parliament and establish liberty of conscience and worship for all. He began his slow march on London. King James's army had either to initiate civil war or retreat. They retreated. William's stately advance (it took him a month to reach London) gave the people time to make up their minds which government they wanted. The king's army began to melt, and James lost confidence. No doubt his father's fate haunted him. So although he joined his troops at Salisbury, it was to face a dwindling morale and the desertion of his leaders to the opposition. Even his daughter Anne threw in her lot with the renegade midland aristocrats.

James was convinced he would be assassinated, and his Catholic friends were hurriedly escaping overseas or hiding on their estates. On 10 December the queen took her infant son and fled to France, and the next day the king tried to follow her. He was detained by some fishermen on the coast and brought back to London, which would have tempted William to have him permanently removed had he not promised his wife that her father would not be harmed. William arranged an opportunity for James to escape, and he took it. He landed in France on Christmas Day and went at once to Versailles; the French court's sardonic verdict was, 'When you listen to him you realize why he is here.'

William, who had staked everything on an unlikely gamble, now found himself regarded as Regent, Protector or Prince Consort of England; in other words, only his wife's husband. He made it clear that he would have the crown or nothing. Mary, dutiful and submissive as ever, agreed, and they became joint monarchs of a land both of them thought inferior to Holland.

The English were never to love their new King, for William

appeared to be a cold, reserved man, though strong-willed and resolute. Few people knew or understood him. Perhaps we have an insight into his personality at secondhand. William apparently spent the first night after the invasion of England at Ford House near Newton Abbot, and this building is haunted by the footsteps of a heavily-booted man, as he walks up and down the corridors and through its rooms, leaving all doors open. William's mind must have seethed with anxiety about the wisdom of his undertaking. He did not like England and had little sympathy with its inhabitants. It would, however, provide him with a useful treasury, though he was to spend as little time as possible in the country during his reign. It is thus ironic that the only known haunting connected with William III should be in the land he disliked.

His wife also left a psychic record of this time. When she followed William to England, she stayed for some time at The Royal Castle Hotel, Dartmouth, waiting for the summons to join him in London. She arrived in England on 12 February 1689, so it seems odd that the haunting is heard only in the autumn, its date varying between September and November, according to Guy Lyon Playfair. It has been heard many times in recent years, first by Mrs Gwyneth Powell, a former manageress, in 1950. The form of the haunting does not vary: it is the sound of a coach and horses drawing up outside the inn, picking up a passenger and driving off into the darkness. The time is always the same, 2.00 a.m. It seems that Mary stayed for several months in safety on the edge of her kingdom before William called her to the capital. Had the political climate changed, she would have been within easy reach of escape by sea.

In the event, it did not change. The couple were granted joint sovereignty, and although in practice Mary deferred to her husband in everything, the system worked. The one blot on Mary's future was her father's resentment. He had disowned her and laid the traditional father's curse upon her. Whether or not this kind of ill-wishing works, Mary did have her trials. She was never to have a child; a rift between her and her sister Anne never healed; and neither she nor her husband settled happily in England.

Guy Lyon Playfair remarks, apropos of this particular anniversary haunting, that it is one case where the triggering emotion seems to have been happiness rather than despair or fear. Certainly a strong positive feeling such as love or delight can result in a spectral echo. The ghost of the love letters at Offord Darcy, Huntingdonshirc (related in *Haunted East Anglia*) is a case in point.

Mary II died of smallpox in 1694, comparatively young, and her husband survived her by only eight years. William's reign was always uneasy, for James II lived in French exile until 1701 and the faction supporting the Stuarts, the Jacobites, was still strong and intermittently active in his former kingdom. Moreover, William was distraught at the death of his wife, and for two months was beside himself with grief. This seemingly cold man astonished his advisers by the passion of misery he displayed at Mary's death. He lived and died with a lock of her hair and her wedding ring next to his heart. He was, as kings go, a singularly faithful man, having had only one mistress, Elizabeth Villiers, whom he married off after his wife's death to one of his military commanders.

William spent little of the rest of his life in England. Military commitments took him back regularly to Holland and, when not in the field, he worked in a purely masculine atmosphere which involved one or two close friendships with his own sex. The Jacobites seized upon this male preference and tried unsuccessfully to make propaganda of it. William died in 1702 as a result of a fall from his horse. He had never been robust (he was asthmatic), and his tireless work for his dominions of the Netherlands, England and Scotland, had left him with little strength. He is remembered in his adopted country for his share in constructing the British Navy, and his gift for choosing the leaders who would head the allied armies under Marlborough in the war which lay ahead.

On the deaths of the childless William and Mary, the throne passed to Princess Anne, younger daughter of James II's first marriage. The beauty traditionally associated with Stuart women by-passed Anne. She did not possess the fine eyes of her sister, Mary, and her features were heavier and more plebeian, even commonplace. She had married a singularly unintelligent man, Prince George of Denmark, and had six children, one of whom was stillborn; the other five died early of hydrocephalus. Anne suffered from dropsy, and although she endured a pregnancy a year, from 1683 to 1700, rarely carried a baby to its full term. In addition to the six children who died, there were twelve miscarriages. Deeply religious, Anne suffered agonies for her part in betraying her father. She had hated her brother-in-law, William, irrationally attaching some blame to him for the guilt she felt.

Her narrow vision expressed itself in the way she chose her associates and ministers; she was much influenced by personal likes and dislikes, seeming more concerned about a person's behaviour than his ability. Her long, emotional friendship with Sarah Churchill, Duchess of Marlborough, and the later dramatic quarrel between them, are an illustration of the queen's lack of regal *savoir faire*. She was dwarfed by the job she had inherited. However, she was lucky in her choice of John Churchill, Duke of Marlborough (Sarah's husband) as her army commander-in-chief, and his successful campaigns in the War of the Spanish Succession – waged primarily against Louis XIV of France – earned Britain a place as a leading European power.

The history of Anne's reign is of political and military struggle, and the still unresolved question of the power-balance between Parliament and monarch. There was also the endless anxiety regarding the succession. Anne's only surviving child, the Duke of Gloucester, died in 1700, and the possible successor now was a descendant of Charles I's sister, Elizabeth, whose daughter Sophia had married the Elector of

Hanover. There was, of course, still a descendant of the main Stuart line living abroad: James, son of James II, whose legitimacy had at one time been in question, waited on the sidelines, his supporters in Scotland and (rather fewer) in England keeping him informed of the situation.

By 1710 the breach between Queen Anne and the Duchess of Marlborough was complete. The queen, ageing and sick, had grown tired of Sarah's bullying, and had found a new, more sympathetic confidante in her lady of the bedchamber, Abigail Masham. Sarah's influence, and that of her husband, Marlborough, was over. The rest of Anne's reign, which had been characterized by a running battle between the Whigs and the Tories, was concerned with ending the European war and securing the bedevilled succession.

The queen fell ill, and it was apparent she had not long to live. Her throne had to go to Sophia of Hanover's son, George, or to James II's son, James III, the Old Pretender. The first was dreaded as a German, a foreigner who could not even speak English, and the second was feared as a Catholic, who might legislate against Protestantism. Anne seems to have hoped that James would turn Protestant, but there was no chance of that; he refused to forsake his creed. The succession question was deadlocked; the country wanted neither the Catholic Stuarts nor a Lutheran and bigoted foreigner. The Privy Council was finally swayed by the Hanoverians among them and, when the dying queen handed the Lord Treasurer's staff to Shrewsbury, he, as leader of the Council, summoned the Elector of Hanover to assume the crown of England.

The queen died at half-past-seven the next morning, 1 August, and the House of Stuart came to its end.

The Jacobites were not disposed to believe it. For so many years they had been passing glasses of wine over water-bowls and toasting 'The king over the water', and the divide between Jacobean England and the imminent Hanoverians was more a chasm than a threshold. The world had changed unrecognizably in a mere twenty-nine years. Between the deaths of Charles II and his niece, Anne, lay the last echoes of the Renaissance and the first brazen rallying notes of modern times.

James Stuart, the Old Pretender, had made an unsuccessful attempt to land in England in 1708. In 1715 he tried again, because George Hanover had been king of Great Britain for a year and the new reign was not proving popular. However, rebellions need good leadership if they are to be successful, and this the Jacobites did not have. Their forces were defeated and the temporary 'King James III' retreated back over the water. The only result was wholesale confiscation of Jacobite property, mainly in Scotland and northern England. One note of alarm sounded in the ears of Hanoverians: the fanatical loyalty the Highland clans had shown to the Stuart cause. Lowlanders had long been more realistic, accepting that prosperity lay with England and English politics; the Stuarts were a luxury they could not afford.

Some politicians paid lip-service to the Hanovers but kept in touch with the Stuart court in France, just in case the unforeseen should happen and they should need to make a choice. Thirty years later, that situation arose, when the Old Pretender allowed his son, Charles Edward Stuart, to land in Scotland in July 1745. The young man, handsome, naive, self-centred but with all the spellbinding charm of his ancestress, Mary Queen of Scots, landed on the white shores of Arisaig with a few middle-aged companions; landed and planted his royal standard at Glenfinnan as a rallying point for his supporters. This Young Pretender appealed greatly to many of the Highland chiefs; he represented their traditions and traditional freedom, the time before Scotland had been bound to English economics or politics. Moreover, the young man was brave, reckless and supremely confident. He asked boldly for their loyalty and many gave it, even against their better judgement, but some declared for the Stuart Prince only out of enmity to clans which had opted for the government. Highland allegiances had always been bitterly tribal. Perhaps, too, the Jacobite clans knew that more was at stake then the Stuart dynasty; they were gambling for the ancient Highland structure which, if the war were lost, would disappear for good.

At first the prince's forces swept all before them on a tidal wave of loyalty, enthusiasm and affection. If his younger supporters ever wondered about the family for whom they fought, it did not hinder their allegiance. They knew the Stuart line to be of Scotland and of the true blood royal. That was enough; that and the crusading fervour of the Bonnie Prince and his entourage. They wore their tartan sashes and white cockades and marched south into England, reaching Derby on 5 December. The momentum petered out when it was learned that one English army awaited them across the Pennines at Wetherby, and that a second under the king's son, the Duke of Cumberland, lurked twenty-four miles to the south-west. A third had begun to assemble at Finchley, north of London.

When Prince Charles faced his Council that night, he wanted to push on to the capital, and jokingly referred to what he would wear when he entered London in triumph. He faced experienced counsellors who pointed out that the English were not rising to support him and no French army had been sent to help, so certain defeat lay ahead. They must turn for home and the safety of the Highlands. So they turned and marched north, fighting rearguard actions as they went. They had one sharp, heart-lifting victory at Falkirk, but then sought the safety of the high hills, the army dwindling as its members dropped off for home.

Early in February the Jacobites crossed the mountains and, at dawn on 16 April, 1746, less than 5000 half-starved and bone-weary men drew up into battle formation on Culloden Moor. Advancing on them from Nairn was Cumberland's disciplined force of 9000, including a company of artillery.

The clash was short and bloody. The Highlanders were cut down by accurate gunfire; they lacked ammunition and some of them were reduced to hurling stones. The clansmen fought heroically, but most died where they stood.

No quarter was given on that field, and the policy of repression invaded the whole structure of Highland life until little was left of it. The English forces fanned out in a systematic search for the young prince, terrorizing anyone thought to know his whereabouts. They had the support of the Lowland Scots regiments. There was a breaking wave of executions in London, Carlisle and York, and many more – men, women and children – died in gaol or on their way to transportation. The old Highland system, mediaeval, feudal, with beauty and terror in its loyalty and emotion, its bonding of son to father and clansman to lord, was torn down forever.

Charles Edward, the Young Pretender, escaped his pursuers and fled overseas, aided by those who loved him. Bonnie Prince Charlie (he had as many endearing nicknames as his ancestress, Mary) lived forty-two years in exile after his wild gamble. He became an elderly drunkard and wife-beater, living only in the memories of his fleeting greatness.

Whatever lives we live leave their traces or imprints in the memories of those who encountered us or in the environment we occupied. So it proved with Charles Edward Stuart.

Some years ago, when I was researching for *The Haunted South*, I stayed overnight in Godalming in Surrey. It is a pleasant town with a strong flavour of the eighteenth and nineteenth centuries – a Jane Austen sort of town, where one might meet Fanny Price going dutifully on some errand for her aunt and cousins, or Mr Collins trotting beside the carriage of Lady Catherine de Burgh. I had not found any ghosts worth reporting in the neighbourhood. I booked in to a local hotel, and here the name of Westbrook Place came up, though the house is now a home for epileptic women and girls, known as the Meath Home.

It is still a handsome building, Palladian in appearance, though mediaeval nails found in the old staircase, bones built into a wall and an underground passage connecting the house with a local church suggest that an earlier dwelling existed. In the mid-eighteenth century it was owned by General James Edward Oglethorpe, founder and one-time governor of the American state of Georgia. The general's daughters were convinced Jacobites, and local tradition says that Prince Charles Edward visited the house, walking in the gardens in the evening, with a grey cloak over his shoulders. Although there is some uncertainty whether the prince's spectre haunts the grounds, the house seems to contain the ghost of a grey lady who, although she appears rarely, is always the harbinger of good news. One of the night staff at the Home had woken to find the grey wraith at the foot of her bed, though the employee may already have been aware of the ghost story before the sighting took place.

Where so renowned a figure as Bonnie Prince Charlie is concerned, it needs only the shadow of a legend and a faint whiff of history to conjure him into being as a full-fledged phantom. But the grey-lady, if she belongs to the eighteenth century at all, is likely to relate to one of the young Misses Oglethorpe, whose excitement and delight at the royal visit must have been intense and lasting.

The prince almost certainly stayed at the County Hotel, Dumfries, probably in 1745, for after that time he was with his army in campaign conditions. Although the evidence for the haunting is slight – the figure of a Jacobite officer materialized from a wall in 1936 – that for its identity is even slighter. It may or may not have been the Bonnie Prince. Unless, that is, he was the only Jacobite who ever stayed there. The phantom does not seem to have made any appearances apart from this 'one-off'.

Culloden, not surprisingly, is deeply and disturbingly haunted. The horror of hand-to-hand fighting was added to in this case by the cold-blooded butchery of the wounded after the battle. On the road from Uig to Portree is a well, known as Prince Charlie's Well. On the day before the battle the spectral figure of a tall young soldier was seen near it, with an expression of great melancholy upon his face. People nearby heard the figure mutter the words 'Defeated, defeated, defeated' before it vanished, leaving a foreboding of disaster. Before the onlookers had recovered, a ghostly army materialized, with drums beating and clashing arms. The prince is said to have drunk from that well the following day. Who was the ghostly soldier? Could it have been an astral projection of the living prince, his *doppelganger* standing beside the well twenty-four hours ahead of the time when his material body would drink from it?

Out-of-body experiences are familiar enough; the division of a person's awareness into a physical and a supra-physical self, each conscious of its separate surroundings and observing life from different vantage points, is a well-authenticated phenomenon. And ghostly armies frequently appear on or near a battle site; though this one turned up precognitively, heralding the battle of the following day. Precognition, too, is a fairly common occurrence, as is the experiencing of events which have yet to occur. Phenomena of this type are studied in my book, *The Mask of Time*.

At Culloden Field, like many another battle area, individual ghosts and fighting armies have been seen, none of which is surprising when one remembers that extreme emotion produces these 'burned-in' images and deeply-imprinted sounds. Emotion, I suspect, is itself electrical, or at least produces heightened electromagnetic effects, the human electrical 'discharge' or 'field' being accentuated by fear, love, horror, hatred, joy. No wonder battlefields hold something of their history.

After the failure of the Forty-five, the Hanoverian dynasty was not seriously challenged. George II succeeded his father in 1727 and reigned until 1760. Although he spoke English fairly well, he preferred Hanover to England. During his reign, the country was involved in yet another European war, that of the Austrian Succession, and George II led his troops at the battle of Dettingen. He was the last British monarch to do so.

All through the reigns of George I and his son there had been the usual English resentment of foreigners as rulers; a situation not helped by the tendency of both men to introduce Hanoverians into their immediate circle, where they were able to influence British affairs. However, royal power was not what it had been under the Tudors. It had been filched from the King and passed over to Parliament.

Abroad, all was struggle and war. This was the century of America's fight for independence and of the conflict between France and Britain over Canada. Towards the end of his reign, George II must have been continually on the alert for news of his fighting forces, and this is borne out by a legendary tale concerning his last illness. The king was at Kensington Palace awaiting important despatches from Hanover. The month was October 1760 and the equinoctial gales were blowing, delaying all ships bound from the Continent to England. The king's health was failing, and he found it hard to tolerate the long wait for news. Frequently he looked out of his window at the weather-vane to see if the longed-for wind change had taken place; after each disappointment he asked plaintively in his strong German accent, 'Vy don't tey kom?' In due course the wind veered and the ships reached port, but too late for George. He died on 25 October, leaving his grandson king of England.

George II had a son, Frederick Louis, who was doomed to the same kind of miserable relationship with his father which George had himself endured. The people of England, though not knowing much about the royal facts, understood family relationships, and in the George v. Frederick affair their sympathies were with the son. The People's prince was invariably referred to by his father's subjects as Poor Fred.

Fred married the Princess Augusta of Saxe-Gotha and a son and daughter resulted from the marriage. Poor Fred endured years of family discord to no purpose. He died in 1751, leaving his thirteen-year-old son, George, heir to the English throne.

George III was twenty-two on his accession and was to reign for sixty years, longer than any British monarch save Victoria. He was good-looking if effeminate, and his youthful portraits show a physical resemblance to the Young Pretender. Unfortunately, he was intellectually mediocre in an age of gifted rulers. Catherine the Great, Peter the Great and the renowned Frederick of Prussia all wielded power in this century. George was quite unremarkable except for his obstinacy and a certain dogged devotion to duty. What greatness there was in England during Georgian times came from his subjects: Fox and Pitt, Burke and Johnson in its early stages; Nelson and Wellington, the Lakeland poets, the painters Constable and Gainsborough, Josiah Wedgwood and Jane Austen, among others, in its latter years.

George seems to have desired a more active part in government than either of his predecessors. He disliked the corruption which had invaded political life, and resented the monopoly of political power by the great Whig families. This, at least, was the view his contemporaries had of the new king. By Victorian times, the interpretation had changed, and he was thought to have been trying to turn back the clock to the times of true monarchical government. This was probably an invention of Whig propaganda, and George's attempts to influence the politics of his day seem to have been altruistic, if misguided. This shift in royal intentions was to produce a decade of instability in government and would ultimately lose Britain the American colonies.

As George III aged, he withdrew from public affairs, becoming more remote as his health failed. He had his first breakdown in 1765 and, although he soon recovered, was alarmed enough to make arrangements for a Regency in case the illness should recur. It did, several times, until it became his permanent state. His subjects and physicians assumed the ailment was mental, a form of insanity, and attributed it to the trials he had undergone from family conflicts, political opponents and rebellious colonists. However, modern medical opinion is that the king's illness was not lunacy but porphyria.

Although regarded with affection by his people, called 'the Good Old King', and 'Farmer George' (the British have always found nicknames for their national figures, especially those of whom they were fond), George III was a man of ordinary mind and few pretensions. He was easy with commoners and kindly and fussy in his manner. This same manner grew steadily more eccentric with age and, when nervous or embarrassed, the king was liable to issue a gunfire of repeated questions: 'Hey? Hey? Hey?' or 'What? What? What?' These foibles were regarded indulgently by his subjects, though not by his eldest son, who was known to entertain his companions of pleasure with merciless mimicry of his father's mannerisms. Towards the end of his life, when his mental instability had become permanent, when the American colonies had gone, the war with Napoleon had ended and his great and trusted minister, Pitt the Younger, was dead, the king was confined in a suite of rooms in Windsor Castle. Occasionally he would hear the approach of the Castle guards and the sound would return him to enough normality for him to take their salute as they passed.

Peter Underwood states that after the king died on 29 January 1820, and while his body still lay in state elsewhere in the castle, the guard took its normal route past the sovereign's old rooms and its commander, without thinking, looked up to see the figure of the old man standing in its place at the window. The officer issued his customary command 'Eyes Right' and, as the troop obeyed, the figure gave its usual response. In great old age, the officer concerned, William Knollys, told the story to the future George V.

This is an excellent example of appearance by the dead

shortly after decease. I have met many instances of this type, as though the newly-dissociated consciousness continued to follow its former life-routine out of habit. Such appearances may occur just once or twice after death, or may continue for a considerable time. These occurrences are of the 'surviving, decision-making' kind, and quite different from pattern-haunting. Elsewhere in Windsor Castle, George III has been encountered muttering 'What? What? What?' as he did in life. However, if genuine, this haunting does belong in the 'pattern' rather than 'survival' category.

After the death of the Good Old King, his crown passed to his eldest son, who had been Prince Regent during the last years of his father's life. Whatever nicknames the British people were about to bestow on George IV, the Good Old King and Farmer George were not likely to be among them.

CHAPTER TEN

The Nineteenth Century

In order to understand the strange paradox which was George IV, one needs to look at the lad from whom he had grown. In childhood the boy had been subjected to that perennial trial of princes of Wales, too-high parental expectations. Little George's parents were good-living, God-fearing, dutiful and conscientious middle-class folk in an upper-class situation, and they expected their children – particularly their eldest son – to obey the stringent rules laid down for their kind of household.

Unfortunately, no one had taken into consideration either the necessity for childish *lebensraum* or the influence of heredity. The little prince was given no space in which to develop naturally, but was forced from an early age to obey impossible rules. For his eighth birthday his mother gave him a pocket-book, accompanied by a note exhorting him to 'Abhor all vice, in private as well as in publick, and look upon yourself as obliged to set good examples. Disdain all flattery . . . Do justice unto everybody and avoid partiality.' There was more to the same effect, but it is doubtful whether the little boy understood a word of this maternal birthday message. However, through all his childhood and adolescence, the tone and expectations did not vary; and when young George showed signs of not reaching perfection, there were wails of disappointment and disapproval from his parents.

The princely ideal held up to him would have been out of reach even if he had not carried within him seeds of a very different temperament. But with a heredity which included the sexuality of the Stuarts and beyond them the Plantagenets, and a delight in sensual gratification which was part of the social atmosphere of his time, there was little chance of his becoming a sober, religious and ascetic princeling. By the time the boy was twelve, the king had discovered that his son was sly and a liar. And by the time he was seventeen the lad had fallen in love with the actress, Mrs Mary 'Perdita' Robinson and written her a series of extravagant letters which, when he had tired of her, the lady used as a blackmail weapon. His father, deeply shocked by the incident, had to arrange for payment of £5,000 before the compromising documents were released. It was to be the first of many such shocks for the king.

What kind of prince was this who, brought up in an atmosphere of dutiful respectability, showed such early signs of raffishness? The portrait painted by Matthew Brown in 1790, when the Prince of Wales was twenty-eight, shows a tallish, handsome young man, his plump smooth cheeks and broad physique already pointing to future corpulence. The expression is amiable, self-satisfied and with a trace of arrogance. There is also something of indefinable charm, although the full lips, hooded eyes and already blurred features speak of an indulgence unlikely to be restrained by conscience. What would have benefited the youth was either the discipline of work or a purpose in life. He was given neither, and had only a distant hope of one day succeeding his father as king. To fill the long empty days and nights between that hope and its attainment, there was nothing but pleasure and entertainment. So the prince, 'Prinny' to his friends, gambled, got into debt, got drunk, over-ate and womanized. And when he was not engaged in these activities, he made undesirable friends among the Whig Party which had for years been in opposition, and which his father regarded with distrust. Prince George Augustus Frederick was proving a great disappointment to his parents.

The situation was polarized when the Prince was finally given his own establishment and allowance. In 1783 he began to transform Carlton House, near St James's Palace, into an elegant home, and it was here that his own rather than his family's abilities began to be displayed, for young George prided himself on his elegant taste. When the place was ready, he gave a gigantic party at which the electoral colours of his Whig friends, 'buff and blue', were lavishly displayed. The king, passing the end of his son's gardens on his way to open Parliament, was not well pleased by the sight. Buff and blue had been the colours of the victorious rebel army recently commanded by George Washington in America. The prince's next move was to acquire a seaside property in Brighton, and an old farmhouse there was turned into a Pavilion, a new focus for his dissipated parties.

The amorous adventures continued indiscriminately until he met a young widow, Mrs Maria Fitzherbert. A ludicrous mini-replay followed of Henry VIII's sarabande with Anne Boleyn. The lady professed virtue and refused to surrender it without marriage. The gentleman, unused to being thwarted, accepted the bargain with the intention of keeping it just so long as was expedient. The pair went through a form of morganatic marriage, to which George was reasonably faithful until, pressured by huge debts, he felt the need to apply to Parliament (not for the first time) for financial assistance. He had little chance of this unless he could offer something in return, and his concession was to marry a royal bride and, with luck, provide the country with an heir. The official bride was his cousin, Princess Caroline of Brunswick, and the marriage was disastrous. It resulted in the birth of one child, Princess Charlotte, and a series of quarrels and recriminations between the parents which brought about a national scandal and eventual separation. George was reunited with Maria Fitzherbert for a few years after the failure of his marriage, and they seem to have lived comfortably together.

One psychic reminder remains of Maria, said by some to be the legendary 'lass of Richmond Hill'. Between Salisbury and Winchester lies the straggling market town of Stockbridge and a mile or two beyond is a house once owned by George after his accession. The place is now Redrice School and is approached by a long well-wooded drive. From time to time the spectre of Mrs Fitzherbert has been seen in the driveway, perhaps taking the air alone when her 'husband' was otherwise engaged. When I visited the area, I was unable to find any word-of-mouth tradition which would relate the ghost story to historical event, though a haunting is frequently an echo of a factual incident.

Prinny is said to haunt the subterranean passage under his Royal Pavilion, though there have been no recent sightings. The ghost which has been seen in the State Rooms of the Pavilion is that of a dumpy elderly woman. A caterer in charge of arrangements for a banquet there between the wars called in late the night before the affair to check that all was in order. He made a few minor alterations to floral arrangements when, chancing to look up, he saw 'a dark rotund shape' come from the kitchen direction, tour up and down the tables laid out for the banquet, and cast an anxious look in the direction of the head of the top table. The caterer followed her, wondering what business the woman had there, but was not able to get nearer to her than twenty or thirty feet. The figure disappeared through a door and the watcher ran after it, only to find the corridor on the farther side empty. He hurried to the next entrance and asked the attendant if he had seen an old lady leave, but the man assured him no one had passed that way in the last hour.

Later the percipient described the figure to a friend, as having worn a long, 'bunchy' skirt, a triangular shawl and a large bonnet, and this suggested the Regency period to them both. It was not until they leafed through a collection of old Brighton prints and cuttings that they found the facsimile of the ghost. The caterer recognized her at once. 'That's her,' he said, 'Bonnet and all!' She was a certain Martha Gunn, the Brighton Bather, and was said to have bathed Prince George when he was a child. But why should she visit the Royal

Pavilion when that building had nothing to do with the prince's childhood? I feel there may be some other explanation for Martha Gunn's appearance in Prinny's Pavilion than seeking her lost charge. That is, if the ghost *is* of Martha Gunn and not of some ancient housekeeper once employed in the prince's service.

The prince's relationship with his wife deteriorated beyond repair, and Caroline was accused of profligacy almost as great as his own. She was now not received by George III and the various shades of scandal concerning her were made painfully public. Yet popular feeling surprisingly championed the princess against her husband for, if she had behaved disgracefully and with sexual abandon, had he not set the example? The family squabbles rumbled on, in a bright glare of publicity. By 1811 the king was again a sick man, and finally a Bill was passed appointing the Prince of Wales Regent of the United Kingdom. He was almost fifty, and at last had a recognizable job.

During his Regency years the Prince showed concern for and patronage of the arts, discovering that superb architect Nash, recognizing the gifts of Jane Austen, Byron and Walter Scott and proving himself a good judge of Dutch painting, English china and French furniture. He also took a genuine intelligent interest in the conduct of the war against Napoleon. In 1812 the French Emperor was defeated by the Russian winter and on 6 April 1814, Bonaparte signed an act of abdication. A temporary peace fell on Europe like a damp but welcome blanket. And after peace came the festivities, orchestrated in England by the Prince Regent. Whenever the prince attempted a role both adult and dignified, some mischance always undid him. On this occasion he was completely outshone by his distinguished guests, the Tsar of Russia, the King of Prussia and Prince Metternich of Austria. The adulation went to the Europeans and George, unfairly, once more looked a slightly ridiculous figure. The situation was repeated when Wellington returned home after Waterloo;

the conquering hero outshone his prince.

In 1817, Princess Charlotte, daughter of the Prince Regent, died in childbed. Hers had been a love-match with Prince Leopold of Saxe-Coburg, and the nation, which had been charmed by the romance, took the news badly. Charlotte's son was stillborn, and the grief-stricken Regent was thus deprived of daughter and grandchild at one blow. The succession was again in jeopardy. His three bachelor brothers – Kent, Cambridge and Clarence – now hurried to marry, although all were well into middle age. The future sovereign seemed unlikely to come from the Regent's marriage, since he and Princess Caroline were still at drawn daggers.

Even in royal circles, life tends to run in one particular pattern for several years, then when one assumes it to be set permanently it changes; the pieces are shaken as in a kaleidoscope and the picture is never the same again. In October 1819, King George III, sixty and permanently deranged, with the added handicaps of deafness and blindness, suddenly grew tired of eating and gave up the habit. Within three months he was dead and his eldest son had become George IV. There followed undignified wrangles as to whether his wife was to be known as queen, whether or not she should be included in the coronation (she was not), and whether or not she was to be divorced for adultery. The King's matrimonial problems were solved by Caroline's death in 1821.

From then until his death in 1830, George IV occupied himself by interfering in politics, building and rebuilding his various houses and by patronizing the arts. Buckingham House was turned into a palace, Windsor Castle completely modernized, the British Museum was given the seventy thousand volumes which had belonged to George III in order to make the King's Library; and the nucleus of the National Gallery was established at the new sovereign's prompting. He also made the acquaintance of his brother's small daughter.

The Duke of Kent had died shortly after Princess Victoria was baptized in 1819, and the king seems to have seen his niece at intervals; she referred to him as 'Uncle King'. From 1824 on George was not in good health, and in the last year of his life suffered a series of strokes which culminated in his death at Windsor Castle in the early hours of 26 June 1830. The Duke of Wellington was surprised to see a miniature gleaming on the monarch's breast; it was of Maria Fitzherbert and was buried with him at Windsor. His one-time 'wife', now an elderly widow, wept when she was told the story.

'Prinny' was one of the many elder royal sons whose lives were spoiled by delayed hopes, under-employment and the too-high expectations of parents. That he added colour and style to the age in which he lived is indisputable; it would have been remarkable had he also added dignity and wisdom. However, he gave his name and image to an age, the Regency; perhaps he would have been pleased by that kind of immortality.

Apart from the paranormal echoes which remain in the Royal Pavilion at Brighton (which in the latter years George rarely visited), he seems to have had psychic ability. He was invited to stay at Houghton Hall in Norfolk as a guest of the Walpoles, and was given the State Bedroom. According to legend he was awakened by the appearance of the famous 'Brown Lady', said to be the unhappy spirit of Dorothy Walpole (sister of England's former Prime Minister, Robert Walpole) who had been married to the second Viscount Townshend. Though a charming woman in life, she had been frivolous and extravagant and apparently the marriage was unhappy. This spectre, named for the brown brocade dress in which it is always seen, has most often materialized at Raynham Hall, where Dorothy's children were brought up by their paternal grandmother. The figure appears on the stairs and has even shown up in photographs. The Prince Regent's remedy for ghostly disturbance was simple: he asked to be moved to another bedroom.

The sons of George III attracted scandal as a magnet draws iron filings. If the Prince of Wales was the most intelligent, and Frederick, Duke of York, the one most loved by his father, perhaps the fifth son, Ernest, Duke of Cumberland, was the strangest. Reputed to be a pervert and possibly incestuous, by some accounts he also possessed an ungovernable temper (see *The Life and Times of George IV* by Alan Palmer). This last fact may throw some light on a curious haunting in St James's Palace. The ghost is said to be one of the Duke's valets, named Sellis, who was found in his bedroom early one morning in 1810 with his throat cut. At the same time the duke emerged from his rooms, bleeding from sabre wounds and crying out that someone had tried to murder him.

The fresh scandal in the royal family set the country by the ears and, since the Duke of Cumberland was both unpopular and feared, it was not surprising that there were two versions of the Sellis incident. The duke said he had attended a concert on the evening of 30 May and been dressed for the occasion by Sellis, whom he had then dismissed for the night. Later that evening one of the maids had heard someone creeping through the state apartments connecting the valet's bedroom with his master's suite. The duke returned home just after midnight and was asleep by one, but in a statement later he said he was awakened by a series of blows to the head and in his half-asleep condition thought a bat had got in and flown against him. Although a lamp was lit, he did not see anyone. He got up and went towards the door leading to the room of the second valet, Neale, calling out to him for help. It was at this point, said the duke, that he received a sabre wound in his thigh, and was rescued from worse by the arrival of Neale. Other servants were roused and made a search of the nearby rooms. The duke's regimental sword, covered in bloodstains, was discovered on the threshold of the door to the state apartments. In Sellis's bedroom the searchers found the valet's body with its throat cut; according to some reports, a bloody razor was lying within reach of the valet's hand. The contrary version said the razor was found a considerable distance from the body.

The faction hostile to the duke interpreted the story as the murder rather than suicide of Sellis. The duke, said the whisperers, had seduced Sellis's wife (or daughter, according to another variation), and been attacked by Sellis in revenge. The valet had been promptly despatched by the duke, who had afterwards raised the alarm. Both these versions would have driven Scotland Yard to a nervous breakdown had there been a Scotland Yard; both were full of discrepancies. The valet had attacked the duke with a knife; or with the duke's own sabre. The duke felt the blows to his head as the buffetings of a bat, but his brain could be seen pulsing through one wound. The razor which was said to have killed Sellis was near the valet's hand; or it was many feet away and out of reach. Sellis had cut his own throat, but his head was almost severed from his body: a circumstance more likely to have been caused by a sword than a razor. So it went on; Cumberland's wounds were reported by one faction as too slight to be caused by a sabre and by the other as severe, his thumb being almost severed.

The truth will never be known now and was possibly impenetrable at the time, given the loyalty of the royal servants to their employers. What is known is that the ghost of a smallish man (Sellis) has been seen many times in the room he once occupied. It always appears with its throat cut and, according to some sources, with an overpowering smell of fresh blood.

The inquest on Sellis gave a verdict of suicide. It could hardly have produced any other. However, even now this case is as unsatisfactory as it is unsavoury. All that can be said about Sellis's ghost is that hauntings often arise as a result of violent deaths, and that part of St James's Palace must have a thoroughly uncomfortable atmosphere.

*

The crown passed to the Duke of Clarence, who became William IV, after the death of the childless George IV. History has dubbed him the Sailor King, which innocuous term is a sure sign that he was kindly, ineffectual and harmless. Melbourne, his Home Secretary, said of him, 'He hasn't the feelings of a gentleman; he knows what they are, but he hasn't them.' William felt at a continual disadvantage when faced with his ministers, recognizing, perhaps, his intellectual inferiority. Even his homely buffoonery vanished once he became king, and he grew morose and ill-tempered towards the end of his life. He died of heart failure on 20 June 1837 and, since he had no issue, apart from a tribe of turbulent bastard children, the crown passed to his niece, the Princess Victoria, daughter of his brother, the late Duke of Kent.

The young princess's mother, the Duchess of Kent, although in some ways self-important and foolish, had been careful in one particular; she had shielded the princess from the more disreputable side of her relatives' lives. The corollary of this was that Victoria was over-protected, leading a life amost exclusively under feminine influence, while being aware that she was the heir to the throne and therefore of importance. There was conflict between William IV and the Duchess of Kent over the control of the young girl, and still further conflict between Sir John Conroy, who as the duchess's secretary influenced his employer greatly, and the princess's governess, Baroness Lehzen. The atmosphere of animosity resulted in a degree of caution and distrust on Victoria's part.

That Victoria grew rapidly in stature was due largely to her Prime Minister, William Lamb, Lord Melbourne. Forty years older than the princess, he combined a shrewd knowledge of the world with a rare warmth of heart; political wisdom and an understanding of human nature enabled him to guide the young girl, whose simplicity was backed by a strong will, forthright opinions and a leaning towards duty and respectability which would give the age its characteristics.

The middle-aged man and the young girl suited each other very well. He provided her with a father figure she could respect; she gave him the flattering attention and affection he needed and which had been denied him in his tempestuous marriage. Lady Caroline Lamb's affair with Byron had rung around London like raucous bells and Melbourne had supported the unstable Caro long after Byron had shattered and left her. We do not know how much of Melbourne's sufferings was understood by the young queen, but it is clear that there was a rapport between the monarch and her Prime Minister, and that it developed into an affectionate regard which had much of love in it. Both needed and depended on regular contact with the other, and it was not until Victoria's marriage to Prince Albert of Saxe-Coburg (which Melbourne himself advocated) that the bonds began to loosen.

The queen, loving a man of her own age, gradually turned from her ageing, beloved minister until she stood alone with her Consort. When the Whigs lost office, Melbourne ceased to be Prime Minister and lost his precious daily contact with the sovereign. This caused him considerable unhappiness, but it is the fate of teachers to see their pupils outgrow them. Victoria's life was expanding as that of her old friend contracted. Melbourne, a generous-spirited and gentle man, died in 1848, while Victoria was to reign for almost sixty years longer, forty of them as a widow.

There are some illuminating glimpses of the young queen in Lord David Cecil's excellent biographies of Melbourne. Headstrong, partial and obstinate, Victoria was particularly touchy about her royal rights – not in the way the Stuarts were about the divine right of kings, but as an adolescent overwhelmed by her inheritance. When the queen wanted to give Albert precedence over everyone by making him king consort, Melbourne said, 'For God's sake, Ma'am, let's have no more of it. If you get the English people into the way of making kings, you will get them into the way of unmaking them!' The lesson of Charles I had been well learned. Albert became mere Prince Consort, though he was to add enough lustre to the honour to make it memorable.

Although Victoria became a down-to-earth, dutiful wife and mother as well as an imperious ruler, she had a strongly developed intuitive side. This might have held the psychic strain, for there is at least one record of her having seen a ghost. Crathes Castle, Aberdeenshire, was built by the Burnetts in the fourteenth century, and is said to have a Green Lady ghost which appears before a crisis in the Burnett family. It has been seen on many such occasions, gliding across one particular room towards a carved fireplace. Underwood and Alexander both record this haunting. Underwood says that Queen Victoria saw the ghost on one of her many visits, and that, when it reached the fireplace, it bent to lift a ghostly child in its arms before fading from sight.

The hearth of this fireplace was taken up and the skeletons of a woman and a child were found. The conclusion is that the remains were related to the Green Lady haunting, though nothing is known of any story which would fit these facts. Whether the bones were given hallowed burial and whether the phantoms continue to haunt the room at Crathes is not known. Often, when these 'indicative' ghosts have directed attention (usually a mere by-product of the haunting) to the place where their mortal remnants lie, they cease to haunt. Decent burial puts an end to it, though it may be that the mere disturbance of the epicentre of the haunting robs it of its power to 'project'.

There is no record of Queen Victoria's reaction to her sighting, but no doubt she took it calmly. Her interest in the paranormal continued throughout her life and was intensified after the death of her adored husband.

One of the central personal mysteries concerning the queen was her relationship with her Scottish manservant, a brusquely uncouth Highlander named John Brown. Victoria came to rely on him increasingly in the years of her widowhood, and he seems to have developed a fiercely protective, even authoritative attitude towards his employer. Certainly he aroused antagonism in her family and friends, and when Edward VII took over Balmoral, he ordered the destruction of all mementoes of the late John Brown, including sundry statuary. Strange that a monarch should commemorate a servant with a statue.

There were rumours, of course, that Brown had been more than a servant to the widowed queen, even that he had been her lover, but this borders on the ludicrous given Victoria's acute sense of propriety. However, he had some kind of influence over her, and more recent guesses include one that he might have been a practising medium who volunteered to put her in touch with her beloved Albert. This idea might have been attractive to her. Kings and queens, insulated as they were from the toughening influences of social intercourse, must have been susceptible to charlatans, miracle-workers, con-men and high-class magicians. One needs only to recall the effect of Rasputin on the Russian czarina for proof of this. Ultimately the relationship between queen and Highland rough diamond remains inscrutable. Her son's reaction indicates that it was not in the ordinary employer-servant category.

One of the most interesting and amusing recorders of royal affairs in modern times has been the Princess Marie-Louise, Queen Victoria's grand-daughter. Her volume of memoirs *My Memories of Six Reigns*, while amateur in its hiatuses and indulgences, is full of acute observation and sound judgement. She is also instructive about royal experiences of hauntings. Her mother, Princess Helena, was Victoria's youngest daughter and married Christian of Schleswig-Holstein, who once had a spooky experience in his native country. In his youth Prince Christian was an officer in the Cuirassier Regiment and was stationed in a castle at Breslau. Owing to the large number of officers quartered there, Christian shared a sizeable room with a brother officer. One night the young man woke to find a woman in a blue silk dress standing in the room. He noticed an unusual object around her neck – a small coffin suspended on a blue silk cord. Although surprised, Christian was not afraid and watched the apparition with curiosity. The 'woman' looked first at his companion, who was soundly sleeping, then she walked around to the prince's side of the bed. Christian had once vowed that if he encountered anything inexplicable, he would count to thirty before drawing his sword: a careful prince. He began to count aloud – 'one, two, three, four . . .' but he was interrupted by the spectre, who said (though whether in surprise or amusement is not recorded), 'Voici, qu'il commence a compter' and vanished – not with a silvery laugh but with a somewhat baffled smile.

A year later, Prince Christian returned to the castle for a partridge shoot, and was greeted by his host with an apology for not giving him the same room, which had undergone renovations, including the laying of a new floor. A skeleton had come to light; it was of a woman, with shreds of blue silk still clinging to the bones, and around her neck was a small coffin containing the bones of a baby.

Although nothing is known of an historical foundation for this burial and its psychic consequences, an interesting factor in the haunting suggests that this is no mere 'record', no pattern-haunting. The spectre had made a communication which suggested 'she' was surprised by the prince's action. 'Well! he begins to count . . .' Whatever was viewing Christian and being seen by him had the use of its wits, in that *it knew what was occurring at that moment*, and could comment on it. This suggests a surviving entity or consciousness, possession of the ability to think and decide.

Later experiences recounted by Princess Marie-Louise indicate that she might have inherited psychic sensitivity from both sides of her family. She had at least two personal experiences which I describe in the next chapter since they happened in the twentieth century.

One other and most remarkable occurrence remains. It,

too, took place in the present century, but as it refers to Queen Victoria and to events already touched on, I include it here. Some time ago, Mrs Betty Childers* sent me an unusual account of a haunting, if such it can be called, which combines the elements of past and present, the nineteenth and the twentieth centuries. My correspondent thought it happened in either 1954 or 1955, and the time was early evening. She emphasized that this was a time when satire on television was in fashion, and the denigration of establishment figures was a sign of trendiness and advanced thinking.

'These broadcasts', Mrs Childers wrote, 'made me feel highly indignant.' She wrote a complaint to Cliff Michelmore of the BBC, the 'anchor man' of the programme which irritated her. These satirical items were regular and soon the Victorians came under the hammer for their habit of covering table- and piano-legs out of a sense of propriety. 'Then,' Mrs Childers continued, 'they arrived at Queen Victoria and her friendship with John Brown, the suggestion being that the friendship was not entirely innocent. I remember feeling highly indignant and generally disgusted with the general trend.'

On the evening in question, Derek Hart, a television newsreader of the time, paused and exclaimed 'in an excited and incredulous voice . . . "Queen Victoria!" I was not aware,' said Mrs Childers, 'that . . . the BBC had the privilege of looking into our homes. Nevertheless I looked in the direction of his gaze and to my amazement standing there, dressed in black, was Queen Victoria.' She was apparently in the Childers's living-room.

Mrs Childers's astonishment increased when the figure said words which sounded like 'I am so tard.' Tard? Was this the queen's way of pronouncing 'tired'? Mrs Childers was frightened, but conveyed to the figure mentally that 'she' might rest where 'she' was. The percipient seems to have

* A pseudonym.

glimpsed the figure out of the side of her vision, because her gaze was mainly focused on the screen. However, she was aware of a strong sense of presence and this continued, although when she got up to make the evening snack at 9.00 p.m. she was certain that she and her husband were once more alone.

I asked her whether her husband had seen the figure, or if she had discussed what she had experienced with him. She said that her husband was an agnostic, and she had not wanted to risk his scepticism by telling him.

This is the kind of case most parapsychologists can knock enough holes in to furnish a colander. The 'apparition' might have been self-suggested, arising from the television reference; it could have come from Mrs Childers's memories of a statue of the queen which she had seen in Worcester when stationed there with the WAAF; it might even have come from her indignation at the denigration perpetrated by television, and been a kind of projection of those feelings. It seems to me, however, that all these possibilities are just as incredible as the suggestion they challenge. Mrs Childers makes the point that she was not particularly interested in or sympathetic towards Queen Victoria. She is also a Catholic from a devout background, and anything in the nature of spiritualism would have been abhorrent to her. The experience seems to have been spontaneous, unexpected and unsought.

One factor which seems to indicate its authenticity is the sentence, 'I am so tard.' The words were clear enough. Had Mrs Childers conjured them from her mind, she would surely have produced something more intelligible. She was mystified by their meaning and says of the apparition, 'I would have dismissed it from my mind, except that she spoke in a normal voice those few words, "I am so tard".' This is indeed a strange example of ghostliness, certainly no common haunting. A 'one off' with no connection with the building where it occurred or the person who witnessed it. What connection there is seems to be with the medium of television. I have once or twice encountered this type of phenomenon, and it is certainly not unknown for a spectral face to take over the television screen by obliterating what is on it. But the apparition was apart from the set, and Mrs Childers said the figure was 'standing in our sitting room. Where she was standing in relation to the television set – my chair was facing the set and she appeared to be on my left hand side and *facing* the set and sideways on to myself.'

Is the queen, eighty-five years after her death, still concerned about the reputation she cherished during her lifetime as queen? Or was the incident produced by the personality of the percipient? Or by the television medium? I have no answer.

CHAPTER ELEVEN

The Twentieth Century

One would imagine that the discords and conflicts of the twentieth century would have banished all ghostly presences from their traditional places. Can ghosts exist in the midst of urban noise or hauntings continue in competition with the screech of traffic and the smell of lead-burdened petrol? They can and do. Ghosts, at least of the pattern-haunting type, function around particular sites, the scenes of their activities in life; unless those sites deteriorate to the stage where their 'activating point' or 'recorder' is destroyed, they continue to function no matter what happens in the neighbourhood. The essence of many, perhaps most, hauntings, is that they retain their own time around them and continue to operate in it, oblivious to what year is on the calendars. Their past is an eternal present.

Where the ghost is not part of a mechanically operating event, a recording, but is an active survival of a human consciousness, the case is different. The presence appears not only to understand what goes on around it, but occasionally to be aware that it has been supplanted by a younger time and newer generation. This type certainly is less common than the pattern-haunter as far as long-term hauntings are concerned. Over the short term, semblances of the newly-dead frequently occur for limited periods after death, appearing in the places and to people they had known in life. When such a place has a long history, it is not easy to be sure of the identity of a ghost attached to it.

Clarence House adjoins the Palace of St James in London, and was built in 1825 for William IV when he was still Duke of Clarence. Since then it has been the London residence of Queen Victoria's mother, the Duchess of Kent, her second son the Duke of Edinburgh and his brother, the Duke of Connaught. In addition it was the official residence of Queen Elizabeth II at the time of her accession and the home of Queen Elizabeth the Queen Mother; and at one time of Princess Margaret.

The haunting of this fine old house involves none of these eminent figures. Its story was told me by Mrs Sonia Marsh, who knew the building in the 1940s, when it was used by the British Red Cross Society, for whom she worked. Mrs Marsh, after saying that the building was then both dowdy and grubby, went on

> At the time, single women with no family commitments were obliged to work long hours, Saturdays included, totalling if I remember aright fifty-odd hours. Some of us managed to reduce Saturday working by arriving fifteen minutes earlier on other days; staying on the odd half-an-hour in the afternoon; or cutting short one's lunch hour. But on the occasion in question, I had mismanaged my hours because of a series of social engagements, and found myself having to work those *hated* extra hours on Saturday afternoon.
>
> It was a dank, dark autumn afternoon, possibly October or November. Everyone else had departed, but there I was, resentfully doing my bit, all alone in the vast first-floor, erstwhile ballroom. There were twin fireplaces, and spaces for paintings above, columns and spacious windows, now incongruously blacked out, except for my small patch with desk and typewriter. The ballroom had bare nondescript floors where once was possibly polished parquet. Metal filing cabinets stood guard, telephones and desks and other office panoply held command.
>
> Minding my own business, with head down, I was suddenly aware of 'a presence'. *Imagination, of course.* In the

dark recesses of the curtained room, I felt sure someone was lurking. I turned and saw some sort of greyish, swirling, triangular, smoky mass, oddly without *feet* – bobbing, receding and advancing alternately. I didn't go much on it. In fact, I was *petrified*! I leapt up from my desk, barking my shin on an open filing-cabinet drawer, and deciding to flee the building. I closed the curtains obediently, thus plunging myself into further terrifying darkness, and raced out of the door and down the stairs, without waiting to put on my coat until I was in the sanctity of the courtyard outside. Prior to that I had heard doors opening and closing outside the ballroom and several times had been out to discover who else, like me, was working on late, on Saturday afternoon. (Perhaps it was merely the caretaker checking.) Whatever it was, I didn't dawdle in trying to get away.

Next day, I recounted my story to my colleagues. It was a five-minute wonder. Society ladies who didn't bother with other than their own kind, came asking me about it. I told them what happened. 'Probably the old Duke of Connaught' said one, but it was all Greek to me, as I had never even heard of him. I was, you see, something of an oddity, I think, as I was not brought up in Britain, but had lived in Soviet Russia for ten years, and was therefore divorced from normal contacts and British customs. (I lived in Russia between 1931 and 1941, returning to England when I was 16½, so I was probably 18+ when the event described happened.)

This is a detailed description of what is probably an active ghost, though at the time Mrs Marsh had no idea what she had seen – only that she was afraid of it. She asked me in a later letter what the amorphous 'something' was; 'some sort of greyish, swirling, triangular, smoky mass – bobbing, receding and advancing alternately'. And *without feet*. The lack of feet is a particularly interesting aspect to any self-respecting ghost-hunter!

These foggy apparitions, which never get beyond a 'ball of mist' or 'amorphous blob' probably represent an early stage in the materialization process, a stage beyond which the intending materializer is not able to proceed. Why would this happen? My own theory, which seems to be substantiated by at least some of the available evidence, is that in order for any parapsychological activity to take place a supply of energy is needed. This may take the form of electricity, heat or mere human energy (i.e. electromagnetic, since this is the type of force field we produce). Frequently, in the neighbourhood of a haunting, one of these energy forms will be affected. It is common for lights to go out – or occasionally switch on; for cold spots or a general fall in temperature to occur immediately before a haunting; or, most interesting of all, for an observer to feel cold and shivery as he (presumably) loses heat to the paranormal event.

Going on from there, if one supposes that the early stages of certain types of haunting are the appearance of mist – and there are many instances of this kind – the later stages seem to be a development into a distinct impression of a human or animal form. This may be so realistic, so three-dimensional and coloured, that it is mistaken for a living being. In between the amorphous and the realistic can be stages where the mist translates itself into a transparent but recognizable shape; where it partially solidifies but remains grey (or black or white) without attaining colour; and the penultimate stage where it achieves apparent solidity without colour. Colour seems to be the last quality to appear.

Now, when one looks at these sequences, it is obvious that the metamorphoses require a considerable supply of energy. In the case of Mrs Marsh's greyish smoky mass, the transition seems to have petered out before shape could be achieved. I have known several cases where the 'ghost' was a ball of mist which eventually translated itself into a human face but nothing more. The Clarence House haunter was vague, 'triangular and swirling . . . bobbing, receding and advancing alternately' as though unable to proceed to the whole semblance of a human being.

Something must already have been known of this spectre because Mrs Marsh's colleagues said, 'Probably the old Duke of Connaught', as though some legend were known to them. If they referred to the Connaught who was Queen Victoria's brother, he was a very old duke indeed, and the older the ghost is in terms of spectral existence, the less energy it retains for materialization, if 'retaining' is a correct description. The fact that this percipient had heard doors opening and closing all afternoon when there was some doubt about anybody else being in the building may add weight to the validity of the haunting. A strange little episode, and one which might have occurred more than once in Clarence House, though I have found no other reports.

Psychic ability was perhaps common property among the human race in its early days, before the brain's left hemisphere took over the lion's share of activity. The two hemispheres are distinct in function, the left being responsible for logic, language, analytical and deductive ability and the right for intuitive and creative activities. In western man the left brain has become predominant, while in more primitive societies the right brain has been the chief functionary. The ideal, which the human race has not yet achieved, is a perfect balance between the halves, logic and intuition feeding and co-operating to produce harmony.

Psychic ability is possibly in the right hemisphere's functioning, although the medium for experiencing *psi* seems to be one of the four wavelengths which the brain uses, the *alpha* rhythm (the others are known as *beta*, *delta* and *theta*). *Alpha* is of a frequency of 8–13 cycles a second, and is the brain's 'idling gear'. It is associated with a relaxed state of mind when mental activity is not concentrated in any particular direction.

Perhaps most people once possessed and used the so-called psychic function, doing so without self-consciousness or thinking its possession extraordinary or shameful and a sign of credulity. These strictures are typical of the left-brain's processes, but the *psi* function has operated throughout history, in spite of civilization's attempts to suppress it. It is thus not surprising to find it as frequently in royal as in other families, cropping up with potency in some, as does the tendency to short sight, asthma, artistic ability, blue eyes, long legs and a host of factors handed down through tribal genes.

A particularly gifted individual in modern times seems to have been one of Queen Victoria's grandchildren, the Princess Marie-Louise. In her autobiography, the princess says firmly that she had no supernatural gifts and then proved the contrary with anecdotes of a convincingly 'supernatural' kind.

Her favourite brother, Prince Christian Victor, died in the South African War. The princess also had her vicissitudes; her marriage failed and she took a small house in South Kensington. Shortly after the removal, she was arranging books in her sitting room when she saw the door open and Christian Victor walk in and seat himself beside the fire. The princess (using his pet name) immediately said, 'Oh, Kicky, how nice to see you again!' To which he replied, 'I just came to see that you were all right and happy.' She noticed then that his favourite dachshund was seated on his knee. The pair talked for a while, then he rose and, instructing her not to follow him downstairs, said that all was well and happy with him. He left, closing the door behind him. The princess returned to reality. She remembered with surprise that although her brother was in khaki he was not wearing his medal ribbons; then recalled that during the South African War officers had been forbidden for identification reasons to wear these decorations. It was only then that she recollected with shock that this beloved brother had died eighteen months previously and was buried in South Africa, but she was cheered rather than depressed by the experience.

An encounter of this nature is easily self-created. Had it been so, the princess would surely have seen her brother as she might have expected to see him: wearing his decorations and not as he had been at the time of his death. Neither would she have remembered his death only *after* the experience ended.

Several other incidents in which Princess Marie-Louise was involved suggest that she was a sensitive of marked psychic ability. The same cannot be said of her cousin George V, who inherited the throne following the death of his elder brother, the Duke of Clarence. George was yet another Sailor Prince, not prepared by upbringing for kingship, but undertaking it with commitment and a stern devotion to duty.

The prince's interests had been the country pursuits of fishing, stalking, shooting, visiting friends, meeting and talking with tenants on his estates and memorizing as much as he could of their lives. He would occasionally stop the village children on their way from school to question them about their work, teasing them (with a mildness he could not have shown to his own boys) about their answers. Over and above these interests, George was a lover of the sea, and a product of the naval training then, as now, considered suitable for a prince of the blood. His elder brother, Prince Albert Victor, was a serving cadet when Prince George, aged sixteen, joined him, and in 1881 both boys set out on a world voyage with a squadron of naval warships, *HMS Bacchante*, *Inconstant*, *Tourmaline* and *Cleopatra*. They were to call at several European, African and Far Eastern ports on a goodwill mission, and the young men were delighted to be joined by their cousin, Prince Louis of Battenberg. On the outward voyage they were all together on the *Bacchante*, but on the return only the two young Britons were to travel on the *Inconstant*.

By early July the squadron was off Australia, docking at Melbourne on the sixth for a visit of some days. The princes took shore leave, but by 10 July were once more at sea, headed for Sydney. It was a fine, warm day with very little breeze and since these were sailing ships they made only slow headway. Night fell with the barometer still forecasting fine weather, and when Prince George went on deck to take the night watch the ocean was calm as a harbour, with only the white wakes of the four ships breaking the surface. A night of full moon gave clear visibility for a great distance.

By dawn, young George had been on watch for five hours, an uneventful time, and he turned in his seat to gaze out across the port bow. He was riveted by the sight that greeted him. A great ship was approaching the *Inconstant* and sailing slowly abreast and past it, glowing with an unearthly phosphorescent light. George stared incredulously. He had glanced to port five minutes before and there had been no ship between him and the horizon. Yet there it was, and just beyond it were other ships of his squadron. He could not look away from the vessel – a three-masted brigantine, aglow from stem to stern, sails to sealine, with eerie light. He was in no doubt at all that he was watching the dreaded *Flying Dutchman*, which was a herald of ill-luck. The young prince, knowing the legend and the strange history of such sightings, prudently called the Officer of the watch, who also saw and recognized the eerie, majestic vessel with its empty decks and lifeless appearance. Thirteen sailors saw *The Dutchman* in that early morning, but by the time all crews had been alerted and had tumbled on deck to view the gleaming legend, she had vanished, as abruptly as she had arrived. Prince George entered in the log for 11 July 1881. 'At 4 a.m. *The Flying Dutchman* crossed our bows . . .' It was an extraordinary occurrence and one the youth would remember all his life.

The ill-luck came later, both to the squadron and to individual members of it, in terms of damage and death. Prince Albert Victor, George's elder brother and heir to the throne, died in 1892, aged 28, leaving George next in line of succession. But in 1881 the young prince had no thought of ruling the British Empire. His elder brother had been groomed to succeed Edward VII, who himself had waited an unconscionable time before wearing the crown. Edward VII's apprenticeship had been long and wearisome; not only had his mother lived to be eighty-two but she had spent sixty-four years on the throne. Even in the dark years of her early widowhood, she had shown no desire to abdicate in Edward's favour, and indeed mother and son were not close. Victoria seems to have disliked her son's lifestyle and distrusted his political judgement, which caused her to isolate him from the part the heir-apparent would normally play in his country's affairs. Perhaps she blamed him (the reaction is not unknown) for not being his father, or for not emulating his father. Edward, a man of charm, as George IV had been a man of charm, and with all that ancestor's self-indulgent sensuality, waited restlessly and fretfully in the wings, with no useful employment. Inevitably, he followed Prinny into the paths of pleasure. He was perhaps only saved from public opprobrium by a comparatively early death, following which, on account of his interest in foreign affairs and influence on his more aggressive foreign relatives, he became known as Edward the Peacemaker. He died in 1910, to national mourning. His eldest son had been dead for eighteen years and it was his second son, George, who now succeeded.

George V had his second brush with the paranormal after his accession. He was the guest of the Duke of Devonshire, owner of Bolton Abbey (actually a priory), and the story of the hauntings was told in the king's hearing. When a boy on holiday from Eton, the duke's son, the Marquis of Hartington, had joined a grouse-shooting party at the Abbey, and had been given accommodation at the Rectory, which occupied the site of the old Priory guest house. The lad retired to bed at 11.15 p.m., but before he reached his bedroom door he saw a dark figure standing beside it. He noticed that the individual was 'more or less clean-shaven' and wore nondescript clothes. He stood open-mouthed for a few seconds at the top of the stairs, then dashed down to fetch another light, although it apparently did not occur to him that he was gazing at a ghost. On his return, the apparition had disappeared.

This spectral character had apparently been seen on a number of earlier occasions, and several times by the local clergyman. Both the witnesses thought the man had an unusually round face, an unshaven appearance and wore long dark robes; the young marquis believed the figure was that of an elderly person and 'as solid as an actual man'. King George V seems to have been intrigued by this story, suggesting that it should be written down for future reference. As it happens, the ghost has made such a record unnecessary, for it continues to appear on the same site, having been seen several times in the sixties. All the sightings have been in or near the Priory, the most recent occurring in the month of July. From time to time the Rector's family have also heard the slap-slap of sandalled feet in the rooms of their home. This is just one more instance of a long-established lifepattern replaying itself. Eventually the energy or force powering it may weaken and the haunting cease.

Here is one last echo of George V, if it *is* George V, for the matter is open to some doubt. One of many who wrote to me about royal hauntings was Mrs M. E. Bulcock of Blackburn, Lancashire. In 1974 the Bulcocks and their two children visited Hampton Court, although the tastes of the family were somewhat divided since their daughter was not interested in royalty. Once in the garden they walked along a straight path, bounded by a wall on one side and trees on the other, but deserted apart from an elderly gentleman slowly approaching. They noticed that the man was small, slim and wore a khaki-coloured gaberdine. He carried a walking stick and wore a pointed beard. They thought he was about seventy years old. As the two parties drew level, the elderly gentleman gazed at them with 'a most wonderfully kind expression'. Something in his appearance, expression or the vivid blue of his eyes struck the family forcibly, for they all stopped to watch the stranger pass out of sight; which he did at the far end of the lane (Mrs Bulcock stresses that he did not 'disappear'). The Bulcocks compared notes. Both parents and their elder daughter thought they had passed either the ghost of King George V or a living man impersonating him. Even the younger girl was sure she had seen him in photographs, though she could not name him.

A few years later Mrs Bulcock was impressed by a written description of Nicholas II, the last czar of Russia, whose strong likeness to King George V was constantly remarked on during their lifetimes. 'His eyes were kind and he had a truly gentle expression. I got the impression that he was a simple, frank and talkative person. Sometimes I felt that he was going to speak to me. He looked as if he would like to talk to us.' The writer of those words was one of the guards of the Russian royal family. The Bulcocks had unconsciously echoed the guard's sentiments when the mysterious elderly man walked past them. 'He looked as if he would like to talk to us.' Could he have been Nicholas II?

In reply to my questions, Mrs Bulcock said there had been no drop in temperature (often a sign of a parapsychological occurrence) at the scene. The family did 'consider the probability that this was someone impersonating the late king, but the likeness was so extraordinary, especially the brilliant blue eyes, that we concluded it must at least have been a close relative, maybe living in retirement in a grace-and-favour house on the estate. The likelihood of the mystery man being Nicholas II scarcely arises, since the person seen by the Bulcocks was at least seventy and slightly stoopd. The last czar had by then been dead for many years, killed with his family at the end of his country's revolution. In spite of some intriguing possibilities, Mrs Bulcock is of the opinion that what her family saw at Hampton Court was no living man but the ghost of King George V.

A strange case, far from conclusive, but with enough flavour of paranormality to make it worth reporting. As the percipients admit, the stranger could equally well have been a living man with an amazing resemblance to the late monarch, but this was not their conviction at the time, and immediate reactions are of some value.

As we have seen in earlier chapters, many Scots appear to possess a marked psychic ability. Non-Celtic peoples, for example the English, are apt to refer disparagingly to 'Celtic twilight' when discussing such matters as clairvoyance, second sight and psychic sensitivity in general. One suspects that the English feel more comfortable with the material than with ideas, unlike the Welsh, Irish, Scots and Cornish, who tacitly accept that every 'reality' has its psychic shadow; that life is a duality of the physical and the spiritual.

Royalty is as human in this as in all else, so one would expect those of Celtic descent to be gifted with psychic ability. Reports seem to bear this out, for the Bowes-Lyons, the family of Queen Elizabeth the queen mother, not only live in a strongly-haunted Scottish castle but have produced at least one member in modern times who has 'the gift'. The youngest brother of the queen mother, David Bowes-Lyon, is reported to have seen one or two of the Glamis ghosts when he was a boy. He is said to have called them 'the grey people' and to have been able to describe their costumes in some detail. However, this 'seeing' ability is hardly surprising in a sensitive child living in surroundings as highly-charged as Glamis Castle.

On one occasion David's clairvoyance was connected not with his home but with the family itself. His elder brother Michael, an officer in the First World War, was reported killed in action, and the family at Glamis were plunged into grief shared by many families throughout Europe at that time. David refused either to mourn or to believe the report, and insisted that he had twice seen Michael and that his brother was seriously ill with head wounds. He was, said David, in a large house surrounded by many trees. An interesting feature of Sir David Bowes-Lyon's assertion is that he actually 'saw' the bandage around Michael's head. How the rest of the family reacted to this announcement is not recorded. Perhaps by then they were used to David's clairvoyance and had learned to trust it. Certainly in this instance he was proved right: several months afterwards news came through to Glamis that the eldest son had been wounded in the head and was in a German prison hospital.

With this degree of sensibility in a family, it would be surprising not to find it recurring in later generations. The problem is that the country's religion, Anglican Christianity, requires the sovereign to swear to uphold the Established Church. And the Established Church, through most of its career, has regarded certain forms of spiritual awareness as dangerously threatening to its precepts. In recent years, some of the archaic mist surrounding such thinking has been dispersed by more progressive intellects within the church, and an organization known as the Churches' Fellowship for Psychical and Spiritual Research has been set up. This body has done and continues to do remarkably enlightened work of an open-minded, investigative nature into the psychic and spiritual qualities of humankind.

It is surely time that the hidebound attitude which requires the sovereign (and by implication, all members of the royal family) to accept the dictates of a church still rooted in mediaeval doctrine and beliefs, should be reviewed. If the monarch's subjects are allowed to examine the theories of modern philosophers, scientists and parapsychologists and to accept or reject them according to informed judgement, surely that privilege should belong also to the sovereign. It is a hypocritical and nonsensical situation. I suspect that the pressure on the royal family arises as much from the attitudes of diehard academics, particularly scientific academics, as from official church conformism. Elsewhere in the world – including the USA, Canada, Russia, Sweden, Holland, Australia – there is a genuine mood of enquiry among scientists; parapsychology is regarded as a legitimate branch of science and in some countries government money is being spent on research and on supporting the researchers. But when the Prince of Wales braved tradition and spoke in favour of a Chair of Parapsychology in Britain, he was greeted with as many arrows of reproach, regret and ridicule as downed the French at Agincourt. The professorship was not likely to cost the government and taxpayers a fortune, for it had already been funded by the will of the late Arthur Koestler. Since then, although the prince has not retracted his forward-thinking and intelligently-declared interest, he appears to have been muzzled, as far as expressing further progressive opinions is concerned, having had publicly to deny concern for that aspect of spiritual life which borders on parapsychology.

The prince's courage bore fruit, however, for the Chair of Parapsychology has been accepted by the University of Edinburgh, and its first holder is Professor Robert Morris, formerly of Syracuse University, New York State. In the meantime, various specialist magazines have reported Prince Charles as being not only interested in spiritualism, but as having attempted to 'make contact' with his late uncle, Earl Mountbatten, via séances. Of the truth of this I have no knowledge, but the matter is surely the prince's affair. Prince Charles, a friend of one of the most spiritually enlightened men of our time, Sir Laurens van der Post, seems to possess a strong awareness of the duality of life and of man's nature: spiritual and physical, temporal and eternal, positive and negative are, I suspect, more than mere words to him.

I am sure royalty do not buy haunted houses more often than the rest of us. If they appear to do so, this is possibly because they tend to seek houses of age and history, buildings which are more likely to have witnessed dramatic happenings than the suburban semi-detached, the detached bungalow or the four-bedroom executive home. The interest in royal connections with hauntings is therefore not only what ghosts haunt royal property but how their members deal with them.

After their marriage Prince and Princess Michael of Kent decided to settle in Gloucestershire, and found a seventeenth-century mansion in the village of Nether Lypiatt, near Stroud. Whether they knew of the rumour that a previous owner had seen a frock-coated ghost at her dinner-table is not known. If the tale reached them, it did not alarm them enough to prevent their buying the house. Another one-time owner reportedly said that there was certainly a ghost at the manor, and that 'he' appeared every year and was charming.

Local inhabitants believe the haunter to be a young blacksmith, hanged long ago by a proprietor of this much-owned building, a certain Judge Charles Coxe. The restless wraith of the blacksmith rides around the manor courtyard on a white horse on each anniversary of his death. He has a chilly annual canter, for he was executed on 25 January. The national press was quite delighted with this story, when it came to light before the royal couple moved in; particularly so when the cast was joined by an exorcist (an official Church of England appointee), a second Anglican clergyman and a Roman Catholic priest, the two latter performing a ceremony reported to have involved prayer and the sprinkling of holy water.

When interviewed on television by Maria Aitken, Princess Michael laughingly referred to the house's ghosts, implying that she knew the stories but was merely intrigued by them. But later she tartly acknowledged an enquiry from me by saying that both she and her husband resent the popular belief that Nether Lypiatt is haunted and that they, their family and friends all feel comfortable there. They 'wish the ghost stories would evaporate as definitely as the so-called ghosts have obviously done'.

Yes.

Althorp Park in Northamptonshire is the home of the Spencers, the family of the Princess of Wales. It is an attractive country mansion, dearly loved by those who have lived in it. From conversations I have had with members of the family who were young there when the century was young, it is clear that Althorp has unusual charm and serenity derived from age and the long rhythms of years, generations of security and gracious ways, happy expectations.

The Spencer family have a history of court service and traditions of sensitivity and marked musical ability; it has boasted several talented pianists. Another hereditary strain has been a striking lack of interest in horses and horsemanship, a quality unusual in the old landowning caste. The Spencers seem always to have inspired loyalty in their servants, from distant to modern times, and an unusual example of this gave rise to the Althorp ghost story.

While paying a visit to the house, a clergyman, Mr Drury, was playing billiards late at night with Lord Lyttleton, Earl Spencer's son-in-law. When the two men decided to retire, a servant asked them to be extremely careful about extinguishing all lights, as the earl was nervous about the fire risk. Shortly after falling asleep, Mr Drury was awakened by a bright light shining on his face. He was startled to see that he was no longer the only occupant of the room; a man in a flat cap and striped shirt was standing at the foot of the bed, quietly regarding him. The lantern he held had shed the intrusive light which had woken the sleeper. Thinking that some domestic crisis had arisen, possibly fire, Mr Drury sharply demanded an explanation, but the man was silent. The perturbed guest lost his temper and threatened to tell Earl Spencer of the intrusion. The visitor still made no reply, merely lowering his lantern and turning away towards the dressing-room. Drury called out in exasperation that he would find no exit in that direction, and then – and this is a curious reaction indeed – turned over and fell asleep once more, without waiting to see what action the man would next take.

The following morning the clergyman told Earl Spencer's daughter, Lady Lyttleton, of the occurrence, remarking that the man he had seen in his room must certainly have been drunk, though nothing specific in his behaviour had suggested it. The lady's reply probably shocked him. She said without hesitation that he must have seen the ghost of her father's favourite groom who had died only two weeks earlier. It had been his regular duty to patrol the house when its occupants had retired to bed, to see that all lights had been extinguished. He had instructions to enter any room where a candle or lamp still burned, to make sure that the occupant was still awake. The house's careful owner had passed on his obsession to a faithful servant to such a degree that he carried his duty over from life into death.

Instances of this kind are not uncommon and may arise from one of two sources. Either the impetus comes from a deeply-ingrained habit established in life and carried on into the post-death state 'through force of habit', or the mere regular exercise of the duty has established a pattern of action recorded by a part of the surroundings and regularly played and replayed until the original psychic 'record' is worn out; at which time it will cease. Such repetitions of regular life-actions often occur immediately after death, as though the newly-dead still felt alive and bound to continue his accustomed sequence. This usually peters out quickly, rarely lasting more than a week or two following the death. There has been only this one report of the Althorp haunting, so I imagine the occurrence was a singleton.

One of the many strange features about the phenomenon of haunting is that where the background is a building, the haunting may be affected by alterations or repairs. Often a mild haunting is exacerbated by such domestic activities to the extent where it becomes quite lively. In other cases, tinkering with the physical structure by adding or removing sections may result in a haunted building no longer being haunted. In my experience this is the more usual effect. I came across one much-haunted rectory in Northamptonshire which had been reproducing all the effects of an occupation by Cromwell's cavalry during the Civil Wars: horses neighing and stamping, men shouting, the noise of armaments being dropped and heavily-booted feet tramping up and down the stairs. Until the ancient house roof began to leak and architects advised its replacement. A new roof was installed and, as though at the flick of a switch, ghostly manifestations ceased.

A similar story but with the opposite effect was told to me by a senior member of the royal family. Having listened to my account of the haunting of the Northamptonshire rectory and its abrupt cessation, she asked if I knew that Sandringham House had recently been extensively renovated. I did. 'The extraordinary thing', she said, 'is that we now seem to have a haunting where there was none before.' The alterations were completed (an old part of the building had been replaced by modern kitchens) and the workmen had left. During a house-party, a woman guest was awakened in the early hours by a light in her bedroom, and was astonished to see a small boy carrying a long pole with some kind of contraption on its end. He walked around the walls, raising his pole every few yards to what must once have been sconce level, carefully either lighting or snuffing invisible candles. The guest watched the activity for some time before the boy vanished.

The royal lady asked my opinion about this occurrence, and I suggested that the guest had watched a scene from the house's past. The fact that no one had reported seeing it before does not, I think, affect its validity. The significant factor is that the scene began only when part of the building had been altered or, in Sandringham's case, removed.

The theory behind such effects is that our old friend 'the recorder', faithfully holding the equivalent of an historical tape, may be any physical property, from a door to a floor, a chimney breast to a ceiling. In the case of the Northamptonshire rectory, the recorder was obviously the roof. In Sandringham House it might have been any part of the demolished section of the building. Had this last been constructed *in front* of the original recorder of the small boy's activities no 'broadcast' could have been received because of the wall(s) blocking it. Once remove the barrier, however, and there was nothing to prevent the recorder putting out its message. A perfectly logical and mechanistically simple operation, easily demonstrable in terms of projector and screen. Obscure the projector and a picture cannot appear. Remove the obstruction and – hey presto! a young pageboy snuffing or lighting candles just as he did in the house's youth.

My royal auditor found this explanation intriguing and, I think, satisfying. I do not know whether the little page has been seen again, but this is one more example of how so-called hauntings may be records of the history of their surroundings. Sometimes in the process of replaying themselves they give us a clearer indication of times past than all the history books. A 'photographic' record; a 'televised' recording; a picture of an actual event imprinted upon a material object and involuntarily run through again and again, as film through a projector. Perhaps it occurs continually, whether or not anyone is there to intercept its message. It is a strangely wonderful idea and one which bears much more investigation. We are still in the very early stages of research into this fascinating subject, and hauntings are only the ozone's breath and the white spray of that deep and remarkable sea which we refer to as the paranormal. A time will come, perhaps, when we accept it as perfectly normal, part of the immense human experience which is the heritage of us all.

Bibliography

ALEXANDER, Marc	*Haunted Castles*	Muller
	Phantom Britain	Muller, 1975
	Haunted Inns	Muller
ALICE, Princess, Duchess of Gloucester	*Memoirs of Princess Alice*	Collins, 1983
ASHE, Geoffrey	*The Quest for Arthur's Britain*	Pall Mall Press, 1968
ASHTON, Robert	*James I and His Contemporaries*	Hutchinson, 1969
BARDENS, Dennis	*Ghosts and Hauntings*	Zeus Press
BARNETT, Corelli	*Marlborough*	Eyre Methuen, 1974
BARRACLOUGH, Geoffrey	*The Crucible of Europe*	Thames and Hudson, 1976
BRADDOCK, Joseph	*Haunted Houses*	Cedric Chivers, 1956
BRIGGS, Katherine M.	*Sampler of British Folk Tales*	Routledge Kegan Paul, 1970
BROWN, R. Allen	*English Castles*	Batsford, 1954
BRYANT, Arthur	*Makers of the Realm*	Collins
CECIL Lord David	*Melbourne*	Constable/Reprint Soc.,1955
DAY, J. Wentworth	*Here are Ghosts and Witches*	Batsford
DE BLACAM,	*Gaelic Literature Surveyed*	Talbot Press
DOUGLAS, David C.	*The Norman Fate*	Eyre Methuen
FORMAN, Joan	*Haunted East Anglia*	Hale, 1974
	The Haunted South	Hale, 1978
	The Mask of Time	Macdonald and Jane, 1978

FRY, Plantagenet S	*Roman Britain*	David and Charles, 1984
FULFORD, Roger	*Royal Dukes*	Pan Books, 1948
GOOCH, Stan	*The Paranormal*	Fontana, 1979
GOODMAN, Jean	*Royal Scotland*	Debrett/Webb and Bower, 1983
HACKETT, Francis	*Henry the Eighth*	Cape, 1929
HAINING, Peter	*The Monster Trap*	Severn House, 1980
HALIFAX, Lord	*Lord Halifax's Ghost Book*	Bles. 1936
HARVEY, John	*The Plantagenets*	Batsford
HELM, P.J.	*Exploring Saxon and Norman England*	Hale, 1976
HERM, Gerhard	*The Celts*	Weidenfeld, 1976
HIPPISLEY-COXE, A.	*Haunted Britain*	Hutchinson, 1973
HOLE, Christina	*Haunted England*	Batsford, 1940
HOPKINS, R.T.	*Ghosts over England*	Meridian Books, 1953
	Cavalcade of Ghosts	World's Work, 1956
HUMBLE, Richard	*The Fall of Saxon England*	Arthur Barker, 1975
IVERSON, Jeffrey	*More Lives Than One*	Souvenir Press 1976
JORDAN, W.K.	*Edward VI. The Threshold of power*	Allen and Unwin, 1970
KEAN, M.H.	*England in the Late Middle Ages*	Methuen,
KENDALL, Paul Murray	*Richard III*	Sphere, 1972
KETTON-CREMER, W.	*Norfolk in the Civil War*	Gliddon Bks. 1985
KIGHTLY, Charles	*Folk Heroes of Britain*	Thames and Hudson, 1982
LAING, Jennifer	*Britain's Mysterious Past*	David and Charles
LAVER, James	*A Concise History of Costume*	Thames and Hudson
LESLIE, Shane	*Ghost Book*	Hollis and Carter
MACKENZIE, Andrew	*Apparitions and Ghosts*	Arthur Barker

MANNING-SANDERS, Ruth	*Scottish Folk Tales*	Methuen, 1976
MARIE-LOUISE, Princess	*My Memories of Six Reigns*	Evans, 1956
MARSHALL, Dorothy	*Eighteenth Century England*	Longmans, 1962
MARWICK, Arthur (Ed.)	*Dictionary of British History*	Thames and Hudson, 1980
MATTINGLY, Garrett	*Catherine of Aragon*	Cape, 1942
METCALFE, Leon	*Discovering Ghosts*	Shire Publications
MITCHELL, W.R.	*Haunted Yorkshire*	Dalesman, 1969
NASH, Roy	*Buckingham Palace*	Macdonald, 1980
NORMAN, Diana	*Stately Ghosts of England*	Muller, 1963
O'DONNELL, Eliot	*Haunted Places in England*	Sands, 1919
	Haunted Britain	Rider, 1948
	Scottish Ghost Stories	Jarrold, 1981
PALMER, Alan	*Life and Times of George IV*	Weidenfeld, 1972
PEPPER, Elizabeth and WILCOCK, John	*Magical and Mystical Sites*	Weidenfeld, 1976
PETRY, Michael J.	*Herne the Hunter*	Wm. Smith, Reading
PLAYFAIR, Guy Lyon	*The Haunted Pub Guide*	Harrap, 1985
PREBBLE, John	*The Lion in the North*	Secker and Warburg, 1971
ROSS, Charles	*The Wars of the Roses*	Thames and Hudson, 1976
SCATTERGOOD, V.J.	*Politics and Poetry in the 15th Century*	Blandford, 1971
SCOTT, A.F.	*Every One a Witness*	Scott and Finlay, 1976
SCULLARD, H.H.	*Roman Britain*	Thames and Hudson, 1979
SELLEY, W.T.	*England in the 18th Century.*	A. and C. Black, 1934
SERGEANT, P.W.	*Historic British Ghosts*	Hutchinson

STEADMAN, G. and ANKER R.	*Ghosts of the Isle of Wight*	I.W. County Press, 1977
STEINBERG and EVANS	*Dictionary of British History*	Edward Arnold, 1970
THOMPSON, Francis	*Ghosts, Spirits and Spectres of Scotland*	Impulse Books
TREVELYAN, G.M.	*English Social History*	Longman, 1944
UNDERWOOD, Peter	*This Haunted Isle*	Harrap, 1984
	Haunted London	Harrap, 1944
WEBSTER, Graham	*Boudicca*	Batsford
WHITE, R.J.	*The Age of George III*	Heinemann, 1968
WILLIAMS, E.N.	*Life in Georgian England*	Batsford, 1962
WILLIAMSON, Hugh Ross	*The Gunpowder Plot*	Faber, 1951

Additional Publications

Tales from Scottish Lairds		Jarrolds, 1981
King Arthur, Tintagel Castle		Ronald Youlton
Prisoners in the Tower	Elizabeth Jenkins	Hamish Hamilton, 1978
Official Guide to Oundle		Brit. Publ. Co., Gloucester, 1973

Parish Magazine, Westhorpe, Suffolk, 1980
The Daily Mail, 30 Oct. 1984
The Spritualist Gazette, May, 1984
Daily Star, 8 Jan. 1981
Daily Express, 28 Jan. 1984
Daily Express, 27 Jan. 1984
The Spiritualist Gazette, July, 1984

Index